QUICK ESCAPES®
BOSTON

Help Us Keep This Guide Up-to-Date

Every effort has been made by the author and editors to make this guide as accurate and useful as possible. However, many things can change after a guide is published—establishments close, phone numbers change, facilities come under new management, and so on.

We would love to hear from you concerning your experiences with this guide and how you feel it could be improved and be kept up-to-date. While we may not be able to respond to all comments and suggestions, we'll take them to heart, and we'll also make certain to share them with the author. Please send your comments and suggestions to the following address:

> The Globe Pequot Press
> Reader Response/Editorial Department
> P.O. Box 480
> Guilford, CT 06437

Or you may e-mail us at:

> editorial@globe-pequot.com

Thanks for your input, and happy travels!

QUICK ESCAPES®
BOSTON

Second Edition

25 WEEKEND GETAWAYS
FROM THE HUB

BY

SANDY MacDONALD

The
Globe
Pequot
Press

GUILFORD, CONNECTICUT

Photo credits: p.1: Steven Ziglar; p. 19: Thomas Neill © Old Sturbridge Village; p. 28: Edith Wharton Restoration Inc.; p. 39: © Plimoth Plantation; p. 106: Robert Dennis courtesy Maine Office of Tourism/NMC; p. 119: Gary Pearl courtesy Maine Office of Tourism/NMC; p. 132: Tom Hindman courtesy Maine Office of Tourism/NMC; pp. 139, 146: Maine Office of Tourism/NMC; p. 155: David Brownell/State of NH Office of Travel and Tourism Development; p. 159: Arthur J. Boufford/State of NH Office of Travel and Tourism Development; p. 182: Bob Grant/State of NH Office of Travel and Tourism Development; p. 191: Luc-Antoine Couturier; p. 197: J-F Bergeron, Enviro Foto; p. 205: Waterbury Tourism Council; p. 211: courtesy Gary Hall; p. 223: Jon Fox © Billings Farm & Museum; p. 245: © Jim McElholm, courtesy Newport County Convention & Visitor's Bureau; pp. 261, 266: Michael Melford/Connecticut's Mystic & More!; p. 281: Litchfield Hills Visitors Bureau; p. 295: Coastal Fairfield County CVB; p. 301: © Mick Hales, courtesy the Metropolitan Museum of Art, New York, The Cloisters Collection, 1925.

Text design by Nancy Freeborn
Maps by M.A. Dubé

ISBN 0-7627-2200-2

Manufactured in the United States of America
Second Edition/First Printing

For John Devaney, Laurel Devaney, Clover and Geoff Bell-Devaney, and a child we can't wait to welcome—a family I love to escape with, whenever and wherever.

CONTENTS

ACKNOWLEDGMENTS

Innumerable tourism officials and independent publicists—most notably, Glenn Faria and Bill DeSouza—have helped acquaint me with the more rewarding byways of New England. Not that I needed much motivation to hit the road, but various magazine editors did provide added incentive. I'm most grateful to Dan Okrent—founding editor of *New England Monthly*—for honing my critical edge, and for seeing some potential in the first place. Among my excellent editors at NEM were Julie Michaels and Alexandra Kennedy, currently editorial director of *FamilyFun*. For the past several years I've enjoyed comparing notes with colleagues and neighbors David Lyon and Patricia Harris.

INTRODUCTION

When Oliver Wendell Holmes dubbed Boston's state house "the hub of the solar system" in an 1858 issue of the *Atlantic Monthly*, his semifacetious tribute alluded primarily to the reach of the city's intellectual and social influence. However, the sobriquet is geographically apt as well. If you were to use a compass to inscribe a radius of roughly 250 miles from Boston's epicenter (a 1737 stone marker denotes the spot, on tiny Marshall Street near Faneuil Hall), the arc would span New York City; Burlington, Vermont; and Bar Harbor, Maine. All of New England, save the wilds of northern Maine, are within easy reach. Not only does Boston itself offer a refreshing escape from the typical rigors of big-city life, it affords ready access to a unique region steeped in history, some of it still in the making.

Different areas lend themselves to different tastes and predilections. Forks, Maine, doesn't offer much in the way of nightlife or cultural enlightenment. But then again, there's no white-water river rafting in ultracivilized Newport. For each destination discussed in the book, I've tried to include pleasures both corporal and intellectual. The former category is a cinch to fill, so widespread is the culinary revolution that gave us inventive, flavorful New American fare to supplant "the bean and the cod." No matter how far you roam, you're likely to eat well—and sleep well, too, in one of the hundreds of small, charming inns that capture the romance of the region.

Reservations are a must, even in off-season (the so-called shoulder seasons are becoming so popular, there's no longer a clear distinction). Most inns require a deposit, and for weekends there's usually a two-night minimum— three if a holiday's involved. If you're hesitant to commit to a particular restaurant site—and menu—unseen, consider dining at an absurdly early hour (sixish) or after 9:00 P.M., *a la español*. You can get a pretty good idea of what you're in for by requesting literature ahead of time from the tourist boards and chambers of commerce listed under **For More Information** at the end of each escape and also by visiting web sites, when available. The establishments featured are my personal favorites, but you'll find equally good alternatives

under **Other Recommended Restaurants and Lodgings,** after each itinerary. Innkeepers are usually excellent sources for restaurant recommendations,
provided you're specific as to your preferences: four-star luxe, for instance,
versus basic lobster shack. Both, of course, have their appeal.

These twenty-five excursions are arranged so that they can be linked—or
each can be pleasantly accomplished in the course of a weekend, provided
you select among suggested options to suit your taste. As a travel writer I tend
to take very type-A trips, trying to fit in every worthwhile attraction. But
occasionally I have landed in a place so lovely, so relaxing, that I had no
choice but to pull out a book and dazedly dream, lolling on the porch or by
the fire. I hope that in your journeys you'll encounter such lacunae of leisure.
Sometimes you need to escape from the escape itself, to find the peace that
truly refreshes.

Getting the Car Ready

Topography and climate demand a few extra steps in addition to the usual
pretrip maintenance precautions (checking fluids, hoses, lights, tires, wiper
blades, etc.):

If you're planning to drive through the mountains in summer, particularly in
   Vermont and New Hampshire, have your radiator checked before you go.
   Older ones often fail in the heat of a long uphill haul, and the inconve-
   nience—especially with dealerships few and far between—could put a real
   crimp in your trip.

Winter driving usually calls for a ton of windshield wiper fluid, to wash away
   the salt used to de-ice the roads. Make sure the squirter nozzles are clear
   before you hit the road, and always carry a spare jug.

If you're not accustomed to driving on snow and ice (black ice, scarcely visible at night, is the scariest), put off your trip until conditions improve. The
   New England states are generally very good about clearing the roads, but
   sometimes precipitation is so heavy and swift that road crews can't keep up.
   Stay tuned to the weather, and heed all advisories. At a minimum take
   along an ice scraper, shovel, and sack of sand for traction. If your efforts to
   rock the car out of a rut (by gently switching from forward to reverse,
   repeatedly) come to naught, quit before you dig yourself in deeper, and tie
   something onto your antenna to attract help.

The dangers don't dissipate with winter. Mud season poses hazards of its own, so don't even attempt a dirt road (maps usually signal them with a broken line) until everything's good and dry—sometimes not till May.

Because some of these destinations are quite remote, membership in a comprehensive, one-call auto club, such as AAA, could be a godsend—as would be a cellular phone.

Handy Take-alongs

There's no glory to traveling light if you end up depriving yourself of essential creature comforts. In our years of gallivanting around New England, we've evolved a basic checklist of necessities:

A two-liter soda or seltzer: The empty bottle can be refilled with cool water (see note on radiators, above)

Healthy snacks such as fruit and vegetables or low-fat munchies (the bag you bring them in will come in handy for garbage)

A roll of paper towels, for general cleanup and emergency use as tissue

A detailed map that includes back roads (state tourist boards generally offer them for free)

Sunglasses, for both driver and shotgun passenger

Umbrellas and/or ponchos (the weather can be capricious)

Jumper cables, and a combination flare/flashlight/tire inflator that plugs into the lighter

A first-aid kit

A Swiss Army–type knife or pocket tool kit (include a corkscrew if you're planning alfresco picnics with wine)

Less essential, but nonetheless useful are:

Pillows and blankets for all passengers, plus amusements—toys, games, tapes, puzzles—for the children

A camera, with extra film and spare batteries

Binoculars: You never know when you'll spot an interesting bird, or perhaps whale.

Suggested Clothing and Footwear

Seasonal differences make for wildly divergent packing lists, but you'll probably want some version of the following, whatever the time of year:

A jacket and tie for men, for those rare restaurants that require them

A dressy outfit for women, ideally one that travels well

Running shoes or hiking boots, depending on the terrain

A hooded, waterproof windbreaker or raincoat

A sweater, even in summer, especially if you plan to be near the water or up in the mountains

Getting In and Out of the City

There's really only one cardinal rule: In summer, don't even think about heading out to Cape Cod on Friday afternoon or evening, or heading back during the same time span on Sunday. Only two bridges—a total of four lanes—offer access, and the traffic can back up for miles (and hours). Juggle your schedule, do whatever you have to, to avoid joining the bottlenecks.

The northerly routes—I–95 into Maine, I–93 into New Hampshire—are usually bearable outbound (except perhaps during the usual after-work rush hour); however, even they can clog up at the end of a weekend, when everyone's funneling home. We have yet to encounter any significant slowdown along Vermont's I–89 or I–91, and the Mass Pike (I–90) usually moves right along. Keep in mind, however, that at fall foliage time the roadways may be littered with leisurely leaf peepers.

Most of the major radio stations issue rush-hour traffic reports. SmarTraveler (617–374–1234, or toll-free ★1 on cellular phones) offers a comprehensive, round-the-clock menu of traffic information for all the major routes fanning out from Boston.

MASSACHUSETTS
ESCAPES

The North Shore

TREASURES OF THE SEA

2 NIGHTS

Seaside mansions • Nautical art • Antiques shops • Beaches
Nature preserves • Whale watching

Often delegated to secondary status as "the other Cape," Cape Ann and the rest of the North Shore enjoy a rugged beauty more akin to Maine. Despite a scattering of sandy beaches, the landscape tends more to dramatic rocky outcroppings and has attracted its share of contrarians—not to mention outright eccentrics. From the prosperous sea captains who left their mark in the form of elegant Federal houses to the creative types who later flocked here for inspiration, the residents have tended to uphold a tradition of free-spirited industry. Yet, with its galleries, restaurants, and curiosity shops, this also remains a prime spot for slacking off, especially in summer.

Encircling the Cape and the contiguous coastline, this itinerary includes opportunities for edification as well as enjoyment. You don't have to know a whole lot about the area's past, though, to appreciate its present charms.

DAY 1

Morning

Brave the tacky gauntlet of Route 1 north to reach Route 128 eastbound; exit at Route 114 east, and follow it into **Salem** via North Street. Take a left on Norman, which leads to Derby Street and the center of town. Ditch your car where you can (there are plenty of garages if on-street space is scarce) and pick up the **Salem Heritage Trail**—a painted footpath similar to Boston's Freedom

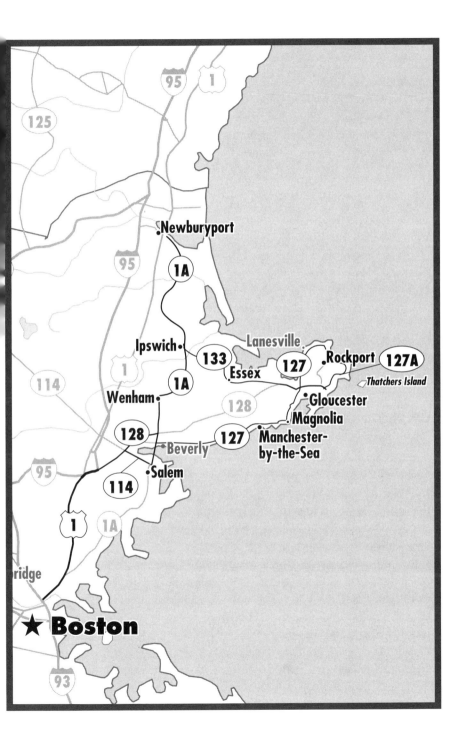

Trail. Although a great many of Salem's attractions appear, alas, to be geared to unexacting tourists, a select few warrant seeking out. Start with the **Witch Trials Memorial Site,** a stark little beauty of a park where incised quotes from the victims of mass hysteria conjure the tragedy vividly. Just up the street, at East India Square, is the well-endowed **Peabody Essex Museum** (978–745–9500 or 800–745–4054; www.pem.org), offering a world-class collection of maritime artifacts as well as treasures from the China trade. A block eastward is its homelier cousin/annex, the **Essex Institute,** whose local-history exhibits may be a bit musty but are nonetheless alluring, especially the original documents dating from the witch hunt. Hours for both are Monday through Saturday, 10:00 A.M. to 5:00 P.M., and Sunday noon to 5:00 P.M.; closed Monday from November to late May.

At the end of the block, turn right on Hawthorne Boulevard—named for Nathaniel Hawthorne—and follow it down to the harbor. To your left, on Derby Street, you'll see the elegant **Customs House** where the as-yet-unsuccessful novelist clerked to support his fledgling career. Farther along, on the right, is the birthplace he immortalized as the **House of the Seven Gables** (978–744–0991; www.7gables.org). The only way to view the interior is by group tour, but the docents are singularly adept at evincing the history of both author and subject. The hours are 10:00 A.M. to 5:00 P.M. year-round.

LUNCH: The Grapevine, 26 Congress Street, Salem; (978) 745–9335; www.grapevinesalem.com. Robust and superlative New American/North Italian fare.

Afternoon

Reclaiming your car, head northeast on Route 1A through Beverly, then follow scenic, coastal Route 127 to **Manchester-by-the-Sea,** where, weather and crowds permitting, you could take a dip at **Singing Beach:** the superfine sand actually squeaks underfoot. (Parking can be a problem; nonresidents usually park in town, about a mile away, and walk.) About 2½ miles farther east along 127, bear right to pass through **Magnolia** (another well-heeled little town with appealing shops), and continue straight along Hesperus Avenue for about 2 miles until you spot **Hammond Castle** (978–283–2080; www.hammondcastle.org). Inventor John Hays Hammond Jr.—whose legacies include the remote control—built this Frankensteinian medieval mansion in 1929 with architectural elements salvaged abroad. The hours are 10:00 A.M. to 3:30 P.M. daily in season, and one visit per lifetime will probably suffice. (It's a lugubrious space: you keep expecting Vincent Price to pop up.) It's interesting, though, to see what deep pockets could dish out in those days.

On the other side of harbor, past the working port of **Gloucester**—now a tourist destination in its own right, post-*Perfect Storm*—and south on Eastern Point Boulevard, is another splendiferous folly from the roaring twenties: **Beauport** (978–283–0800; www.spnea.org), a forty-five-room mansion decorated to the hilt—and then some—by influential interior designer Henry Davis Sleeper. Modern sensibilities might find the compulsive color scheming and general de trop-ness oppressive, but it can't be denied that he had an eye, as well as the foresight to hoard Early Americana while the pickings were primo. Hourly tours are offered 10:00 A.M. to 4:00 P.M. weekdays mid-May to mid-October, as well as from 1:00 to 4:00 P.M. weekends mid-September to mid-October, when the museum closes for the season.

Returning to Atlantic Road, cruise the southeast stretch of the Cape (Route 127A), keeping an eye on the horizon for the twin lights at **Thatchers Island,** site of a legendary Colonial shipwreck. Continue along the coast through picturesque Rockport, taking time out to plunder the better shops.

DINNER AND LODGING: Yankee Clipper Inn, 96 Granite Street, Rockport; (978) 546–3407; www.yankeeclipperinn.com. Well removed from the touristy hordes (it's about a half-mile north of town), this charming hostelry consists of a cluster of handsome Federal houses set along a rocky bluff; its heated saltwater pool is most refreshing. The in-house restaurant, the **Verandah,** turns out accomplished New American cuisine highlighting the ocean's bounty. Note: Rockport has been a dry town since 1856, when septuagenarian Hannah Jumper took an ax to local saloons, but you're welcome to bring your own wine.

DAY 2

Morning

BREAKFAST: Yankee Clipper Inn. A beauty, enhanced by fresh-baked pastries.

Get an early start if you'd like to get a jump on the nature lovers flocking to **Halibut Point State Park and Reservation** (978–546–2997; www.state.ma.us/dem/parks/halb.htm.), a sixty-six-acre promontory that contains a cored-out granite quarry, or the mountain bikers and hikers exploring **Dogtown,** a 3,600-acre conservation area that contains the cellar holes of an abandoned Colonial settlement. Driving along Route 127 you'll pass through sleepy **Lanesville,** clustered with browse-worthy antiques shops, and arrive

back in Gloucester. There seek out the **Cape Ann Historical Museum** at 27
Pleasant Street (978–283–0455; www.cape-ann.com/historical-museum), a relatively small but astute assemblage of decorative and primarily fine arts of local
significance; the hours are 10:00 A.M. to 5:00 P.M. Tuesday through Saturday.
The rather florid Fitz Hugh Lane is the town's hugest success story, with can-
vases now fetching millions, but Winslow Homer and Milton Avery also summered here. John Singer Sargent spent his boyhood nearby, and the **Sargent
House Museum** at 49 Middle Street (978–281–2432)—a gracious Georgian
abode—has some of his clumsy early sketches on display, noon to 4:00 P.M. Friday through Monday in season.

At the eastern edge of town, you'll find the **Rocky Neck Art Colony**
(978–283–7878; www.cape-ann.com/rocky-neck), a score or so of fishing
shacks-turned-studios clustered along a picturesque peninsula. Active since the
1890s, Rocky Neck claims to be the oldest such enclave in the country. Amid
the current output—rather mediocre, as a rule—you may happen upon such
treasures as the minuscule **Weiler Photo Gallery** at 77 Rocky Neck Avenue
(978–281–6443; www.seasidetrade.com/Joseph_Flack_Weiler.html). Specializing in photographs and prints, also check out the delightful **English Bookshop** at number 22 (978–283–8981), where a warren of crammed shelves
bulges with fascinating tomes, both old and new.

LUNCH: Passports, 110 Main Street, Gloucester; (978) 281–3680. This
lively, welcoming international bistro is a perfect embodiment of the New
Gloucester.

Afternoon

If you have yet to go watch whales, it's a must, and Gloucester is well situated
for visiting both Stellwagen Bank (the Northeast's first National Marine Sanctuary) and nearby Jeffreys Bank, another favorite feeding spot. Trip lengths
vary, depending who has been spotted hanging out—the onboard naturalists
can identify individual whales from their distinctive tail patterns—but the
norm is about an hour to get out there, an hour to poke around, and another
to get back. If you're lucky, you might come upon a baby frolicking with its
mother, or a couple of adolescents showing off. Like most such operations,
Yankee Fleet Whale Watch (75 Essex Avenue; 978–283–0313 or 800–
WHALING; www.yankeefleet.com) contributes a portion of its proceeds to
cetacean research and offers "guaranteed sightings," which doesn't mean that
the creatures are contracted to show up on cue—merely that if the ship fails

to track one down, you can go out again for free. You're likely to debark yearning for another encounter in any case.

DINNER: The White Rainbow, 65 Main Street, Gloucester; (978) 281–0017. Polished Continental fare in a romantic granite-walled cellar.

LODGING: Addison Choate Inn, 49 Broadway, Rockport; (978) 546–7543 or (800) 245–7543; www.cape-ann.com/addison-choate. This historic 1851 hostelry is set right in the center of Rockport (only 4 miles away), so you'll have a chance for one last stroll.

DAY 3

Morning

BREAKFAST: Addison Choate Inn. The morning buffet features wonderful home-baked treats.

With time running out, you'll have to make a tough choice between shopping or sunbathing, but you might be able to fit in a bit of both, if you concentrate on only one of two top spots: **Ipswich/Essex** or **Newburyport,** up the coast. Better get your sunning done early in the day—ideally starting at 8:00 A.M., as soon as the paid lots open (they tend to max out quickly). Locals know to avoid the beach from mid-July to mid-August, when the greenhead flies are insufferably voracious.

Otherwise, the top swimming spots are pristine **Crane Beach,** off Argilla Road in Ipswich (978–356–4354; www.thetrustees.org), 4 miles of silken sand and gentle surf arrayed beneath the grand 1927 mansion of Castle Hill, and 10 miles of mostly conservation land on **Plum Island** off Newburyport.

If the weather is uncooperative, or you'd rather collect than catch rays, antique your way through Essex. Among the dozens of shops lining Route 133, keep an eye out for **Howard's Flying Dragon** (978–768–7282), for stock that's truly recherché, and the atmospheric **White Elephant Shop** (978–768–6901). Acquisitive appetites whetted, you might want to continue on to Newburyport, the very model of a Federal-era town. Its beautifully renovated 1830s brick Market Square now houses all manner of enticing shops, imaginatively stocked.

LUNCH: Woodman's, on Main Street, Essex; (978) 768–6451; www. woodmans.com. This is the rustic birthplace—back in 1915—of the beloved fried clam. Or **Ten Center Street,** Newburyport; (978) 462–6652. This pub, fashioned from a 1790 bakery, dishes out sophisticated, yet substantial fare.

Afternoon

Heading home, make one last stopover in the quaint inland town of **Wenham.** Anyone who was ever been or is now a child will find the contents of the tiny **Wenham Museum** at 132 Main Street (978–468–2377; www.wenhammuseum.org) irresistible. Viewable Tuesday through Sunday 10:00 A.M. to 4:00 P.M., the collection comprises thousands of dolls, toy soldiers, and other evocative playthings. Prepare to be flooded with fond memories.

TEA: To fortify yourself for the journey back to Boston (only an hour hence), head across the street to the **Wenham Tea House** (978–468–1398), which was opened by the civic-minded ladies of the Wenham Village Improvement Society in 1916 and has changed very little since. After perusing the tasteful gift shop for some suitable keepsakes, from decorative to delectable, linger over a pot of tea and perhaps some "cottage pudding." The years, even decades, will melt away as you observe this timeless ritual of civilized camaraderie.

THERE'S MORE

Boating. The *Thomas E. Lannon,* a 1997 replica schooner (978–281–6634; www.schooner.org), sets out from Gloucester several times a day in summer. From Rockport Harbor you can catch a ferry to Thachers Island (978–546–2326); adventurous types are even welcome to sleep out. Essex River Cruises and Charters out of the Essex Marina at 35 Dodge Street (978–768–6981 or 800–748–3706; www.essexcruises.com) offers a narrated voyage past beaches, marshes, and shipyards. The self-propelled might prefer to canoe the placid Ipswich River through nature preserves and past grand estates: rentals, with an upstream drop-off, can be arranged through Foote Bros. Canoes in Ipswich (978–356–9771). Essex River Basin Adventures, based at the Story Shipyard off Main Street in Essex (978–768–3722 or 800–KAYAK–04; www.erba.com), organizes guided sea-kayaking tours along tidal estuaries, by day or moonlight, with or without clambake.

Diving. Its frigid waters notwithstanding, Cape Ann abounds in scenic dive sites. Whether you prefer to snorkel or scuba, Cape Ann Divers, located at 127 Eastern Avenue in Gloucester (978–281–8082; www.capeanndivers.com), can steer and/or accompany you to the most promising spots. Get a lobster license and you can grab lunch.

Theater. The North Shore Music Theater at 62 Dunham Road in Beverly (978–922–8500; www.nsmt.org) mounts high-caliber musicals—mostly—in the round. The Gloucester Stage Company, occupying a rehabbed fish-processing plant at 267 East Main Street in Gloucester (978–281–4099; www.cape-ann.com/stageco.html), specializes in modernist, working-class dramas. The Firehouse Center for the Performing & Visual Arts in Market Square, Newburyport (978–462–7336; www.firehousecenter.com), is a dazzling complex, strong on family fare.

Treats. At the Harbor Sweets factory at 85 Leavitt Street in Salem (978–745–7648; www.harborsweets.com), visitors are welcome both to taste and to tour. Goodale Orchard at 143 Argilla Road in Ipswich (978–356–5366) offers seasonal pick-your-own opportunities, from strawberries to apples, as well as an exemplary—and effortless—traditional farmstand.

SPECIAL EVENTS

May to October. Myopia Hunt Club, South Hamilton; (978) 468–7956. Sunday polo matches draw spectators and picnickers.

June. Rockport Chamber Music Festival; (978) 546–7391; www.rcmf.org. International musicians convene for weekend concerts.

Last weekend in June. St. Peter's Fiesta, Gloucester; (978) 283–1601; www. stpetersfiesta.org. This nautical celebration includes a blessing of the fleet, fireworks, parades, and contests such as a greasy-pole competition.

Late August. Crane Beach Sand Blast, Ipswich; (978) 356–4351. A festive, free-form sand-sculpture contest open to all ages.

Early September. Newburyport Waterfront Festival; (978) 462–6680; www. newburyportchamber.org. International foods, plane rides (from vintage to ultralites), and continuous entertainment, including a New England song-writers competition.

Mid- to late October. Haunted Happenings, Salem; (978) 744–0004; www.salem-chamber.org. Family-oriented festivities, including pumpkin-carving classes and costume parades.

OTHER RECOMMENDED RESTAURANTS AND LODGINGS

Beverly

Wild Horse Cafe, 392 Cabot Street; (978) 922–6868. A New American dinner destination.

Yanks, 717 Hale Street; (978) 232–9898; www.yanksrestaurant.com. A chic American bistro in a former Cadillac showroom.

Gloucester

The Franklin Cape Ann, 118 Main Street; (978) 283–7888. David Du Bois's storefont bistro—sibling to the Boston original—lends Gloucester some real style.

Grange Gourmet, 457 Washington Street; (978) 283–2639 or (800) 236–2639; www.grangegourmet.com. A deli/cafe with topnotch takeout.

Ipswich

Chipper's River Cafe, 24 Market Street; (978) 356–7956. A congenial waterside cafe, with home-baked pastries.

The Inn at Castle Hill, 290 Argilla Road; (978) 356–7774; www.theinnat castlehill.org. A fabulously updated 1840 farmhouse amid 2,100 acres of glorious grounds.

Stone Soup Cafe, 20 Mitchell Road; (978) 356–4222. A corny little brick box creating a buzz with Southern Italian cuisine.

Newburyport

Fowle's Newburyport Coffeehouse, 17 State Street; (978) 463–8755. A genuine 1932 soda fountain, where you can get old-fashioned flavored Cokes or newfangled flavored coffees.

Glenn's 44, Merrimac Street; (978) 465–3811. Adventurous international cuisine, in a smartly pared-down former shoe factory, often with a side order of live blues.

Rockport

Emerson Inn by the Sea, 1 Cathedral Avenue; (978) 546–6321 or (800) 964–5550; www.emersoninnbythesea.com. A substantive 1839 hotel (where Emerson did stay), updated with a restaurant called the Grand Café, a salt-water pool, and a day spa.

The Seaward Inn, 44 Marmion Way; (978) 546–3471 or (877) 4SEAWARD; www.seawardinn.com. A cottage complex right by the sea, with an appealing restaurant, Seagarden.

Salem

Finz, 76 Wharf Street; (978) 744–8485. Progressive seafood on Pickering Wharf.

Hawthorne Hotel, On the Common; (978) 744–4080 or (800) 729–7829; www.hawthornehotel.com. A nicely refurbished and conveniently located 1920s beauty, with a polished restaurant, Nathaniel's.

Red Raven's Love Noodle, 75 Congress Street; (978) 745–8558. A splashy bistro boasting a tripartite menu: spa, bourgeois, and *gastronomique.*

FOR MORE INFORMATION

Cape Ann Chamber of Commerce, 33 Commercial Street, Gloucester, MA 01930; (978) 283–1601 or (800) 321–0133; www.cape-ann.com.

Greater Newburyport Chamber of Commerce, 29 State Street, Newburyport, MA 01950; (978) 462–6680; www.newburyportchamber.org.

Massachusetts Office of Travel & Tourism, 10 Park Plaza, Boston, MA 02116; (617) 973–8500 or (800) 227–MASS; www.massvacation.com.

Rockport Chamber of Commerce, 3 Main Street, Rockport, MA 01966; (978) 546–6575 or (800) 323–0133; www.rockportusa.com.

Salem Chamber of Commerce, 32 Derby Square, Salem, MA 01970; (978) 744–0004; www.salem-chamber.org.

MASSACHUSETTS

The Pioneer Valley

HISTORY AND THE HIPOISIE

2 NIGHTS

Historic settlements • Authors' abodes
Colonial to contemporary crafts • A haven of hipness
Blasts from the past

In heading west from Boston, you'll be pretty much following in the footsteps of the early colonists who soon found Boston and "Newtowne" (Cambridge) a mite crowded. They kept fanning out until they happened upon a fine home-steading site in the fertile alluvial plains flanking the Connecticut River, which doubled for the next several centuries as a kind of nautical interstate.

In retracing their path, you can catch glimpses of the forces that helped shape not only this landscape, but our nation. The route takes in the nearby Revolutionary battle sites in Lexington and Concord (a day trip many Bosto-nians find they never get around to); the extraordinary antiques cache that is Deerfield; the ineffably hip town of Northampton, where the avant-garde thrives in a Hopperesque retro setting; and the living history village of Stur-bridge, where time is willfully suspended circa 1830. It's a somewhat jerky time-travel excursion back and forth among the past three centuries. Take your pick of the sights and sensations covered, and enjoy history a la carte.

DAY 1

Morning

Head out on Route 2 from Cambridge, exiting at Lexington Street for a quick and scenic drive-through of **Lexington** and **Concord,** home to

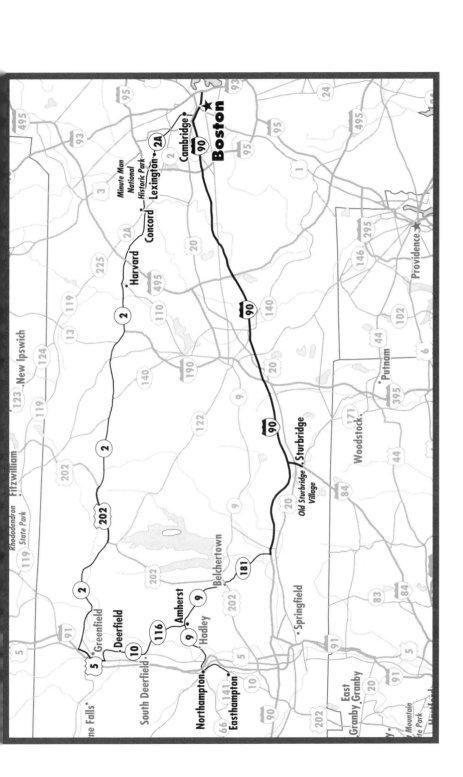

Revolutionary firebrands and, two generations later, idealistic transcendental-ists. Most of their hangouts require a full guided tour, so on this pass, just scope out those worth a lengthier visit—such as the circa 1709 **Buckman Tavern** (781–862–5598; www.lexingtonhistory.org) on Lexington's village green, where, on the night of April 18, 1775, as Paul Revere raced through the coun-tryside, the Minutemen retired for refreshments, convinced that nothing was cooking. Dawn proved them wrong, of course, and it was rumored that the very first bullet fired—for which neither side ever claimed credit—issued from this public house.

Farther west along Route 2A, amid the **Minute Man National Historic Park** (978–369–6993; www.nps.gov/mima), is the "rude" **North Bridge**—or rather, a replica thereof—where the farmer-soldiers stood their ground and, though outnumbered five to one, prevailed. Overlooking the battle-ground and Daniel Chester French's famous statue *The Minute Man* is the **Old Manse** (978–369–3909; www.thetrustees.org), the 1770 farmstead of Con-cord minister William Emerson, whose grandson, Ralph Waldo, would in the mid-nineteenth century turn this rural village into a world-renowned capital of literature and philosophy, with the help of such friends as Nathaniel Hawthorne—who honeymooned at the Manse before buying the **Wayside** (978–369–6975; www.nps.gov/mima/wayside), next to the Alcotts' **Orchard House** (978–369–4118; www.louisamayalcott.org), up the road—and the influential ascetic Henry David Thoreau. The interior of Thoreau's Walden Pond cabin, along with a study moved intact from the **Ralph Waldo Emer-son House** (978–369–2236), is recreated in the **Concord Museum** (978–369–9763; www.concordmuseum.org) at 200 Lexington Road, a must-visit open Monday through Saturday 9:00 A.M. to 5:00 P.M., Sunday noon to 5:00 P.M., with reduced hours January through March. Those longing to commune further with these visionaries might want to take a quick detour north on Bedford Road, out of the center of town, to visit **Authors' Ridge** within the Sleepy Hollow Cemetery (978–318–3230), an eerily evocative setting. Oth-ers, by this point, may find themselves longing for corporeal sustenance.

LUNCH: Guida's Coast Cuisine, 84 Thoreau Street, Concord; (978) 371-1333. The top lunch spot in town, tucked away in the loft of the commuter train station, serves contemporary/Mediterranean fare.

Afternoon

Regaining Route 2, head about 15 miles west and take a short detour to the

Fruitlands Museums (978–456–3924; www.fruitlands.org) at 102 Prospect Hill in Harvard, where the Concord utopians embarked on a short-lived agrarian commune, and Shakers later made a better go of it. The complex, which also includes a fascinating collection of Native American artifacts, is open mid-May to mid-October, daily from 10:00 A.M. to 5:00 P.M.

Your ultimate destination for the day is another 55 miles west on Route 2, then 5 miles south on Route 5. **Historic Deerfield** (413–774–5581; www.historic-deerfield.org) comprises a preserved mile-long Main Street showcasing over a dozen eighteenth- and early nineteenth-century houses packed to the gills with priceless antiques of the appropriate period. Before picking a house or two (each has its distinctive treasures) for a docent-guided tour, pop into **Hall Tavern,** open daily from 9:30 A.M. to 4:30 P.M., for an interesting audiovisual introduction to the town's colorful history.

DINNER: Deerfield Inn, Main Street, Deerfield; (413) 774–5587 or (800) 926–3865; www.deerfieldinn.com. Operated by the same foundation that maintains the houses, the beautifully appointed inn serves an elegant dinner, on the traditional side but with some sophisticated flourishes. Dedicated foodies may prefer to make a 5-mile pilgrimage south to enjoy the highly acclaimed regional/fusion cuisine served at **Sienna,** at 6B Elm Street in South Deerfield (413–665–0215).

LODGING: Deerfield Inn. The twenty-three spacious rooms, all with every modern convenience, are attractively decorated in a neo-Colonial style.

DAY 2

Morning

BREAKFAST: Deerfield Inn.

Time permitting, take a stroll down Main Street, imagining the sights and sounds of daily life two centuries ago—all the easier to do, the earlier you get up. (Cars kind of spoil the mood.) If yesterday's old-house tour left you craving more, venture into one or two (the recommended daily max, to prevent sensory overload). Or press on to **Amherst** (about 5 miles south on Route 5 and another 10 southeast on Route 116) to visit the **Emily Dickinson Homestead** on Main Street (413–542–8161; www.dickinsonhomestead.org), where the celebrated recluse produced her extraordinary oeuvre; forty-five-minute tours are offered by reservation, March through early December. Poke around this college town for a bit if you like, but save the bulk of your time for **Northampton**—aka, "the Paris of New England" or, perhaps more appropriately, "Harvard Square West"—just 5 miles southwest, where you'll find a more vibrant mix of sights, shops, and eateries.

LUNCH: The unofficial center of town is **Thornes Marketplace** at 150 Main Street (413–584–5582; www.thornesmarketplace.com), a warren of trendy boutiques wedged into an imaginatively retrofitted old mercantile building. At its heart is **Paul and Elizabeth's** (413–584–4832), a hippie-holdover vegetarian cafe that's enduringly popular.

Afternoon

First you'll probably want to peruse the alternative retail array. Start your walking/browsing tour with the Guild Art Centre's **Hart Gallery** at 43 Center Street (413–586–4278 or 800–479–6343, www.newenglandart.com), which showcases the work of local luminaries (some 1,500 artists are said to reside in the region). At the foot of Main Street at the **Don Muller Gallery,** number 40 (413–586–1119) carries some rather dazzling crafts: Northampton is the acknowledged epicenter of New England artisanship. Across Main Street, at 1 King Street, a snazzy 1928 art deco bank houses **Silverscape Designs** (413–584–3324; www.silverscapedesigns.com), offering the largest assortment of fine handmade jewelry in the region. Two blocks up, **Ben & Bill's Chocolate Emporium** at 141 Main Street (413–584–5696) tempts with delectable treats made on the premises, as advertised by the shop's seductive aroma. **Pinch!** at 179 Main Street (413–586–4509; www.epinch.com) is a must-visit source of contemporary crafts.

When you've had enough of Mammon, head for **Smith College** on the western edge of town (a pleasant walk) for an aesthetic refresher. The campus is basically a 125-acre botanical garden, designed by Frederick Law Olmsted of Central Park fame; at its heart, on College Lane off Elm Street, is the **Lyman Plant House** (413–585–2740; www.smith.edu/garden), a charming complex of 1890s greenhouses harboring species from around the world. Also visit-worthy is the **Smith College Museum of Art** (413–585–2760; www.smith.edu/artmuseum). This staggering collection sweeps from the Middle Ages to le dernier cri and includes major holdings of French impressionism. Either or both of these peaceful hideaways (call for hours, which vary month to month) would make for a romantic retreat on a blustery afternoon.

DINNER: Spoleto, 50 Main Street, Northampton; (413) 586–6313; www.fun dining.com. Northampton has scores of inviting restaurants, but this is the one not to miss. Chef-owner Claudio Guerra turns out updated Italian classics in a jazzy fishbowl of a contemporary cafe.

LODGING: Hotel Northampton, 36 King Street, Northampton; (413) 584–3100 or (800) 678–8946; www.hotelnorthampton.com. A fine example of the kind of mini-grand hotel that a first-class traveler could expect to come across during the prosperous twenties, this hotel offers seventy-two rooms, recently renovated, and you're mere steps from all the entertainment options in town.

Evening

Find out who's playing at the legendary **Iron Horse Music Hall** at 20 Center Street (www.iheg.com), an intimate space featuring national headliners, or at the Calvin Theatre at 19 King Street (www.calvintheatre.com), an ornate 1924 movie palace turned performing arts center. Tickets can be obtained at the Northampton Box Office in Thornes Marketplace (413–586–8686 or 800–THE–TICK). For other goings-on, consult *The Valley Advocate,* a free alternative weekly (413–247–9301; www.valleyadvocate.com).

DAY 3

Morning

BREAKFAST: Hotel Northampton. Enjoy a bountiful spread in the hotel's eighteenth-century Wiggins Tavern, while debating how to spend the day.

Getting out into the countryside would be a good way to start. You might bike the 17-mile (round-trip) **Norwottuck Rail Trail** (413–586–8706; www.state.ma.us/dem/parks/nwrt.html), linking Northampton, Hadley, and Amherst; or consider boating along the sheltered shore of the big, broad Connecticut, an ideal playground for recreational canoers and kayakers. For rentals and recommendations, call **Wildwater Outfitters** (413–253–5500) on Route 9 in Hadley. If you'd rather explore on foot, two spots are especially appealing. Located on a scenic oxbow in Easthampton, about 4 miles southwest of Northampton (go figure), the 650-acre **Arcadia Nature Center and Wildlife Sanctuary** (413–584–3009; www.massaudubon.org) organizes wildflower walks and hawk watches, as well as guided canoe trips, or you can just meander at will. Or when heading back toward Boston along rural Route 9, you might take a short detour a few miles past Belchertown—much prettier than it sounds—to visit **Quabbin Reservoir** (413–323–7221; www.centralquabbinarea.org), dammed in 1939 to meet Boston's water needs, at the cost of four flooded towns. While exploring the shores, keep an eye out for ancient cellar holes and nesting bald eagles.

LUNCH: Cedar Street Restaurant, 12 Cedar Street, Sturbridge; (508) 347–5800; www.cedarstreetrestaurant.com. Regional fare, adventurously tweaked.

Afternoon

Though **Old Sturbridge Village** (508–347–3362; www.osv.org), with forty vintage buildings spread across 200 acres, may look like a classic New England town circa 1830, it's actually an amazing amalgam pieced together by the Wells brothers, local antiques lovers, starting in the mid-forties. Now a nonprofit educational institution, it does an extraordinary job of conveying the sights, sounds, smells, and even tastes of a bygone era. Costumed interpreters are on hand to demonstrate period crafts and industries, explaining as they go and patiently answering every last question. Each building—gathered from the four corners of New England—has its own appeal, from the stark schoolhouse incised with ancient graffiti to the fancy Federal-style Towne House, a compact farmstead presiding grandly over a reconstituted common. Special events, such as candlelight dinners and "gossips' tours," are held throughout the year; you can call ahead to plan your trip around a particular interest, or just take pot luck and check the computerized list updated daily on the walking map that comes with admission (in-season hours, April through October, are 9:00 A.M. to 5:00 P.M. daily; winter hours are 10:00 A.M. to 4:00 P.M. daily). Mid-afternoon on is actually a great time to wander around and immerse yourself in the past, as the shadows lengthen and the tourist hordes disperse, leaving you alone with history and the props and people that bring it to life.

THERE'S MORE

Ballooning. Pioneer Valley Balloons (413–584–7980; www.pioneervalley balloons.com) takes off daily from Northampton Airport for sunrise and sunset flights.

Kid Stuff. Six Flags, New England's largest amusement park, is located a few miles west of Springfield, at 1623 Main Street in Agawam (413–786–9300

Shoemaking at Old Sturbridge Village

or 877–4–SIXFLAGS; www.sixflags.com): the old "woody" roller coasters are world-class. The Children's Museum at Holyoke Heritage State Park, located at 444 Dwight Street (413–536–KIDS), will also give young bodies and minds a fun workout—as will the interactive exhibits at Springfield's Naismith Memorial Basketball Hall of Fame (413–781–6500; www.hoop hall.org), at 1150 West Columbus Avenue off Route 91.

Museums. Gritty, industrial Springfield might not seem the most enticing of destinations, but for its Quadrangle, or Quad, of exceptional museums at 220 State Street (413–739–3871; www.quadrangle.org), all open Wednesday through Friday from noon to 5:00 P.M. and Saturday through Sunday 11:00 A.M. to 4:00 P.M. The sciences get their due at the Springfield Science Museum, whose interactive exhibits will appeal to all ages. The arts, from fine to decorative, are well represented by the Springfield Museum of Fine Arts, which features American folk art (e.g., portraits by the itinerant painter Rufus Porter) as well as contemporary work; by the George Walter Vincent Smith Art Museum, showcasing the international finds of an obsessive nineteenth-century collector; and by the Connecticut Valley Historical Museum, home to historical artifacts, including outstanding Colonial and Federal furniture.

Performing Arts. Northampton's Academy of Music on Main Street (413–584–8435; www.academyofmusictheatre.com) is among the oldest theaters in the United States. Though it's a little too late to catch the likes of John Barrymore or Anna Pavlova, you might chance upon a traveling troupe or, more likely, the latest art film. Another performance site in town is the Northampton Center for the Arts, just off Main at 17 New South Street (413–584–7327; www.nohoarts.com). It's also worth braving the Brave New World complex that is University of Massachusetts–Amherst to catch headliner performing artists at the Fine Arts Center there (413–545–2511; www. umass.edu/fac).

Riding/Skiing. The Rocking M Ranch (508–248–7075), at 120 Northside Road in Charlton, about 5 miles northwest of Sturbridge on Route 20, converts its bridal paths to cross-country ski trails come winter; either way, they cover 100 rural acres.

SPECIAL EVENTS

Late February. 1704 Weekend, Historic Deerfield; (413) 774–7476; www. historic-deerfield.org. Costumed English Puritans, French soldiers, and Native Americans demonstrate the crafts and customs of the day.

Mid–May, mid–July, and mid–September. Brimfield Outdoor Antiques Show; (413) 283–6149 or (800) 628–8379; www.brimfieldshow.com. The largest flea-market in the country attracts thousands of dealers, and exponential crowds.

Early August. Teddy Bear Rally, Amherst; (413) 549–5165. The town green is overrun with toy bears, plus their owners, collectors, sellers, and healers.

Mid–August. Taste of Northampton; (413) 584–1900; www.northampton uncommon.com. Sample local delicacies, as well as music, crafts, and more.

Mid–October. Paradise City Arts Festival, Northampton; (413) 527–8994; www.paradise-city-com. Crafts/music/food fairs that bring out this creative community's best.

Early November. Northampton Film Festival; (413) 586–3471; www.noho
film.org. Creative types converge for this alternative cine-fest.

December 31. First Night, Northampton; (413) 584–7327; www.nohoarts.
org. The city erupts in close to a hundred performances.

OTHER RECOMMENDED RESTAURANTS AND LODGINGS

Amherst

Allen House Victorian Inn, 599 Main Street; (413) 253–5000; www.allen
house.com. A bold resurrection of William Morris's aesthetic style in an 1886
Queen Anne manse.

Lord Jeffrey Inn, 30 Boltwood Avenue; (413) 253–2576; www.lordjeffrey
inn.com. A comfortable, rambling hostelry offering good regional cuisine.

Concord

Concord's Colonial Inn, 48 Monument Square; (978) 369–9200 or (800) 370–
9200; www.concordscolonialinn.com. A Victorian hotel superimposed on
a 1716 homestead, offering New American cuisine and afternoon tea.

Florence

The Miss Florence Diner, 99 Main Street; (413) 584–3137. Not a whole lot
has changed since 1941; the cream pies are still homemade.

Montague

Blue Heron, 442 Greenfield Road (off Routes 63 and 47); (413) 367–0200.
Creative Americana within an 1834 sawmill turned bookstore.

Northampton

Eastside Grill, 19 Strong Avenue; (413) 586–3347. Exuberant New Orleans–
style bistro fare.

Green Street Café, 62 Green Street, Northampton; (413) 586–5650. Fran-
cophilic New American fare.

La Cazuela, 7 Old South Street; (413) 586–0400; www.lacaz.com. Exceptional
Mexican and Southwestern cuisine.

Northampton Brewery, 11 Brewster Court; (413) 584–9903; www.
northamptonbrewery.com. A spiffy microbrewery offering bountiful eats.

Pizzeria Paradiso, 12 Craft Avenue; (413) 586–1468; www.fundining.com. A
Spoleto satellite.

Springfield

Student Prince and Fort Restaurant, 306 Westfield Street; (413) 734–7375;
www.studentprince.com. A classic German beer hall, pre–World War II.

Sturbridge

Oliver Wight House, Route 20; (508) 347–3327; www.osv.org. A ten-room
1789 Federal inn operated by Old Sturbridge Village.

West Brookfield

The Salem Cross Inn, Route 9; (508) 867–8337; www.salemcrossinn.com. A
1705 ordinary (tavern) that replicates hearth cookery on a massive scale.
Inquire about the drover's roasts held in late summer.

FOR MORE INFORMATION

Greater Northampton Chamber of Commerce, 99 Pleasant Street,
Northampton, MA 01060; (413) 584–1900 or (800) A–FUN–TOWN;
www.northamptonuncommon.com.

Massachusetts Office of Travel & Tourism, 10 Park Plaza, Boston, MA 02116;
(617) 973–8500 or (800) 227–MASS; www.massvacation.com.

MASSACHUSETTS

The Berkshires

A CULTURAL OASIS

2 NIGHTS

Mammoth mansions • Music alfresco
Off-off-off-Broadway theater • Venerable inns • Natural wonders

Prized for its relatively cool summer air (a real premium pre-air-conditioning), this swath of smallish mountains has attracted seasonal rusticators since the 1820s, when local literata Catherine Sedgwick put it on the map by drawing Hawthorne, Emerson, et al. to her backwoods salon. Wherever art flows freely, money inevitably follows, and by the turn of the century the area boasted scores of baronial "cottages" (one such humble abode boasted a hundred rooms, another a porch a mile long). Denizens proudly referred to their retreat as "the inland Newport."

Today the Berkshire region is still known for its residual cache of gargantuan mansions—some have since become museums or luxury inns—and, of course, for its cultural smorgasbord come summer. It's easy enough to zip out along the Mass Pike to catch a specific event (it's only a two-hour trip), but you really need to linger to get the feel of the place and fall under its spell. Just be sure to reserve everything—from tickets to lodging—far enough in advance so you don't get squeezed out by the hordes already enraptured.

DAY 1

Morning

Your objective today will be to reach the northern end of the range, so head westward for about 90 miles along comparatively pretty Route 2; eventually

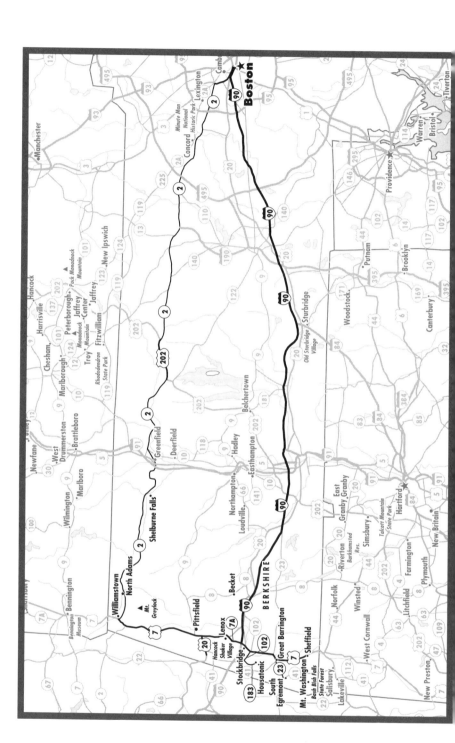

it turns into the **Mohawk Trail,** a scenic park-lined route that evolved from a native footpath. About 10 miles past Greenfield, bear left for a de rigueur detour through the seemingly enchanted village of **Shelburne Falls,** where the Deerfield River has carved out a cascade of granite "potholes"—rounded whirlpools that offer a refreshing, if frigid dip. Stroll around town, stopping in the **Salmon Falls Artisans Showroom** at 176 Ashfield Street (413–625–2544), a handsome former granary turned emporium for fine crafts, and cross the **Bridge of Flowers,** a decommissioned 1908 trolley bridge which local green thumbs have turned into a dazzling aerial garden.

LUNCH: Copper Angel, 2 State Street, Shelburne Falls; (413–625–2727). This celestially themed natural-foods cafe is perched over the garlandlike bridge. Alternately, recherché picnic fixings can be found across the street at **McCusker's Market** (413–625–2548).

Afternoon

Continuing west about 20 miles, you'll descend a dizzying hairpin turn (pull over to take in the view) before entering the postindustrial town of **North Adams,** which now has something major to offer tourists in the form of the **Massachusetts Museum of Contemporary Art** at 87 Marshall Street (413–MOCA111; www.massmoca.org), a thirteen-acre arts center and dotcom-incubator transformed from an electric factory in 1999. It's open daily from 10:00 A.M. to 6:00 P.M. Stop by to see what's shaking—invariably something interesting—then press on to **Williamstown,** where two more extraordinary art museums, both free, await. The **Williams College Museum of Art** on Main Street (413–597–2429; www.williams.edu/wcma) covers the ages from classical to contemporary, paying particular attention to twentieth-century American artists; the hours are Tuesday through Saturday 10:00 A.M. to 5:00 P.M. and Sunday 1:00 to 5:00 P.M. The more expansive **Sterling and Francine Clark Art Institute** at 225 South Street (413–458–2303; www.clark.williams.edu), open Tuesday through Sunday 10:00 A.M. to 5:00 P.M. (daily in July and August), focuses primarily on the past two centuries, and especially the French impressionists. Having plundered these collections, wander along Spring Street, Williamstown's downtown, where shops like **The Library Antiques** at number 70 (413–458–3436) may better suit your acquisitions budget.

DINNER: Main Street Café, 15 Water Street, Williamstown; (413) 458–3210. Join the local cognoscenti for delightful Mediterranean fare.

LODGING: The Orchards, 222 Adams Road, Williamstown; (413) 458–9611 or (800) 225–1517; www.orchardshotel.com. Though not optimally located (on a commercial strip east of the campuslike town center), this neo-country inn features fifty luxurious, antiques-lavished rooms, plus a spa and outdoor pool.

Evening

After enjoying a night of superlative drama at the **Williamstown Theatre Festival** (413–597–3400; www.wtfestival.org)—a must in-season—you can unwind along with the actors, from unknowns to quite well-knowns, at a postplay cabaret at Williams College's nearby Goodrich Hall.

DAY 2

Morning

BREAKFAST: The Orchards. Most delectable in bed.

View seekers will want to ascend **Mount Greylock,** at 3,491 feet the highest peak in Massachusetts. You can enter the 12,000-acre Mount Greylock State Reservation (413–499–4262; www.state.ma.us/dem/parks/mgry.htm) by way of Notch Road off Route 2 just east of Williamstown, climb the 100-foot thirties-deco tower on top, and exit about 4 miles southwest onto Route 7 in Lanesborough.

Museum lovers have their pick of several in this area, including **Arrowhead** at 780 Holmes Road off Route 7 about 20 miles south in **Pittsfield** (413–442–1793; www.mobydick.org). Here, from 1850 to 1862, while landlocked in a predominantly female household, Herman Melville labored mightily over *Moby-Dick,* drawing on Greylock's hulking profile for inspiration. (Half-hour tours take place daily from 10:00 A.M. to 4:00 P.M. in season.) The small but pleasant **Berkshire Museum** at 39 South Street in Pittsfield (413–443–7171; www.berkshiremuseum.org) encompasses history and natural science exhibits as well as artwork, with an emphasis on eighteenth-century portraits and Hudson River School landscapes; in-season hours are Tuesday through Saturday, 10:00 A.M. to 5:00 P.M., and Sunday 1:00 to 5:00 P.M.

For a fascinating side trip back a century or so, detour 5 miles west on Route 20 to visit **Hancock Shaker Village** (413–443–0188 or 800–817–1137; www.hancockshakervillage.org), founded in 1790 by followers of Mother Ann Lee. Though practitioners in the United States now number in the single digits (the inevitable outcome of a creed requiring celibacy), admirers maintain this 1,200-acre, twenty-building utopian farming community with showcase herb gardens and a round stone barn (as handy for the occasional art or antiques show as it was for feeding and mucking cows). In-season hours are 9:30 A.M. to 5:00 P.M. daily; off, 10:00 A.M. to 3:00 P.M.

Although "'tis a gift to be simple," as the Shaker hymn goes, 'tis surely sometimes a treat not to be, and in **Lenox,** about 7 miles south of Pittsfield on Route 7, you can segue effortlessly into the all-out luxe of Gilded Age indulgence.

LUNCH: Church Street Cafe, 65 Church Street, Lenox; (413) 637–2745. This charming contemporary bistro with outdoor deck offers light, lyrical, New York-level cuisine.

Afternoon

Troll the shops in town, including **R. W. Wise** at 81 Church Street (413–637–1589; www.polygon.net/~rwwise) for sleek contemporary jewelry; **Mary Stuart** at 69 Church for recherché home goods and baby gifts (413–637–0340); **Michael Charles Cabinetmakers** at number 53 (413–637–3483; www.michaelcharles.com) for custom wood furniture; **Tanglewool** (413–637–0900) and **Evviva**! (413–637–9875), both on Walker Street, for city-slicker takes on country chic. Take in a **Tanglewood** rehearsal or concert—see Special Events, below—or just wander about the estate's gorgeous grounds. The **Museum of the Gilded Age** at 104 Walker Street (413–637–3206; www.gildedage.org) is itself a survivor of the era: Ventfort Hall, an 1893 Arthur Rotch concoction, was saved from the wrecker's ball to showcase Lenox's glory days (tours are offered at 11:30 A.M., 12:30, 1:30, and 2:30 P.M. in season). A crenelated Elizabethan Revival monstre sacré, it's mirrored—and mocked—by **The Mount** (413–637–1899; www.edithwharton.org), on Plunkett Street a short drive south of town. Built in 1902 by New York socialite Edith Wharton, an avatar of interior design and budding novelist, this handsome Classic Revival manse represented her retort to the stylistic excesses of the day. Acolytes are welcome on hour-long tours 9:00 A.M. to 5:00 P.M. in season.

DINNER AND LODGING: Wheatleigh, Hawthorne Road, Lenox; (413) 637–0610 or 800–321–0610; www.wheatleigh.com. This Palladian palazzo, built in 1893 for an American-born contessa (evidently one of Wharton's title-collecting "buccaneers"), fulfills every possible princessly yearning—at an admittedly regal price. The nineteen rooms are drop-dead dreamy, especially one replete with carved cupids; the nouvelle cuisine, positively transcendental.

The Mount, built by Edith Wharton, is a comparatively modest "cottage."

Evening

You'll probably want to head out to partake of the area's cultural offerings—perhaps more music at nearby Tanglewood, or stellar summer theater at the **Berkshire Theatre Festival** in Stockbridge (413–298–5536; www. berkshiretheatre.org), or modern dance at **Jacob's Pillow** (413–243–0745; www.jacobspillow.org) in Becket, about 10 country miles east. But it's awfully tempting just to stay put and revel in utmost luxury.

DAY 3

Morning

BREAKFAST: Wheatleigh. Abed again, or, if you're feeling sociable, among your fellow connoisseurs in the dining room with its massive tiled hearth.

Lest you turn elitist, it's time to soak up some good old Americana at the **Norman Rockwell Museum,** about 1 mile southwest on Route 183 in Stockbridge (413–298–4100; www.nrm.org). Much of the popular illustrator's work, plus his studio, transported, can be found within this spiffy, site-appropriate museum designed in 1993 by Robert A. M. Stern. Whatever you think of the artist going in, your estimation is sure to inch up several notches once you've seen the range of his oeuvre—some of it confrontational rather than commercial. Hours are 10:00 A.M. to 5:00 P.M. daily (to 4:00 P.M. in winter).

Just down the road, on Williamsville Road off Route 183, is another artist's shrine, **Chesterwood** (413–298–3579), longtime summer home to the nation's preeminent public sculptor, Daniel Chester French. Among his more notable works were Concord's *The Minute Man* and Washington's Lincoln Memorial. Today the house and studio are open for touring (the studio can even be rented for overnights), and the beautifully landscaped grounds showcase French's and other, more modern, work, from 10:00 A.M. to 5:00 P.M. in-season.

Though no artist ever resided at **Naumkeag** (413–298–3239; www.thetrustees.org) on Prospect Hill Road about 1 mile northwest of Stockbridge's town center—it was built in 1885 for a wealthy attorney/diplomat—an artist did design this gabled Gilded Age mansion: the renowned, indeed notorious architect Stanford White. The house is packed with Chinese export treasures, and tours are offered in-season daily 10:00 A.M. to 5:00 P.M. The gardens manage to outshine the house, with lovely environments such as the peony terrace and the famous Birchwalk, a delicate braid of stairways, grottos, and pale trees.

All this sightseeing has earned you rocker time on the porch at the **Red Lion Inn** (413–298–5545 or 800–876–6123; www.redlioninn.com), for two hundred years the social center of Stockbridge. Nonguests are welcome to explore the antiques-appointed common rooms, highly evocative of a bygone era, and those planning a little home improvement of their own will want to browse the **Country Curtains** shop within the inn (413–243–1300 or 800–937–1237; www.countrycurtains.com). A little mews just down Main boasts two vintage jewelry shops: **Heirlooms** (413–298–4436) and **Greystone Gardens** (413–298–0113). If you'd rather stretch your legs than your budget, look for Park Street two blocks south, and follow it and then signs to the **Ice Glen,** a scenic ravine that remains spookily cool straight through the summer.

LUNCH: Jacks Grill, Main Street, Housatonic; (413) 274–1000; www.jacksgrill.com. If your taste runs to trendy-casual, head to this Red Lion Inn

satellite within a milltown just beginning to discover its own retro charm. Here, amid various kitsch collections, a toy train zips overhead as patrons enjoy jazzed-up comfort food. Or head southwest another 10 miles—through increasingly trendy Great Barrington—to **South Egremont,** to enjoy a leisurely, inventive brunch in the garden at **John Andrew's** on rural Route 23 (413–528–3469).

Afternoon

If you lunch in Housatonic, you could follow up with a walking tour of the galleries beginning to sprout like mushrooms in the old mill buildings. A South Egremont repast, on the other hand, will leave you perfectly situated to scavenge the dozens of excellent antiques shops here and in **Sheffield** to the southeast. The one not to miss is the **Splendid Peasant** on Route 23 at Old Sheffield Road in South Egremont (413–528–5755; www.splendidpeasant. com), a museum-quality repository of country primitives and folk art. Fancier finds are likely at **Darr Antiques and Interiors** at 28 South Main Street in Sheffield (413–229–7773).

Or you could use your few remaining hours before heading home to explore the naturally artful countryside. Twelve miles southwest of South Egremont is **Bash Bish Falls State Park** (413–528–0330; www.state.ma. us/dem/parks/bash.htm), where a roaring 60-foot torrent funneled between granite cliff faces and deep woods invite clambering and roaming. To catch the sunset piercing the falls' eternal mist is to have some idea of the marvels that awaited westward-bound adventurers centuries ago.

THERE'S MORE

Crafts. A great many artisans have sought shelter in these hills, and their output is ubiquitous. You can visit Undermountain Weavers (413–274–6565) and the Berkshire Center for Contemporary Glass (413–232–4666; www. berkshireweb.com/bcfcg) in the pretty village of West Stockbridge. Amid the reclaimed factories of Housatonic you'll find Great Barrington Pottery (413–274–6259; www.greatbarringtonpottery.com) and Vigneron Design Studio (413–274–6619), as well as many others.

Historic houses. Maintained by the Trustees of Reservations (413–298–3239; www.thetrustees.org), the 1739 Mission House on Stockbridge's

Main Street features period furnishings and a colonial garden. A somewhat younger Society for the Preservation of New England Antiques property, the brick-walled Merwin House at 14 West Main Street (413–298–4703; www.spnea.org) is a fine example of late Federal style, down to the delicate fanlight. Old-house hunters will also want to seek out the 1750 Bidwell House at 100 Art School Road in Monterey (413–528–6888; www.berkshireweb.com/bidwellhouse) and the 1735 Colonel John Ashley House on Cooper Hill Road in Ashley Falls (413–298–3239; www.thetrustees.org), thought to be the Berkshires' oldest abode.

Kid stuff. Restive young travelers will appreciate a swoop down the alpine slide at Jiminy Peak in Hancock (413–738–5500 or 888–4–JIMINY; www.jiminypeak.com) and a splash in the cooling waters of the Sand Springs Pool in Williamstown (413–458–5205). There's a dazzlingly beautiful waterfall swimming hole within Wahconah Falls State Park off Route 9 in Dalton (413–442–8992; www.state.ma.us/dem/parks/wahf.htm).

Museums. If you've already done the basics, consider the Crane Museum on South Street off Route 9 in Dalton (413–684–2600; www.crane.com), an 1844 stone mill covering the history of American paper-making, including currency.

Nature walks. The region is rife with lovely preserves, from smallish Monument Mountain in Great Barrington (413–298–3239) to Bartholomew's Cobble off Route 7A in Ashley Falls (413–229–8600; www.thetrustees.org), which consists of a natural rock garden covering nearly 300 acres and harboring over 700 species.

Outdoor adventures. Undermountain Farm on 400 Undermountain Road in rural Lenox (413–637–3365) offers guided trail rides, as does Horsesense at 87 Golden Hill Road in Lenoxdale (413–637–1999; www.goldenhillfarm.com). Berkshire Mountain Llama Hike in Lee (413–243–2224; www.bcn.net/llamahike) and Moon Mountain Llamas in Great Barrington (413–528–5056) offer an Andean assist, plus companionship. Berkshire Sculling at 43 Roselyn Drive in Pittsfield (413–496–9160; www.berkshiresculling.com) offers rentals and instruction by appointment. Or you could join Zoar Outdoor (413–339–4010 or 800–532–7483; www.zoaroutdoor.com) in various white-water rafting, canoeing, or kayaking excursions along the scenic rivers of the region, from April to mid-October; Zoar also offers rock-climbing clinics. In winter, four local ski areas will satisfy the needs of novice-to-intermediates: Butternut (Route 23 in Great Barrington; 413–528–2000; www.skibutternut.com); Catamount (Route 23 in South Egremont; 413–528–1262 or 800–342–1840; www.catamountski. com); Brodie (Route 7 in New Ashford; 413–443–4752; www.skibrodie. com); and Jiminy Peak (37 Corey Road, between Routes 7 and 43 in Hancock; 413–738–5500 or 800–882–8859; www.jiminypeak.com).

SPECIAL EVENTS

Mid-May to mid-September. The Guthrie Center Summer Concert Series, Great Barrington; (413) 528–1955; www.guthriecenter.org. Singer-songwriters flock to the interfaith church founded in Alice's former abode—the 1829 Trinity Church—by Arlo Guthrie.

Mid-May through October. Shakespeare and Company, Lenox; (413) 637–3353; www.shakespeare.org. The reliably radical theater troupe honors contemporary playwrights as well as the Bard.

Late May to early September. Berkshire Opera Company, Great Barrington; (413) 443–1234; www.berkop.org. From classics to world premieres, presented in the Mahaiwe, a 1905 movie palace.

Late June. Williamstown Film Festival; (413) 458–2700; www.williamstown filmfest.com. New American indies, plus tributes to classics.

Late June to early September. Tanglewood Music Festival, Lenox; (413) 637–5165 or (800) 274–8499; www.bso.org. The 200-acre state comes alive with the sounds of the Boston Symphony Orchestra.

Mid-July to early August. Aston Magna Festival, Great Barrington; (413) 528–3595; www.astonmagna.org. Early music is performed on period instruments at the St. James Church.

Mid-July to mid-August. Berkshire Choral Festival, Sheffield; (413) 229–8526; www.choralfest.org. Avid choristers from around the country work with outstanding conductors and soloists to put on weekly concerts.

Early August. Monument Mountain Climb, Great Barrington; (413) 442–1793. Aficionados replicate the outing—complete with picnic—made by Herman Melville and Nathaniel Hawthorne in 1850.

Mid-August. Hancock Shaker Village Antiques Show; (413) 443–0188 or (800) 817–1137; www.hancockshakervillage.org. A good excuse to visit the village and perhaps export some of its atmosphere.

Early September. A Taste of the Berkshires, Great Barrington; (413) 528–1947. Over fifty restaurants show their stuff, to benefit local charities.

Mid-September. Tub Parade, Lenox; (413) 637–3646 or (800) 255–3609; www.lenox.org. Continuing a Gilded Age tradition, ladies and children drive flower-strewn "tubs"—two-wheeled pony carts—through the streets of town.

Early October. Harvest Festival, Stockbridge; (413) 298–3926; www.berkshire botanical.org. All the traditional fixings: a pancake breakfast, fresh-pressed cider, farmer's market, hayrides.

Early December. Main Street at Christmas, Stockbridge; (413) 298–5200; www.stockbridgechamber.org. This all-American town reverts to its Norman Rockwell image with decorations and antique cars.

OTHER RECOMMENDED RESTAURANTS AND LODGINGS

Great Barrington

Marketplace Kitchen at Guido's, 760 South Main Street; (413) 528–5775 or (888) 5–CHEFS–4; www.marketplacekitchen.com. A highly glorified farmstand with terrific prepared food.

Thornewood Inn, 453 Stockbridge Road; (413) 528–3828 or (800) 854–1008; www.thornewood.com. A tastefully appointed Dutch Colonial home whose restaurant, Spencer's, serves a Sunday jazz brunch.

Union Bar & Grill, 293 Main Street; (413) 528–6228. A modernist satellite of the elegant John Andrew's, this brushed-steel box is aggressively chic, a lively, high-tech temple of world cuisine.

Verdura, 44 Railroad Street (Route 7); (413) 528–8969; www.verdura.net. Chef/co-owner William Webber (once of Wheatleigh) provides polished North Italian *cucina rustica*.

Lanesboro

Bascom Lodge, at the summit of Mount Greylock; (413) 443–0011, www.outdoors.org. This stone lodge built by the Civilian Conservation Corps in the 1930s offers a rare opportunity to rough it—comfily—in the Berkshires, with two hearty communal meals and the option of nature programs and art workshops.

Lee

Applegate, 279 West Park Street; (413) 243–4451 or (800) 691–9012; www.applegateinn.com. Six spacious rooms in a 1920s pillared Colonial with pool amid a six-acre orchard.

Devonfield, 85 Stockbridge Road; (413) 243–3298; www.devonfield.com. Once the summer home of Queen Wilhelmina of the Netherlands, this expanded Federal manse is as homey as it is elegant; amenities include a heated in-ground pool, tennis court, and bicycles.

Lenox

Birchwood Inn, 7 Hubbard Street; (413) 637–2600 or (800) 524–1646; www.birchwood-inn.com. A gracious Colonial overlooking Lenox village.

Bistro Zinc, 56 Church Street; (413) 637–8800. Very chic, down to the salmon leather banquettes, with a citified sensibility.

Blantyre, 16 Blantyre Road (off Route 20); (413) 637–3556; www.blantyre.com. Mock Tudor grandeur on eighty-five manicured acres, including a world-class croquet court. Dinners are befittingly baronial.

Canyon Ranch, Bellefontaine, 165 Kemble Street; (413) 637–4100 or (800) 742–9900; www.canyonranch.com. New England's most luxurious spa centers on an 1890s cottage modeled on Le Petit Trianon.

Kemble Inn, 2 Kemble Street; (413) 637–4113 or (800) 353–4113; www.kembleinn.com. A lovely 1881 mansion hidden in the village, with a view to the mountains.

New Marlborough

Old Inn on the Green and Gedney Farm, Route 57; (413) 229–3131 or (800) 826–3139; www.oldinn.com. Stellar New American cuisine in a restored

1760 stagecoach inn; some suites in the adjoining Gedney Farm, a Norman-style barn, feature whirlpools and flickering fireplaces.

North Adams

The Porches, 231 River Street; (413) 664–0400; www.porches.com. The Red Lion folks took six worker's cottages and turned them into a fifty-room complex—complete with heated pool—a stone's throw from MOCA.

Sheffield

Race Brook Lodge, 684 Undermountain Road; (413) 229–2916; www.rblodge.com. This renovated country barn has a communal country look and a mood to match; it's ideally situated for mountainside hikes.

South Egremont

The Old Mill, Route 23; (413) 528–1421. Creative continental cuisine in a beautifully spare 1797 grist mill.

South Lee

Federal House, Route 102; (413) 243–1824. A grand colonnaded 1824 brick manse, with seven lovely guest rooms and a fine restaurant.

Historic Merrell Inn, 1565 Pleasant Street (Route 102); (413) 243–1794 or (800) 243–1794; www.merrell-inn.com. At this beautifully restored 1792 stagecoach tavern, a birdcage bar lends local color to breakfast; the riverside gazebo is perfect for lazing.

Stockbridge

Inn at Brookside, 1 Interlaken Road (Route 183); (413) 298–3099; www.innatbrookside.com. This 1850 Colonial home adjoins the Berkshire Botanical Garden and extends its beauty.

Once Upon a Table, the Mews, 36 Main Street; (413) 298–3870. A charming little chef-owned cafe.

Taggart House, 18 Main Street; (413) 298–4303; www.taggarthouse.com. An extravagantly appointed Gilded Age mansion with ballroom, billiard room, library—the works.

West Stockbridge

La Bruschetta, 1 Harris Street; (413) 232–7141. Superb regional Italian cuisine served riverside in a charming little town.

The Williamsville Inn, Route 41; (413) 274–6118; www.williamsvilleinn.com. The ten acres surrounding this 1797 farmhouse harbor a pool and clay tennis court; dinner in the tavern earned accolades in *Bon Appetit*.

Williamstown

Field Farm Guest House, 554 Sloan Road off Route 43; (413) 458–3135; www.thetrustees.org. A 1948 American Modern mansion with pool and tennis courts set amid nearly 300 acres of conservation land.

Hobson's Choice, 159 Water Street; (413) 458–9101. A fresh take on New England decor and dining.

River Bend Farm, 643 Simonds Road; (413) 458–3121; www.cycle-logical. com/riverbend. A five-bedroom 1770 Georgian Colonial featuring classic four-posters—including a few authentic rope beds with feather mattresses.

FOR MORE INFORMATION

Berkshires Visitors Bureau, Berkshire Common, Pittsfield, MA 01201; (413) 443–9186 or (800) BERKSHR; www.berkshires.org.

Massachusetts Office of Travel & Tourism, 10 Park Plaza, Boston, MA 02116; (617) 973–8500 or (800) 227–MASS; www.massvacation.com.

Plymouth and the Upper Cape

CRADLE OF THE COUNTRY

2 NIGHTS

Colonial days recaptured • A model factory town
Wild beaches • Breakthroughs in marine biology
A Native American "plantation"

That Plymouth should be considered the nucleus of the United States is questionable: the Pilgrims, after all, first touched down in what is now Provincetown. There's even talk that the authenticity of Plymouth Rock is pure apocrypha, hearsay handed down through the generations. But in erecting a monument around it in 1921, the Daughters of the American Revolution rendered it a shrine—one that attracts more than a million visitors a year to "America's Hometown."

The trick to enjoying Plymouth is ignoring all the tourist hype and immersing yourself in Puritan culture—best achieved at the remarkable recreation that is Plimoth Plantation. A further foray onto the Cape provides a fascinating précis of subsequent developments: the clash between native and Colonial cultures, the onset of the Industrial Revolution, the latest frontiers in oceanic research. And, of course, it doesn't hurt that you're never more than a few miles from some sand to stretch out on.

DAY 1

Morning

Heading Capeward on Route 3, forgo the first Plymouth exit for the one marked **Plimoth Plantation** (508–746–1622; www.plimoth.org). Once

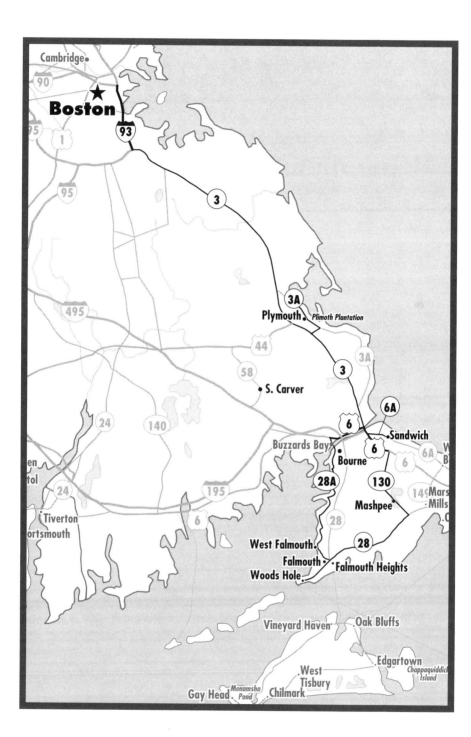

Plimoth Plantation recreates every detail of Colonial life

you've passed through the handsome welcome center designed by Graham Gund (catch the audiovisual show should your Colonial history need refreshing), you're ready to enter into the stockaded village and soak up the sights, sounds, smells, and curious convictions of Puritan life. The skilled actors playing specific colonists of the year 1627 will be busy attending to their tasks, but will gladly explain them, or anything else you have a mind to discuss: whether marriage is a matter for church or state, for example, or what herb best soothes poison ivy. Allow enough time for your self-consciousness to subside, and you can really have an extraordinary experience, fresh every visit. Museum hours are 9:00 A.M. to 5:00 P.M. daily in-season, and a combination ticket will also admit you to the replica *Mayflower,* berthed in Plymouth harbor, about 3 miles northwest on Route 3A.

Clamber about the cramped boat for a bit (it seems unimaginable that the original vessel carried over a hundred "saints and sinners" for a tumultuous two months), then wander about town. Northward on the harbor is the

Cranberry World Visitors Center at 158 Water Street (508–747–2350; www.oceanspray.com), a mini-museum devoted to the history of the profitable crop. A parting sample should give you enough juice to zigzag a couple of blocks southwest to visit the **Pilgrim Hall Museum** at 75 Court Street (508–746–1620; www.pilgrimhall.org), a handsome granite Greek Revival temple designed by Alexander Parris in 1824. Here you'll find real *Mayflower* relics, from John Alden's halberd to elder William Brewster's wooden chair, and the cradle of Peregrine White, born onboard. The town itself is not that enchanting (too many modern incursions), but you can get a more historic perspective by climbing **Burial Hill,** where the Pilgrims interred their dead—half their number, that first harsh winter—by night rather than advertise their dwindling population to possibly hostile tribes. The *Mayflower's* flag—British, of course—waves gaily from the harbor.

LUNCH: Crane Brook Tea Room, 229 Tremont Street, South Carver; (508) 866–3235. It's worth detouring a few miles southwest to lunch at this New American restaurant housed in a former iron foundry.

Afternoon

You'd never guess, pulling into the tidy little town of **Sandwich** (about 20 miles southeast of Plymouth via Routes 3 and 6A), that in the mid-nineteenth century this was an industrial hotbed where dark satanic mills cranked out the first mass-produced glassware accessible to the common citizen. Today the town has reverted to its original New England primness, and Sandwich glass has become something of a holy grail for collectors. You can learn all about its history—the town's, too—at the **Sandwich Glass Museum/Historical Society** at 129 Main Street (508–888–0251; www.sandwichglassmuseum.org), open daily in-season from 9:30 A.M. to 5:00 P.M.

Sandwich is perfectly scaled for strolling. Catercorner from the museum, and opposite the handsome 1834 Greek Revival Town Hall, still in use, stop in at **H. Richard Strand Antiques** at 2 Grove Street (508–888–3230) to view an exceptional cache. Continuing along Grove Street, you'll come upon **Old Cemetery Point** overlooking placid Shawme Pond. It's fascinating to wander among the centuries-old tombstones with their carved death's-heads and stern epitaphs.

Circling back around the pond to the center of town, you'll pass the 1640 **Dexter's Grist Mill** (508–888–4910), restored so that it again grinds corn into meal (available for sale in summer); also at this end of the pond is an artesian well offering cool water of exceptional purity. Should you need more in the way of sustenance, pause for refreshments at the charming British-run **Dunbar Tea Shop** at 1 Water Street (508–833–2485; www.dunbarteashop.com). Further up Water Street, on the pond side, is the **Thornton W. Burgess Museum** (508–888–6870; www.thorntonburgess.org), a sweet little cottage celebrating the works of a prolific local children's author (it's open Monday through Saturday 10:00 A.M. to 4:00 P.M. and Sunday 1:00 to 4:00 P.M. in-season), and the circa 1675 **Hoxie House** (508–888–1173; www.sandwichmass.com), a striking saltbox furnished with Colonial antiques on loan from Boston's Museum of Fine Arts. Hours are Monday through Saturday 10:00 A.M. to 5:00 P.M., Sunday noon to 5:00 P.M. mid-June to mid-September.

Amble down School Street to reach Main Street, then zigzag left and right to reach **Madden & Co.** at number 16 (508–888–6434), a stylish blend of country-primitive antiques and compatible contemporary accessories. Also browse-worthy is the multidealer **Sandwich Antiques Center** at the intersection of Route 6A (508–833–3600).

DINNER AND LODGING: Belfry Inne, 8 Jarves Street, Sandwich; (508) 888–8550 or (800) 844–4542; www.belfryinn.com. A turreted "painted lady" plus neighboring church, converted into luxurious quarters and a bistro serving deft New American fare.

DAY 2

Morning

BREAKFAST: Belfry Inne.

Make your first (open-ended) stop **Heritage Plantation,** a ½-mile drive to 130 Grove Street (508–888–3300; www.heritageplantation.org), open daily from mid-May through October from 10:00 A.M. to 5:00 P.M. This extraordinary seventy-six-acre complex reflects the collectomania of late local benefactor Josiah Kirby Lilly. A replica Shaker round barn houses a fleet of vintage cars, and the folk art collection includes a working circa 1912 carousel with amazing animal mounts; unlimited rides come free with admission. Crisscrossed with foot trails (a jitney serves the tired of feet), the show gardens are gorgeous any time of year, but especially in May and June when hundreds of carefully crossbred rhododendrons burst forth in multicolored bloom.

Heading westward along Route 6A toward Buzzards Bay, you might want to visit the **Aptucxet Trading Post Museum** at 24 Aptucxet Road off Parry

Avenue in Bourne Village (508–759–9487; www.bournehistoricalsoc.org), open Monday through Saturday 10:00 A.M. to 5:00 P.M., Sunday 2:00 to 5:00 P.M. May to mid-October. This on-site recreation of the United States' first store contains a quirky little collection of pre-Colonial artifacts and affords a nice view of the **Cape Cod Canal** and the 1935 **Vertical Lift Railroad Bridge,** an aesthetic as well as engineering feat.

Meandering down tree-lined Route 28A, consider a brief shopping stop in **West Falmouth,** where you'll find international clothing at **Europa,** 628 Route 28A (508–540–7814), and a hodgepodge of antiques at the **Village Barn,** 606 Route 28A (508–540–3215).

LUNCH: **The Chickadee,** 881 Old Palmer Avenue at Saconesset Hill Drive, West Falmouth; (508) 548–4006. A soup or salad plucked fresh from the field will leave you feeling virtuous enough to justify packing away some tasty home-baked pastry.

Afternoon

Continuing down Route 28A, you'll enter the village of **Falmouth.** Take a left on Palmer Avenue to circle the village green, where Colonial militia started training in the mid-eighteenth century—well in time to fend off a British invasion during the War of Independence. On the northern side of the common, at 55–65 Palmer Avenue, are the volunteer-run **Falmouth Historical Society Museums** (508–548–4857; www.falmouthhistoricalsociety.org), open for tours Tuesday through Saturday 10:00 A.M. to 4:00 P.M. in season; it may be enough just to admire the pillared facade of the otherwise modest **Julia Wood House,** built in 1790. Returning to North Main Street via West Main, you'll pass the birthplace of Falmouth's most celebrated native daughter, Katharine Lee Bates, who wrote the poem that became "America the Beautiful."

Press on to **Woods Hole,** where you can catch up on what's new in the watery two-thirds of the world at the **Woods Hole Oceanographic Institute Exhibit Center,** 15 School Street off Water Street (508–289–2252; www.whoi.edu), open Tuesday through Saturday 10:00 A.M. to 4:30 P.M. and Sunday noon to 4:00 P.M. in season (off-season hours vary). If displays of curiosities and videos of amazing voyages whet your appetite for the mysteries of the deep, you could follow up with a free visit to the **Woods Hole Science aquarium** at 166 Water Street (508–495–2000; www.nefsc. nmfs.gov/nefsc/aquarium/ocean.html), open daily in-season 10:00 A.M. to 4:00 P.M., or play researcher yourself and collect actual data during a 1½-

hour hands-on harbor cruise with the nonprofit educational organization **Ocean Quest** (508–385–7656 or 800–376–2326).

After all that salt water, you might want to pause for refreshments at one of the community's atmospheric bars and cafes, such as the rough-hewn **Cap'n Kidd** at 77 Water Street (508–548–9206), where locals hobnob with Nobel scientists. Return to Falmouth along the water, by way of Nobska Road, so you can take in the picturesque sight of **Nobska Lighthouse** and its view of the **Elizabeth Islands.**

DINNER: Regatta of Falmouth-by-the-Sea, 217 Clinton Avenue; (508) 548–5400; www.theregattas.com. Located at the mouth of Falmouth Harbor is one of the finest restaurants on the Cape, as well as one of the prettiest. The all-pink color scheme picks up on some pretty spectacular sunsets, and the New American cuisine is seductive in the extreme.

LODGING: Inn on the Sound, 313 Grand Avenue South, Falmouth Heights; (508) 547–9666 or (800) 564–9668; www.innonthesound.com. Sharing a bluff with other turn-of-the-century shingled manses, this ten-room bed-and-breakfast is breezily chic—and the view toward Martha's Vineyard is simply glorious. The sound of gentle surf will lull you to sleep.

DAY 3

Morning

BREAKFAST: Inn on the Sound. Banana-stuffed French toast, anyone? Or whatever indulgence appears on the carte du jour.

It will be very tempting just to beach it from here, and you're certainly welcome to—right at the foot of the bluff (a popular collegiate scene, it tends to get crowded), or about 10 miles eastward in **Mashpee,** in relative seclusion at the 450-acre **South Cape Beach State Park** (508–457–0495; www.state. ma.us/dem/parks/socp.htm). Mashpee was originally a "plantation" granted in perpetuity to the "praying Indians" of the Wampanoag tribe in 1660. Most of that land was gradually sold off or pilfered, but you can learn a lot about the area's history by conferring with a custodian at the 1684 **Old Indian Meetinghouse** (508–477–0208) on Route 28 just past the superficially pleasant but rather appalling **Mashpee Commons** mall (508–477–5400; www.mashpeecommons.com); within the meetinghouse, be sure to see the schooners inscribed in the gallery by some restless young reprobate of the nineteenth century.

LUNCH: The Flume, Lake Avenue (off Route 130), Mashpee; (508) 477–1456. Earl Mills is not only a Wampanoag chief but an excellent chef, and at his tasteful country restaurant you can feast on such Cape classics as clam chowder, codfish cakes, and what the colonists were happy to adapt as Indian pudding.

Afternoon

You don't want to linger too long, as the homeward-bound traffic quickly turns to sludge. But for one last glimpse of the Cape primeval, visit the **Lowell Holly Reservation** off South Sandwich Road (617–921–1944; www.thetrustees.org). This 135-acre preserve jutting out into the Cape's two largest freshwater lakes shelters not only hundreds of holly trees, but stands of indigenous beeches untouched for several centuries. Prowl the paths looking for rare wildflowers (no picking!) before heading reluctantly home.

THERE'S MORE

Arts and antiques. Collectors will want to stop in at the Woods Hole Gallery, 14 School Street (508–548–4329), and the Falmouth Artists Guild, 744 Main Street (508–540–3304), to check out the best of local talent. Appealing crafts can be found at Woods Hole Handworks, 68 Water Street (508–540–5291). The antique selection at Horsefeathers, 454 Route 6A in East Sandwich (508–888–5298), is leavened with lace and linen.

Bargain Shopping. Don't let the name mislead you: The Christmas Tree Shop (508–888–7010), an overgorwn thatched cottage beside the Sagamore bridge, with several branches elsewhere on the Cape, has little to do with holiday folderol; instead it's a great source of off-price home goods.

Beaches. A 6-mile barrier beach (that is, a peninsula running parallel to shore), Sandy Neck Beach in East Sandwich (508–362–8300) affords the rare opportunity, in these parts, to get away from the crowds if you're willing to hike. Walkable via the Sandwich Boardwalk over the marsh, Town Neck Beach is a bit rocky but a nice vantage point for viewing the canal boat traffic. Falmouth's many sound-side beaches have a bit more surf— though they're nowhere near as thrashing as those of the Outer Cape.

Bike paths. Spanning Bourne and Sagamore, the 14-mile loop flanking the Cape Cod Canal offers a scenic, easy ride. In Falmouth, the 3⅘-mile Shining Sea Bikeway links Falmouth to Woods Hole, hugging the bay, and connects with 24 more miles of marked blacktop. For directions and rentals, visit Holiday Cycles at 465 Grand Avenue in Falmouth Heights (508–540–3549).

Historic houses. A standout among the Cape's many ancient dwellings, the 1641 Wing House at 69 Spring Hill Road in East Sandwich (508–833–1540) has remained in the same family for 3½ centuries, and shows an interesting sequence of decorative styles.

Horseback riding. Haland Stable, 878 Route 28A, West Falmouth (508–540–2552), offers English-style lessons and escorted trail rides through forests and colorful cranberry bogs.

Kid stuff. Built in the late fifties, the eighteen-hole Sandwich Minigolf course at 157 Route 6A (508–933–1905) replicates local architecture and features what may be the world's only floating green. The Cape Cod Children's Museum can be found at 577 Great Neck Road South in Mashpee (508–539–8788; www.capecodchildrensmuseum.pair.com).

Nature walks. Geared as much to horticulturists as to curious children, the Green Briar Nature Center (508–888–6870; www.thortonburgess.org) at 6 Discovery Hill Road off Route 6A about 2 miles east of Sandwich has labeled trails featuring regional flora. (While you're there, sample the output of the Green Briar Jam Kitchen, a cottage industry founded in 1903 and still going strong.) The forty-nine-acre Ashumet Holly and Wildlife Sanctuary at 186 Ashumet Road off Route 151 in Mashpee (508–563–6390; www.massaudubon.org) was originally set aside to preserve a native shrub endangered by its holiday popularity. Here, footpaths wend among some sixty-five species and circle a pretty pond lined with lotus blossoms. The 650-acre Beebe Woods at the end of Depot Road in Falmouth is as popular with mountain bikers as it is with hikers, so stay alert. You'll find further room to roam at the 2,250-acre Waquoit Bay National Estuarine Research Reserve at 149 Waquoit Highway (508–457–0495; www.state.ma.us/dem/parks/wbnr.htm), which includes a 1-mile self-guided nature trail, and the 5,871-acre Mashpee National Wildlife Refuge (978–443–4661; www.northeast.fws.gov/ma/mhp.htm), established in 1995 at the urging of Wampanoag activists.

Performing Arts. The Woods Hole Theater Company (508–540–6525; www.woodsholetheatercompany.org) performs at the 1878 Community Hall on Water Street. The College Light Opera Company (508–548–0668;

www.collegelightopera.com), an ensemble of top student actors from around the country, puts on a repertory of musicals every summer at the Highfield Theatre in Falmouth, a former horse barn. While awaiting its bricks-and-mortar embodiment, the Boch Center for the Performing Arts (508–477–2580; www.bochcenterarts.com) mounts popular concerts at a tent amid Mashpee Commons.

Water sports. To get a barque's-eye view of Plymouth Harbor, sign on for a guided tour at the Billington Sea Watercraft Kayak Center at 14 Union Street (508–746–5444). With their barely-there waves, Buzzards Bay and Nantucket Sound are ideal for windsurfing; for rentals and instruction, contact Cape Cod Windsurfing Academy on Maravista Beach in East Falmouth (508–495–0008). Waquoit Kayak at Edward's Boat Yard, 1209 East Falmouth Highway in East Falmouth (508–548–2216), rents kayaks and canoes for exploring the inlets of Waquoit Bay.

SPECIAL EVENTS

Late May. Rare Breeds and Heirloom Seeds Weekend, Plymouth; (508) 746–1622; www.plimoth.org. A chance to learn about—and acquire—some of Plimoth Plantation's Colonial cultivars.

July 4th weekend. Wampanoag Pow Wow, Mashpee; (508) 477–0208. A national gathering of the tribes, for traditional dances and games.

Mid-July. Barnstable County Fair, Falmouth; (508) 563–3200; www.barnstablecountyfair.org. An old-fashioned agricultural meet, with petting zoo and craft demos.

Early August. Woods Hole Film Festival; (617) 232–4722; www.woodshole.com/filmfest. First crack at some promising indies.

Early October. Bourne Farm Pumpkin Festival, West Falmouth; (508) 548–8484. The 1775 farmstead offers hayrides and pony rides, plus your pick of the crop.

December 31. Last Night, Falmouth; (508) 548–8500 or (800) 526–8532; www.falmouth-capecod.com. Festivities feature popular local performers.

OTHER RECOMMENDED RESTAURANTS AND LODGINGS

Cataumet

Wood Duck Inn, 1050 County Road (Route 28A); (508) 564–6404; www.
woodduckinnbb.com. For those who prefer the Cape countrified and quiet.

East Falmouth

Bed and Breakfast of Waquoit Bay, 176 Route 28; (508) 457–0084 or (800)
894–8816; www. waquoitbay.com. A charming country house on spacious
wooded grounds beside Child's River.

The Coppage Inn, 224 Route 28; (508) 548–3228. A grand old summer home
tricked out with an indoor heated pool, sauna, and hot tub.

East Sandwich

Wingscorton Farm Inn, 11 Wing Boulevard (off Route 6A); (508) 888–0534.
A working farmstead since 1758, with original paneled bedrooms, a 9-foot
hearth, formidable breakfasts, and plenty of four-footed company.

Falmouth

The Clam Shack, 227 Clinton Avenue; (508) 548–2626. Classic fried seafood
with a million-dollar view.

Coonamessett Inn, Jones Road and Gifford Street; (508) 548–2300. A venerable and beloved old inn serving surprisingly sophisticated regional cuisine.

Peking Palace, 452 Main Street; (508) 540–8204. Exceptional Chinese food,
available until 2:00 A.M. in summer for those with late-night cravings.

Tra Bi Ca, 327 Gifford Road; (508) 548–2076. Mediterranean, meaning Italian and even a touch of Morrocan.

Mashpee

Contrast @ the Commons, Mashpee Commons; (508) 477–1299. Edgy cuisine and ambiance amid the mall.

New Seabury

Popponesset Inn, Mall Way off Shore Drive; (508) 477–1100; www.new
seabury.com. This beachside inn turned restaurant has drawn high-steppers
for decades; the cuisine bridges traditional and dernier cri.

Plymouth

Jackson-Russell-Whitefield House, 25 North Street; (508) 746–5289. A beautifully restored 1782 Federal house in the heart of town.

Sagamore

Sagamore Inn, 1131 Route 6A; (508) 888–9707. A roadhouse little changed
since the 1920s, and still a fine place to go the fried clams route.

Sandwich

Dan'l Webster Inn, 149 Main Street; (508) 888–3622 or (800) 444–3566; www.
danlwebsterinn.com. A modern, midsize luxury hotel with three dining
rooms serving above-average cuisine.

Summer House, 158 Main Street; (508) 888–4991; www.capecod.net/
summerhouse. An 1835 Greek Revival house with five large, airy bedrooms and an inviting garden.

West Falmouth

Chapaquoit Grill, 410 Route 28A; (508) 540–7794. Casual eats in a Califor-
nia-style bistro.

Inn at West Falmouth, 66 Frazar Road; (508) 540–7696; www.innatwest
falmouth.com. Peaceful luxury in a sumptuously decorated 1900 Shingle-
style summer house with a tennis court and deck pool overlooking
Buzzards Bay.

Woods Hole

Fishmonger's Cafe, 56 Water Street; (508) 548–9148; www.fishmongerscafe.
com. Natural foods rule at this inviting water-view eatery.

Shuckers World Famous Raw Bar & Cafe, 91A Water Street; (508) 540–3850; www.woodshole.com/shuckers. Primo bivalves, plus outstanding chowder, all served waterside.

Woods Hole Passage, 186 Woods Hole Road; (508) 548–9575 or (800) 790–8976; www.woodsholepassage.com A nineteenth-century carriage house turned stylish inn.

FOR MORE INFORMATION

Cape Cod Chamber of Commerce, Routes 6 and 132, Hyannis, MA 02601; (508) 362–3225 or (888) 332–2732, fax (508) 862–0700; www.capecod.com.

Falmouth Chamber of Commerce, 20 Academy Lane, Falmouth, MA 02540; (508) 548–8500 or (800) 526–8532; www.falmouth-capecod.com.

Massachusetts Office of Travel & Tourism, 10 Park Plaza, Boston, MA 02116; (617) 973–8500 or (800) 227–MASS; www.massvacation.com.

Plymouth Information Center, 130 Water Street, Plymouth, MA 02360; (508) 747–7525 or (800) 872–1620; www.visit-plymouth.com.

The Mid-Cape

A WALK ON THE MILD SIDE

---

2 NIGHTS

Prime antiquing • Aerial thrills • Treasure houses
Exquisite restaurants • Placid beaches • Classic Americana

Though often overlooked in the rush to the action-packed Islands or Outer Cape, the Mid-Cape is far from mediocre. In fact, this is where you'll find most of the money—not that anyone is showing it. It's hidden away along the inlets of Osterville, the tiny lanes snaking toward Barnstable Harbor, and amid the tasteful tidiness that is Chatham. It's true that the favored pastimes here tend to be on the tame side. But for those content to wander and wonder, there's no playground quite so enchanting as Cape Cod Bay at low tide, when the rippled garnet sand stretches for miles, leaving behind all sorts of curiosities, as well as prime kiting terrain.

Despite Hyannis's Kennedy halo, today it's mostly a mall, indistinguishable from its counterparts across the country, and you probably won't want to spend much time there—though visit by all means if you feel you must. Nor is there much appeal in the highly commercialized stretch of Route 28 between Hyannis and Harwich. For local color and the joy of discovery, Route 6A—the bay-hugging footpath that became the Old King's Highway—proves a much richer vein.

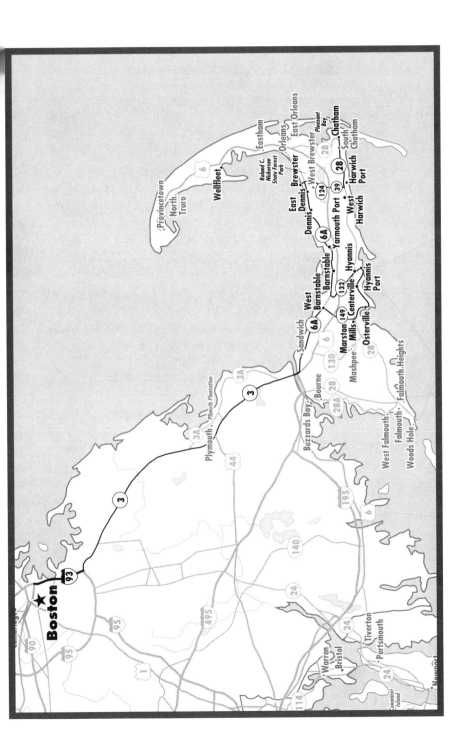

DAY 1

Morning

It should take you less than an hour to zip down Route 3 to Sandwich; from there, follow poky, meandering Route 6A through **West Barnstable,** pausing from time to time to admire—and possibly acquire—some of its notable stash of crafts. First you'll come upon **Black's Handweaving Shop,** 597 Route 6A (508–362–3955), one of the last bastions of custom-designed jacquard-pattern weaving. At 2454 Meetinghouse Way (Route 149), look for the **Tern Studio** (508–362–6077), where A. O. Barbour creates lovely vessels out of found and rare woods, and **West Barnstable Tables** (508–362–2676), where antique planks are creatively recycled. Heading south on Route 149, pause for spiritual and aesthetic refreshment at the **West Parish Meetinghouse,** 1049 Meetinghouse Way (508–362–4445; www.westparish.org), which is not only a marvel of Colonial construction—built in 1717–19, it's the Cape's oldest public building—but an inspiring example of thoughtful renovation.

Continue south and then skyward—via a glider provided by **Cape Cod Soaring Adventures** at the Marstons Mills Airport (508–540–8081), by reservation. A pilot steers, thermal currents provide the uplift, and all you have to do is ooh and aah.

Route 149 will bring you to an as yet undeveloped portion of Route 28; head east about ½ mile, then turn right at South Country Road to reach **Osterville**'s Main Street, the Cape's rural answer to Rodeo Drive. Among the shops that warrant a stop are **The Farmhouse** at 1340 Main (508–420–2400), for antiques ranging from fine to fun; **Oak and Ivory** at 1112 Main (508–428–9425), for authentic Nantucket baskets and neo-Shaker boxes; and, in the center of town, at 877 Main, the **Country Store** (508–428–2097), a classic general store little changed in the past century. Check out the other shops in town for a glimpse of what the rich and resolutely unfamous do with their disposable income (redecorate, apparently), then take Parker Road to West Bay Road to tour the **John Parker House** (508–428–5861; www.osterville.org), a local history museum open in-season Tuesday, Thursday, and Sunday from 1:30 to 4:30 P.M. Continue along Parker Road and then eastward along Seaview Avenue, eventually regaining Main Street by way of East Bay Road. Along the way you'll catch glimpses of roughly half a billion dollars' worth of highly enviable real estate.

Stay on Main until you reach the center of **Centerville,** where a prelunch ice cream cone at **Four Seas** (508–775–1394; wwwfourseasicecream.com), a summertime staple since 1934, might not be amiss. Heading eastward along Craigville Beach Road, you'll pass one of the Cape's more popular—and packed—beaches, as well as a cottage colony that grew out of the revivalist camps of the mid-1800s. Passing through **Hyannisport** by way of Ocean Avenue, withstand the temptation to gawk at the **Kennedy compound** (there is nothing to see past those high green hedges) and head instead down Gosnold then Ocean Street, to the **Kennedy Memorial,** a restful rose garden overlooking **Veterans Beach**—well suited to young waders—and Hyannis's harbor, **Lewis Bay.** Visually, this is by far the most palatable way to sneak into town. You'll probably want to cruise Main Street, and maybe stop in at the **John F. Kennedy Hyannis Museum** at number 397 (508–790–3077; www.hyannischamber.com/jfkmuseum.asp), a primarily photographic homage to Hyannis's most celebrated summerer. In-season hours are Monday through Saturday 10:00 A.M. to 4:00 P.M., Sunday 1:00 to 4:00 P.M.; it's closed Sunday through Tuesday off-season.

LUNCH: Baxter's Boathouse, 177 Pleasant Street, Hyannis; (508) 775–4490. Have a classic fried-clam—or other seafood—feast on a deck jutting into the harbor.

Afternoon

Grit your teeth and gun it, congestion permitting, up the gamut of malls that is Route 132. After about 5 miles, you'll regain soothing Route 6A, the whole of which constitutes a Regional Historic District. One minor anomaly: Just east of the intersection, check the walls of the railroad underpass for the angels that now-celebrated artist Edith Vonnegut (daughter of Kurt) gracefully graffiti'd in her youth.

Another mile or so east, on the left, the **Sturgis Library** at 3090 Route 6A (508–362–6636; www.capecod.net/sturgis) is a must-visit for amateur as well as professional genealogists. If you suspect there was a Pilgrim in your past, this is the place to find out for sure. In any event, it's worth stopping in to see the tallow-stained Bible lugged overseas by town founder John Lothrop in 1639; in fact, the library was built around a portion of his 1644 home, still intact. Hours are quirky (subject to funding), so be sure to call ahead.

As you pull into Barnstable village, you'll see the **Barnstable Superior Courthouse** at 3195 Route 6A (508–375–6684) looming on your right. Like Plymouth's imposing Pilgrim Hall Museum, this 1832 granite Greek Revival edifice was most likely designed by Boston architect Alexander Parris, a

Bulfinch protégé. Court proceedings are open to all comers—it's actually a popular rainy-day pursuit. Others might prefer to contemplate the superior antiques plunder and locally produced art on display at the **Harden Studios,** housed in an early eighteenth-century deaconage just down the street at 3264 Route 6A (508–362–7711). History buffs will enjoy poking around the **Trayser Museum Complex,** up the hill at 3353 Route 6A (508–362–2092; www.barnstablepatriot.com/trayser); displays in the handsome brick customs house built in 1856 recall the region's glory days as shipping capital, whereas the 1700 jail on the premises evokes tougher times. In-season hours are Tuesday through Saturday, 1:30 to 4:30 P.M.

About 2 miles east, you'll enter the charming village of **Yarmouth Port.** Break for an old-fashioned ice cream soda or frappe at **Hallet's,** 139 Route 6A (508–362–3362; www.hallets.com), an 1889 drugstore, and check out the cluster of interior design and antiques stores. The most formidable is **Nickerson Antiques** at 162 Route 6A (508–362–6426), which is constantly restocked with pre-industrial English antiques. At the farther end of town, a stop at **Parnassus Books,** 220 Route 6A (508–362–6420), is de rigueur, despite the proprietor's legendary gruffness. Somewhere in this warren of crammed bookshelves and improvised stacks, you're sure to find just the book you're seeking, especially if it has anything to do with Cape lore.

Just up the road, you'll encounter two historic houses representing very different periods. The **Winslow Crocker House** at 250 Route 6A (508–362–4385; www.SPNEA.org) is a 1780 Georgian beauty packed with extraordinary Early American antiques and the intriguing stories that go with them; it's open for hour-long tours Saturday and Sunday in-season from 11:00 A.M. to 5:00 P.M. Across the street, the 1840 **Captain Bangs Hallet House** at 11 Strawberry Lane (508–362–3021; www.hsoy.org/historic/hallethouse.htm)—open Thursday through Sunday in-season from 1:00 to 4:00 P.M.—offers a dazzling window on the lifestyle of prosperous sea captains at the peak of the China trade, when they had their pick of the decorative riches of the East as well as the finest furnishings that Europe had to offer.

Depending how many stops you've opted for, you might still have time to do some high-end hunting-and-gathering yourself, in the neighboring town of **Dennis.** The **Antique Center of Cape Cod** at 243 Route 6A (508–385–6400; www.antiquecenterofcapecod.com) showcases the goods of over 160 dealers: you can pretty much count on a discovery or two. The **Baksa Studio** at 766 Route 6A (508–385–5733 or 800–357–5733; www.baksa.com) purveys Michael Baksa's fabulous contemporary jewelry, fashioned on the premises, along with alluring alabaster sculptures by Laura Baksa. Time permitting, take a look around at the **Cape Museum of Fine Arts** (508–385–4477; www.cmfa.org), which shares a green meadow with the **Cape Playhouse** and **Cape Cinema** (see Performing Arts, below) at 36 Hope Lane. Open Monday through Saturday 10:00 A.M. to 5:00 P.M. and Sunday 1:00 to 5:00 P.M. in-season, the museum features a small but growing collection of local art dating from the turn of the century, and the contemporary shows are a good place to scout for new talent.

In **East Dennis,** at the far end of Scargo Lake—take a dip, if you're so inclined—seek out **Scargo Stoneware Pottery** at 30 Dr. Lord Road South off Route 6A (508–385–3894), where Harry Holl and his four daughters produce fanciful work in a sylvan setting. For a fabulous all-Cape view, continue circling around the lake, along Scargo Hill Road, and climb tiny Scargo Tower. Farther along Route 6A, **Ross Coppelman** offers another arresting take on contemporary goldsmithing at number 1439 (508–385–7900; www.rosscoppelman.com), and **Webfoot Farm Antiques** at number 1475 (508–385–2334) always has some fabulous pieces, including hard-to-find vintage garden furniture. Another mile east, in **West Brewster,** you'll find the finest crafts in the country gathered at **The Spectrum,** 369 Route 6A (508–385–3322; www.spectrumamerica.com), and some truly outré trouvailles—some in the five-figure range—at **Kingsland Manor Antiques,** 440 Route 6A (508–385–9741 or 800–486–2305).

DINNER: Chillingsworth, 2449 Main Street, Brewster; (508) 896–3640; www.chillingsworth.com. You might also dine among antiques, some dating back as far as Louis XV, at this 1689 Colonial manse, deservedly ranked among the Cape's finest restaurants. Chef Robert Rabin is a French classicist who renders homage to local provender in his elaborate seven-course table d'hôte. (Chillingsworth has a trio of antiques-accoutered rooms if you anticipate feasting unto immobility.)

LODGING: Captain Freeman Inn, 15 Breakwater Road, Brewster; (508) 896–7481 or (800) 843–4664; www.captainfreemaninn.com. This 1866 manse in the center of town has been reno'd to the hilt: some suites feature a four-poster bed, TV/VCR, stocked minifridge, and a sunporch with whirlpool.

DAY 2

Morning

BREAKFAST: Captain Freeman Inn. The poolside breakfast is both healthy and splendiferous.

Start your day by picking up a paper at the century-old **Brewster Store** next door at 1935 Route 6A (508–896–3744) to peruse on a church pew out front, like a regular. Or explore the historic graveyard of the **First Parish Church,** where Louis XVI's rescued dauphin is rumored to be buried among the scores of ship's captains. You could stroll down the road to enjoy the quiet bay beach at **Breakwater Landing** (where packet boats used to unload hordes of tourists in exchange for fresh produce a century ago) or cycle a bit of the 25-mile **Cape Cod Rail Trail** (508–896–3491; www. state.ma.us/dem/parks/ccrt.htm), which extends all the way from Dennis to Wellfleet; this section crosses 2,000-acre **Nickerson State Park** in East Brewster (508–896–3491; www.state.ma.us/dem/parks/nick.htm), with its scattering of freshwater kettle ponds left in the wake of receding glaciers a millennia ago. Or, to get a better understanding of your surroundings, backtrack about 2 miles to West Brewster to visit the **Cape Cod Museum of Natural History** at 869 Route 6A (508–896–3867; www. capecodnatural history. org), which offers a fascinating collection of interactive displays and several self-guided nature trails through variegated terrain; it's open Monday through Saturday 9:30 A.M. to 4:30 P.M., Sunday 11:00 to 4:30 P.M. Circle back by way of pretty Stony Brook Road to check out the amazing **Underground Art Gallery** at 673 Satucket Road (508–896–3757), headquarters of pioneering subterranean architect Malcolm Wells, and the scenic **Stony Brook Grist Mill** at 830 Stone Brook Road (508–896–1734), the last vestige of a booming nineteenth-century factory village.

LUNCH: Brewster Fish House, 2208 Route 6A, Brewster; (508) 896–7344. Its Shaker-plain decor belies its lush inventiveness in putting local catches to brilliant use.

Afternoon

Head back to the center of town and then south on Routes 124 then 39 into **West Harwich,** where any restless kids you happen to be dragging along can cut loose at the **Trampoline Center,** 296 Route 28 (508–432–8717) or at

Bud's Go-Karts, Routes 39 and 28 (508–432–4964)—and, of course, there's no rule that grown-ups can't play.

Farther east in the sweet little town of **Harwich Port,** adults might opt for an elegant tea at the **Augustus Snow House,** 528 Route 28 (Main Street) (508–430–0528 or 800–320–0528; www.augustussnow.com), while children will probably clamor for **Sundae School Ice Cream,** 606 Main Street (508–430–2444; www.sundaeschool.com). Either should tide you over for the roughly 6-mile drive to **Chatham,** a picturesque, all-American town located at the Cape's elbow. Along the way, stop in to admire, and perhaps covet, the handsome sea-motif stoneware at **Chatham Pottery,** 2058 Route 28, South Chatham (508–430–2191 or 800–682–2529; www.chatham pottery.com), and the dazzlingly, often playful output of the **Chatham Glass Company** (508–945–5547; www.capecod.net/chathamglass) at 758 Main Street. If you're so inspired, get airborne there with the **Cape Cod Flying Circus** (508–945–2363), which offers scenic flyovers of Chatham's ever-changing coastline aboard a replica 1927 biplane—an adventure embellished, if you so choose, with loops and rolls.

Pulling into Chatham proper, grab the first parking spot you come across, and take off on a stroll of long, leafy Main Street, lined with enticing shops. **Spyglass** at number 618 (508–945–9686) features amazing optical and/or nautical antiques. **Pentimento** at number 584 (508–945–0178) offers stylish summery gifts, as does **Chatham Cookware** at number 524 (508–945–1550)—along with some irresistible fresh-baked nibbles. Save yourself, though, for the **Chatham Candy Manor** at number 484 (508–945–0825 or 800–221–6497; www.candymanor.com), where you can observe—and taste—chocolates being hand-dipped. Follow Main Street all the way to the end for a scenic ocean view from the foot of the 1828 **Chatham Light**—a beacon still essential to navigating the coastline's ever-shifting shoals. Below it is a brand-new beach, created after a 1987 hurricane cut a breach through Chatham's barrier beach. Currents can still be treacherous, so get your feet wet and little else.

DINNER AND LODGING: Wequassett Inn, 2173 Route 28, Chatham; (508) 432–5400 or (800) 352–7169; www.wequassett.com. This colony of cottages nestled along a cove about 5 miles northwest of town is a peaceful resort on a very personable scale. Rooms are large and handsome, done up in elegant country style. The restaurant in the eighteenth-century Eben Ryder House blends country-club suavity with some rather dazzling regional cuisine.

DAY 3

Morning

BREAKFAST: Wequasett Inn. At the Eben Ryder House, or ask that a basket be sent to your room.

The agenda for the day is to stay put—relatively speaking. Take advantage of the five tennis courts, with attendant pros, or the fleet of sailboards and boats to explore aptly named **Pleasant Bay.** Postpone your departure as long as feasible, given the inevitable Boston-bound bottlenecks, or better yet, be sensible and sign on for another infinitely pleasant day.

THERE'S MORE

Collectors' meccas. Hyannis's Plush & Plunder (508–775–4467), a vintage clothing store at 605 Main Street, draws devotees from as far as Hollywood. Eldred's Auction House at 1483 Route 6A in Dennis (508–385–3116; www.eldreds.com) presents antiques worthy of—and often destined for—Sotheby's and the like. Wisteria Antiques at 1199 Route 6A in Brewster (508–896–8650) is a lavender house lavished with costume jewelry and other baubles—it's a trip. Serious art collectors will want to visit the Munson Gallery at 880 Route 28 in Chatham (508-945-2888; www.munsongallery.com), a former horse barn now stabling some of the foremost contemporary artists in the Northeast.

Harbor tours, etc. To learn more about the aquatic denizens, take a "Sea-fari" aboard the R/V *Tiger Shark* out of Hyannis's Ocean Street Dock (508–775–1730). Off Chatham, the uninhabited—but for the birds—Monomoy National Wildlife Refuge can be reached via the Monomoy Island Ferry (508–945–5450; www.virtualbirder/com/ripryder), which also runs shuttles to the North and South barrier beaches.

Kid stuff. The Cape Cod Melody Tent (see "Performing Arts," below) puts on children's matinees. Kids will also enjoy the very brief tour—culminating in samples—at the Cape Cod Potato Chips factory on Breed's Hill Road just north of Hyannis (508–775–3206). West Yarmouth's eco-sensitive ZooQuarium at 674 Route 28 (508–775–8883) features positive-reinforcement shows by sea lions unable to live in the wild. The evocative 1887 Chatham Railroad Museum at 153 Depot Road (508–945–5199) overlooks a phenomenal "play-a-round" park designed by Robert Leathers. On Friday nights in summer, the bunny-hop set convenes for the celebrated brass-band concerts in Kate Gould Park (800–715–5567; www.chatham.org), which regularly draw admirers in the thousands.

Museums. Though known for its namesake collection of modern Americana, the tiny Cahoon Museum of American Art at 4676 Route 28 (508–428–7581; www.cahoonmuseum.org) warrants a visit for its contemporary shows, and for the setting itself, a pretty 1775 Georgian Colonial farmhouse. Packed with specialized collections, the fourteen-room Centerville Historical Society Museum at 524 Main Street (508–775–0331), viewable only by guided tour, will reward those with a particular interest in Cape history. Housed in the country's first school of navigation, built in 1844, the Brooks Academy Museum at 80 Parallel Street in Harwich's center (508–432–8089) contains a number of interesting collections related to seafaring, cranberry harvesting, and other popular local pursuits.

Performing arts. If there's some famous musician or comedian you've always been dying to see, odds are good that they've been booked into the Cape Cod Melody Tent at the West End Rotary in Hyannis (508–775–9100; www.melodytent.com), a popular tradition since 1950. Strictly amateur, but nonetheless engaging, the Barnstable Comedy Club at 3171 Route 6A (508–362–6333; www.barnstablecomedyclub.com) has been putting on spirited shows since 1922. A splendid straw-hat survivor, the Cape Playhouse at 36 Hope Lane in Dennis (508–385–3911; www.capeplayhouse.com) was envisioned in 1927 as a country counterpart to the Great White Way—and so it remains, still attracting some well-known names. Built in the same complex in 1930, the Cape Cinema (508–385–4477; www.capecinema.com) is an art deco wonder curiously encased in a replica Congregational Church. Featuring black leather armchairs and a proscenium designed by Rockwell Kent, it provides a sumptuous setting indeed for viewing the current crop of art films. The Cape Cod Repertory Theatre (508–896–1888; www.cape rep.org), headquartered at 3379 Route 6A in Brewster, presents Shakespeare and more under the stars—and indoors—on the grounds of a grand old estate. At the Monomoy Theatre at 776 Route 28 in Chatham (508–945–1589), the accomplished Ohio University Players mount musicals throughout the summer.

SPECIAL EVENTS

Late April. Brewster in Bloom; (508) 896–2670; www.brewsterinbloom.com. Spring festivities include a craft fair and flea market, parade, and hot-air balloons.

Mid-May. Spring Fling, Chatham; (508) 945–5199; www.chathamcapecod. org. Clowns and a crazy hat parade highlight this celebratory weekend geared to families.

Mid-September. Cranberry Festival, Harwich; (508) 430–2811 or (800) 441–3199; www.harwichcranberryfestival.com. A week's worth of events to celebrate the tasty crop first domesticated here.

OTHER RECOMMENDED RESTAURANTS AND LODGINGS

Barnstable

Ashley Manor, 3660 Route 6A; (508) 362–8044 or (888) 535–2246; www. capecod.net/ashleymn. Bright and airy, this 1699 Colonial mansion—concealed by towering privet hedges—makes an idyllic country retreat, complete with private tennis court.

Charles Hinckley House, 8 Scudder Lane; (508) 362–9924. A colorful carpet of wildflowers announces this handsome, shipwright-built 1809 Federal house, where breakfasts are a work of art.

Henry Crocker House, 3026 Route 6A; (508) 362–6348. A colonial tavern turned restful guest house.

Brewster

Bramble Inn, 2019 Route 6A; (508) 896–7644; www.brambleinn.com. This intimate 1861 inn is famed for its restaurant, which encompasses several charmingly appointed parlors and explores the rewarding edges of Mediterranean-rim cuisine.

Brewster Farmhouse Inn, 716 Main Street; (508) 896–3910 or (800) 892–3910; www.brewsterfarmhouseinn.com. A formidable Greek Revival facade conceals a peach of a B&B. A heated pool and hot tub await by the backyard.

Cobie's, 3260 Route 6A; (508) 896–7021. An unspoiled 1948 clam shack, right off the Rail Trail.

Old Sea Pines Inn, 2553 Main Street; (508) 896–6114; www.oldsea pinesinn.com. This 1907 Shingle-style mansion once served as a charm school and has held onto its retro charms. Home-cooked dinners on the sunporch are sometimes accompanied by musical or dramatic entertainment.

Chatham

Captain's House Inn of Chatham, 371 Old Harbor Road; (508) 945–0127 or (800) 315–0728; www.captainshouseinn.com. Nineteenth-century luxury—including a silver-service tea—in a pretty compound centered on a Greek Revival manse.

Chatham Bars Inn, Shore Road; (508) 945–0096 or (800) 527–4884; www. chathambarsinn.com. A 1914 hunting lodge turned grand hotel, this waterside compound offers every amenity, including nine holes of rather relaxed (but scenic) golf.

Chatham Wayside Inn, 512 Main Street; (508) 945–5550 or (800) 391–5745; www.waysideinn.com. A handsomely restored—and expanded—1860s stagecoach stop.

Christian's, 443 Main Street; (508) 945–3362. A congenial bistro that tangos engagingly with the latest culinary trends; upstairs, there's a lively, movie-motif piano bar.

Impudent Oyster, 15 Chatham Bars Avenue; (508) 945–3545. A seafood mecca beloved of locals.

Moses Nickerson House, 364 Old Harbor Road; (508) 945–5859 or (800) 628–6972. A picture-perfect B&B in an 1839 captain's house.

Cotuit

Regatta of Cotuit at the Crocker House, 4631 Route 28; (508) 428–5715; www.theregattas.com. Just as sophisticated, as the Falmouth original, this 1790 stagecoach inn serves cutting-edge fusion cuisine.

Dennis

The Cape Playhouse Bistro, 36 Hope Lane; (508) 385–8000. A strawhat Sardi's, run by Chillingsworth.

Contrast Bistro, 605 Route 6A, Dennis; (508) 385–9100; www.contrast bistro.com. A jazzy cafe offering tasty, novel fare.

Isaiah Hall B&B Inn, 152 Whig Street; (508) 385–9928 or (800) 736–0160; www.isaiahhallinn.com. You might find yourself breakfasting with stars—from the nearby Cape Playhouse—at this charming 1857 Greek Revival farmhouse within walking distance of a pretty bay beach.

Red Pheasant, 905 Route 6A; (508) 385–2133; www.redpheasant.com. An eighteenth-century chandlery provides a handsome setting for sure-handed and often superlative regional cuisine.

Harwich Port

Cape Sea Grille, 31 Sea Street; (508) 432–4745; www.seagrille.com. Vivid New American fare in a low-key setting steps from the water.

Winstead Inn, 4 Braddock Lane; (508) 432–4444 or (800) 870–4405. A spiffy little inn right on the beach.

Hyannis

Alberto's Ristorante, 360 Main Street; (508) 778–1770; www.albertoscape cod.com. Roseate and romantic, this new-wave Italian trattoria is among the top spots in town.

RooBar, 586 Main Street; (508) 778–6515. A snazzy contemporary space centered on a "performance kitchen."

Marstons Mills

Inn at the Mills, 71 Route 149; (508) 428–2967. A model of gracious country living, this tastefully furnished 1780 farmstead overlooks a pond and its resident swans.

Osterville

Five Seas Bistro, 825 Main Street; (508) 420–5559. A modern, yet warm source of New American finesse.

Keeper's Restaurant, 72 Crosby Circle, (508) 428–6719. A casual but ambitious, fusiony spot right on the water, amid the historic Crosby Yacht Yard.

South Yarmouth

Captain Farris House, 308 Old Main Street; (508) 760–2818 or (800) 350–9477; www.captainfarris.com. A rare gem just off Route 28, this 1845 house has undergone a restoration worthy of *Architectural Digest,* and the breakfasts are a foodie's delight.

West Barnstable

Honeysuckle Hill Bed & Breakfast, 591 Route 6A; (508) 362–8418 or (800) 441–8418; www.bbonline.com/ma/honeysuckle. At once cozy and romantic—a picture-perfect B&B.

West Brewster

High Brewster, 964 Satucket Road; (508) 896–3636. A countrified idyll perched above a millpond, this 1738 farmstead is known for its exceptional regional cuisine—some of it picked right on the premises. The four rooms in the main house are tiny and cramped (think Colonial), the three cottages are much more spacious.

West Dennis

The Beach House, 61 Uncle Stephen's Road; (508) 398–4575. Set right on the water, this seven-bedroom B&B is optimally set up for families, with kitchen and barbecue privileges, plus its own little playground.

Lighthouse Inn, 4 Lighthouse Road; (508) 398–2244; www.lighthouseinn. com. Seemingly stuck in a 1930s time warp, this seaside resort—built around an 1855 lighthouse—features supervised children's programs and communal dining. The patrons, as well as the owners, go back generations.

Yarmouth Port

Abbici, 43 Route 6A; (508) 362–3501. Brilliant North Italian cuisine served in a 1775 saltbox turned temple to minimalist modernism.

Inaho, 157 Route 6A; (508) 362–5522. A charming and authentic Japanese restaurant and sushi bar camouflaged within a seemingly ordinary clapboard house.

Jack's Outback, 161 Route 6A; (508) 362–6690. A quirky self-service cafe as famous for its cutting wit as for its flavorful, affordable food.

One Center Street Inn, 1 Center Street; (508) 362–8910 or (888) 407–1653. A circa 1824 parsonage, beautifully decorated and near Gray's Beach.

Wedgewood Inn, 83 Route 6A; (508) 362–5157/9178; www.wedgewood-inn. com. A lovely 1812 Federal house and restored barn with all-out romantic rooms.

FOR MORE INFORMATION

Cape Cod Chamber of Commerce, Routes 6 and 132, Hyannis, MA 02601; (508) 862–0700 or (888) 332–2732; www.capecodchamber.org.

Massachusetts Office of Travel & Tourism, State Transportation Building, 10 Park Plaza, Suite 4510, Boston, MA 02116; (617) 973–8500 or (800) 227–MASS; www.massvacation.com.

MASSACHUSETTS

The Outer Cape

A RETREAT FOR RENEGADES

2 NIGHTS

Rough surf • Art rules • Noshing and shopping
The theater tradition • No-holds-barred nightlife

For a century or more before the storm-tossed Pilgrims anchored off what is now Provincetown, the natural harbor at the curled tip of the Cape had attracted its share of summertime visitors—fishing vessels, mostly, come across the sea to plunder the abundant schools of cod that gave the Cape its name. In search of greener pastures, the would-be colonists quickly moved on, leaving this outland to observe its own customs and laws—the foremost being lawlessness. For a long time, the makeshift community went by the name of Helltown, and the uptight colonists of the mainland knew better than to try to meddle. In a sense, their grudging tolerance set the stage for what remains a town in a state of constant creative anarchy, where descendants of the early Azorean fishing clans peaceably coexist alongside iconoclastic artists and out-and-proud hordes of homosexual tourists. Provincetown is gay in every sense, and seemingly in a state of permanent party—at least in-season. (It's lovely, too, when the crowds subside.) Leave your preconceptions home, and you're welcome to partake.

This end of the Cape is also where the great surf beaches are—all fortuitously preserved in the form of the 44,000-acre Cape Cod National Seashore. No high-rises mar the 30-mile stretch of the "back side"—which Henry David Thoreau, wearing his curmudgeonly travel writer hat, admiringly referred to as "this wild rank place." That it still is, and there's nothing quite as revivifying as a primal encounter with the elements—especially when you can plan on segueing to a sumptuous dinner, then lush digs in a luxury inn.

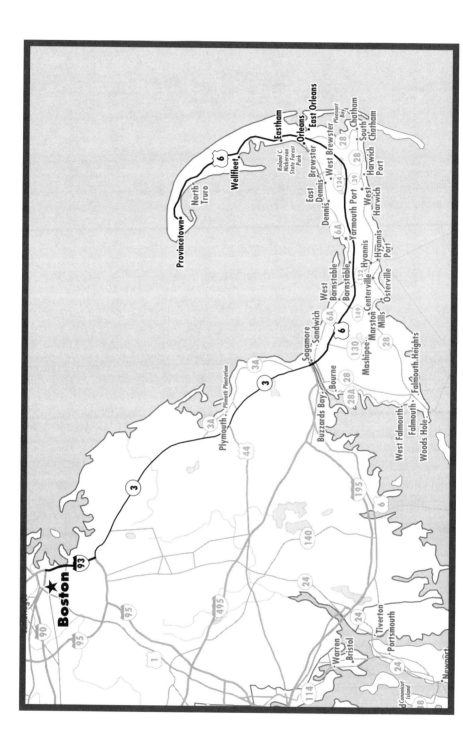

DAY 1

Morning

The sooner you start out, the better your odds of beating the crowds. Follow Route 3 southeast to the Sagamore Bridge, then Route 6 about 30 miles east to **Orleans.** (See the preceding chapter for information on the scenic alternative, Route 6A.) Named for a future king of France who visited the hamlet as an exile in 1797, Orleans still has its airs and expectations; it seems to want to be Hyannis, but fortunately hasn't succeeded so far.

Route 6 will bring you to the center of town, which has a handful of shops worth browsing—notably **Oceana** at 1 Main Street Square (508–240–1414) for nature-motif gifts. Other interesting stores flank Route 28 where it approaches Route 6. Check out the **Addison Art Gallery** at 43 Route 28 (508–255–6200 or 877–291–5400; www.addisonart.com) for an interesting cross-section of area artists. **Peacock Alley Antiques** at 35 Route 28 (508–240–1804) harbors a cache of twentieth-century furniture—the moderne stuff that made us all cringe not long ago. Up the road past the 1720 **Jonathan Young Windmill, Kemp Pottery** at 9 Route 6A (508–255–5853) features large sculptural creations. Also along this stretch, at 36 Route 6A, is the **Bird Watcher's General Store** (508–255–6974 or 800–562–1512; www.bird watchersgeneralstore.com), packed with every conceivable product of appeal to bird-lovers and the objects of their affection.

LUNCH: Kadee's Lobster & Clam Bar, 212 Main Street, East Orleans; (508) 255–6184. Enjoy a casual alfresco feast about a mile east from the center of Orleans. Or stop in at **Fancy's Farm** at 199 Main Street (508–255–1949; www.fancysfarm.com) to select a fanciful picnic to tide you over at one of the Outer Cape's unspoiled ocean beaches.

Afternoon

The closest is **Nauset Beach,** another mile east. The area around the town-run parking lot—where the fee is about $10, pretty much the Cape-wide norm—tends to get congested, but this remarkable barrier beach extends 10 miles, cupping Pleasant Bay all the way down to Chatham; those willing to hoof it can eventually find the privacy they seek. There are several more sunning options up the coast, starting with **Coast Guard Beach** and **Nauset Light Beach** in **Eastham,** both Cape Cod National Seashore preserves with high, scenic bluffs and insistent surf.

Eastham itself is a blink-and-you'll-miss-it town, but newcomers to the area will find a terrific educational resource in the National Seashore's **Salt Pond Visitor Center** off Route 6 (508–255–3421; www.nps.gov/caco), open 9:00 A.M. to 5:00 P.M. in-season, 9:00 A.M. to 4:30 P.M. off-season, which introduces the area's unique ecology and history through audiovisual presentations and a small but fascinating museum. Park rangers lead guided nature walks through a network of trails, all of which hook up with the 25-mile **Cape Cod Rail Trail** (508–896–3491; www.state.ma.us/dem/ccrt.htm), which extends from Dennis to **Wellfleet.** The latter town has its share of beautiful beaches, too, including the National Seashore-supervised **Marconi Beach,** whence in 1903 Italian inventor Guglielmo Marconi sent the world's first wireless communication (complete with typos), and the town-operated **Cahoon Hollow Beach,** a popular surfing spot where an 1897 life-saving station has been revived as a lively live-music bar called the **Beachcomber** (see "Evening," below).

Whichever beach you retreat to, leave an hour or so in the late afternoon to stroll through Wellfleet, a town that combines classic New England charm with world-class art. Robert Motherwell used to show at the tiny **Cherry Stone Gallery** at 70 East Commercial Street (508–349–3026); you'll still find some of his work stashed away, along with that of Jasper Johns, Berenice Abbott, and other avatars, while the walls are given over to tomorrow's stars. Down by the water, the **Cove Gallery** at 15 Commercial Street (508–349–2530; www.covegallery.com) is worth a look. Wellfleet boasts several dozen galleries all told; pick up a gallery guide at your first stop and chart your own itinerary, to taste. Or if you'd prefer to let serendipity be your guide, park behind Town Hall—where you'll find a rustic farmstand, **Hatch's** (508–349–6734), offering superb produce, seafood, and treats like frozen fresh-fruit pops—and do a loop of Main, Bank, and Commercial Streets. En route check out the flowing women's clothing designed by **Karol Richardson,** 11 West Main Street (508–349–6378; www.karolinc.com), and the attractive and unusual home accessories at **Eccentricity,** 361 Main Street (508–349–7554).

DINNER: Aesop's Tables, 316 Main Street, Wellfleet; (508) 349–6450. This former governor's summer retreat is the perfect place to celebrate summer's bounty—with world-renowned oysters straight from the harbor, perhaps, or a locally grown, Monet-inspired salad. Should reservations prove elusive, try the fun, affordable world-beat cuisine at **Painter's,** which occupies a rambling 1750 tavern at 50 Main Street (508–349–3003).

LODGING: Truro Vineyards, 11 Shore Road, North Truro; (508) 487–6200. Oenophiles and just plain sybarites will lap up the ambience here. The slate-floored great room that dominates this 1836 farmstead seems more reminiscent of Provence than hardscrabble New England, and the rooms are sumptuously draped in claret—and cabernet, chardonnay, etc.—tones.

Evening

For a nostalgic treat, take in a double feature at the **Wellfleet Drive-In** (508–349–7176; www.wellfleetdrivein.com), the last of its kind on the Cape. If you've got to dance, the **Beachcomber** at 1220 Old Cahoon Hollow Road in Wellfleet (508–349–6055; www.thebeachcomber.com) is by far the best place to kick loose.

DAY 2

Morning

BREAKFAST: Truro Vineyards. Enjoy a pleasant outdoor repast while gazing out over the vineyards.

Today's mission is to "do" **Provincetown,** a potentially wearying but—with proper planning—rewarding proposition. For a warm-up, stop in at the **Susan Baker Memorial Museum** at 46 Shore Road in North Truro (508–487–2557). It's open daily 11:00 A.M. to 5:00 P.M. from June 1 through Labor Day. Baker's very much alive and kick-ass, and her unique form of folk art earns her critical kudos, as well as avid fans.

Drive north along Route 6A through North Truro's retro-picturesque rows of beach cottages. Few galleries open their doors much before noon, so you might as well start by getting your bearings at the **Pilgrim Monument & Provincetown Museum,** looming above town atop High Pole Hill Road (508–487–1310 or 800–247–1620; www.pilgrimmonument.com). It has parking—at a premium along this congested peninsula. Open 9:00 A.M. to 7:00 P.M. in-season (to 5:00 P.M. off), the smallish museum packs intriguing exhibits spanning Provincetown's Colonial and arts-colony history, and the 253-foot granite tower, modeled after Siena's Torre del Mangia, is a breeze to sprint up—surprisingly easy and cool. From gargoyle height, the town—not to mention the entire Cape and, in clear weather, Boston—is laid out at your feet.

Straight ahead is **MacMillan Wharf,** which offers further public parking, for a price. Named for the peripatetic native son and Arctic explorer, it's now home to several whale-watching fleets—the original, the **Dolphin Fleet** (508–255–3857 or 800–826–9300; www.whalewatch.com) is still the best—and to the **Expedition Whydah Sea-Lab & Learning Center** (941–343–9147; www.naut-res-guild.org/museums/whydah). Here the pirate ship *Whydah,* which lay off Wellfleet from 1717 until Barry Clifford's dramatic discovery in 1984, is slowly being reclaimed from the sea. While some of the exhibits seem unduly sensationalist, on the whole the facility—open 10:00 A.M. to 5:00 P.M. in-season—offers a thoughtful introduction to the fascinating field of marine archaeology.

By now the natives have probably begun to bestir themselves, so it's time to do some plundering of your own. Hugging the shore, **Commercial Street** is a 2-mile gamut of shops and eateries, ranging from the frankly tacky to the divine. Head east to hunt up the latter, seeking out, specifically, the **East End Gallery** (508–487–4745) for promising new work and **Moda Fina** (508–487–6632; www.shopmodafina.com) for sensuous Euro-fashion, both at number 349; **Small Pleasures** at 359 (508–487–3712) for exquisite estate jewelry; the **Halcyon Gallery** at 371 (508–487–9415) for handcrafts, including clothes; **Remembrances of Things Past** at 376 (508–487–9443) for a carnival of twentieth-century kitsch; **Silk & Feathers** at 377 (508–487–2057) for luxury lingerie; **Turning Point** at 379 (508–487–0642; www.province town.com/turningpoint) for tasteful cottons and linen fashions; **Utilities** at 393 (508–487–6800; www.utilitiesp.com) for stylish kitchen stuff; and the **Giardelli/Antonelli Studio Showroom** at 417 (508–487–3016) for simple-lined, locally designed clothing and jewelry. Galleries are ubiquitous, and you're now in the thick of the action. Noteworthy enterprises include **Albert Merola** at 424 Commercial (508–487–4424; www.universalfineobjects.com), **Rice/Polak** at 430 (508–487–1052; www.ricepolak.com), **Cortland Jessup** at 432 (508–487–4479), and **William-Scott** at 439 (508–487–4040).

The real motherlode awaits at the **Provincetown Art Association & Museum,** 460 Commercial Street (508–487–1750; www.paam.org), established by arts colony founder Charles Hawthorne and associates in 1914. Throughout the decades since, the museum has astutely acquired a world-class collection, only some of which is visible at any given time. All the shows—usually pairing old and new—are guaranteed attention-worthy. In-season hours are noon to 5:00 P.M. and 8:00 to 10:00 P.M. daily; off-season hours are noon to 5:00 P.M. Saturday and Sunday. Aficionados will also want to check out the **Schoolhouse Center for Art & Design,** a complex of studios and galleries at 494 Commercial Street (508–487–4800; www.schoolhousecenter.com).

One block north, at 208 Bradford Street, you'll find the influential **Berta Walker Gallery** (508–487–6411) and a half-mile hike east to 286 Bradford will bring you to **dna** (508–487–7700; www.dnagallery.com), a hot spot for up-and-comers. Don't despair if you tire of trekking; you can easily catch these outlying spots tomorrow, on your way out of town.

LUNCH: The Mews, 429 Commercial Street; (508) 487–1500; www.mews.com. Enjoy a sophisticated beachside lunch.

Afternoon

For further refreshment, take the beach route back to the center of town (that's what locals did till the mid-nineteenth century, lacking a street), before assaying the western flank. Duck into the 1878 **Town Hall** at 260 Commercial Street (508–487–7000; www.provincetowngov.org) for a look at some outstanding examples of local art from the colony's heyday; you might even witness a domestic partnership ceremony being celebrated. The **Julie Heller Gallery** at 2 Gosnold Street (508–487–2169; www.juliehellergallery.com) is a mecca for collectors of early Provincetown art. **Marine Specialties** at 235 Commercial Street (508–487–1730; www.thearmynavy.com) is an irresistible hodgepodge of bargain surplus—from ball gowns to ship's bells. **Clifford-Williams Antiques,** upstairs at 225 Commercial Street (508–487–4174), offers the most serious selection in town. There are plenty of stylish home-goods shops at this end of town, including the Zennish **Wa** at 184 (508–487–6355 or 888–779–6355; www.waharmony.com), over-the-top **Forbidden Fruit** at 173 (508–487– 9800), and world-roaming **Roots** at 142 (508–487–8807; www.rootshomeandgarden.com).

DINNER: Martin House, 157 Commercial Street; (508) 487–1327; www.the martinhouse.com. Exquisite taste sensations gathered from the four corners of the earth and conjoined with vibrant local provender amid the rustic/romantic, candle-lit rooms of a circa 1740 Cape—utter seduction.

LODGING: The Brass Key, 12 Carver Street; (508) 487–9005 or (800) 842–9858; www.brasskey.com. In a town with scores of attractive inns, this one soars above the competition, with thirty handsomely appointed rooms surrounding a garden courtyard with lap pool and whirlpool. Not a single luxury has been overlooked, from oversized loaner umbrellas to on-tap lemonade. Several of the quarters feature a fireplace, Jacuzzi, and/or private deck, and the widow's walk, open to all, is ideal for nude sunbathing—or stargazing.

Evening

Evening officially begins mid-afternoon, with the **Boatslip**'s convivial Tea Dance at 161 Commercial Street (508–487–1669; www.boatslipbeachclub.com), followed by a post-Tea Dance at the **Pied Piper,** 193A Commercial Street (508–487–1527; www.thepied.com), and lots more dancing all over town, including the **Atlantic House** at 4–6 Masonic Place (508–487–3821; www.ahouse.com), long considered the nation's premier gay bar. Or take in a drag show: six-foot-tall barkers—seven, counting the bouffant—will clue you as to where to go. Cabaret and comedy abound.

DAY 3

Morning

BREAKFAST: The Brass Key. A buffet of fresh fruit and fresh-baked pastries, best enjoyed poolside.

The day is wide open. You might try viewing Provincetown from another perspective—for instance, on horseback courtesy of **Nelson's Riding Stable** at 43 Race Point Road (508–240–1112). Or you could bike the swooping dunes of the Provincelands to glorious **Race Point Beach,** where sunbathers often spot spouting whales right from shore. You could, reluctantly, get a jump on the Boston-bound traffic—or, if the weather holds, do the smart thing and book another night or two.

THERE'S MORE

Antiquing. A few miles south of Orleans, near the Harwich border, the low-profile Pleasant Bay Antiques at 540 Orleans Road (508–255–0930) is one of the top shops on the Cape, known mostly to cognoscenti. Countryside Antiques at 6 Lewis Road, just off Main Street in East Orleans (508–240–0525) is another trove, stuffed with European imports more accessibly priced. East Orleans Art & Antiques at 204 Main Street (508–240–0525) features a small but select sampling, plus some worthy local artwork. Held on the grounds of the Wellfleet Drive-In, the Wellfleet Flea Market (508–349–7176; www.wellfleetdriven.com) is hardly a sure thing, but who knows what treasure you might find?

Art centers. In addition to its scores of galleries, the tip of the Cape contains two outstanding cultural centers where you can catch not only shows, but readings, lectures, and classes, some accessibly short-term. Send ahead for brochures from the Truro Center for the Arts at Castle Hill, 10 Meetinghouse Road (508–349–7511; www.castlehill.org), and the Fine Arts Work Center at 24 Pearl Street in Provincetown (508–487–9960; www.fawc.org).

Museums. Among the small, local-history museums that warrant a visit—especially on a rainy day—are the 1869 Old Schoolhouse Museum at 6 Nauset Road in Eastham (508–255–0788); the Wellfleet Historical Society Museum, 266 Main Street, Wellfleet (508–349–9157); and the Truro Historical Museum, 6 Lighthouse Road, North Truro (508–487–3397; www.capecod.net/ths/museum.htm).

Nature walks. The 1,000-acre Wellfleet Bay Wildlife Sanctuary off West Road in South Wellfleet (508–349–2615; www.massaudubon.org) has a lovely assortment of trails, spoking out from a state-of-the-art, eco-sensitive visitor center. Only the strong of leg—and savvy about tides—should assay Great Island, a 4-mile barrier beach alongside Wellfleet Harbor that was once a thriving whaling post and is now a welcome wilderness. In Provincetown a trek across the West End breakwater leads to unsullied Long Point, about a 3-mile round trip.

Nibbles. The homemade donuts start emerging at 5:00 A.M. at the Hole-In-One Donut Shop, 4295 Route 6A in North Eastham (508–255–9446); soon the stools fill up with a chorus of regulars discussing the fate of the world. In Provincetown, try the esoteric treats at the Provincetown Portuguese Bakery, 299 Commercial Street (508–487–1803).

Performing arts. Housed in an imposing 1873 town hall, the Academy Playhouse at 120 Main Street in Orleans (508–255–1963; www.apa1.org) puts on creditable strawhat fare, plus the occasional reading and recital. WHAT—otherwise known as the Wellfleet Harbor Actors' Theatre—at 1 Kendrick Avenue near the Town Pier (508–349–6835; www.what.org) mounts an ambitious, highly rewarding season.

Tennis. Among the clay courts accessible to the public (for a fee) are two with special charm: the Chequessett Yacht & Country Club on Chequessett Neck Road (508–349–3704) and Oliver's at 2183 Route 6 (508–349–3330), both in Wellfleet.

Water sports. Surfers can stock up, while getting the latest word on the waves, at the Pump House, 9 Route 6A in Orleans (508–240–2226). The Goose

Hummock Shop, next door at number 15 (508–255–0455; www.goose. com) can rent you the means—canoe, kayak, sailboard, etc.—for getting out on the water, as can Flyer's Boat Rental at 131 Commercial Street in Provincetown (508–487–0898; www.sailnortheast.com/flyers).

SPECIAL EVENTS

Mid-June. Provincetown International Film Festival, Provincetown; (508) 487–6992 or (800) 648–0364; www.ptownfilmfest.com. Hand-picked films, plus all-out fun.

Mid-August. Carnival Week, Provincetown; (508) 487–2313 or (800) 637–8696; www.ptown.org/carnival. Nonstop parties take to the street during the gay community's seasonal shindig.

Mid-September. Harbor Swim for Life & Paddler Flotilla, Provincetown; (508) 487–3684; www.swimforlife.org. A race to raise funds for local AIDS organizations is accompanied by community-building celebrations.

Provincetown Art Association and Museum Annual Consignment Auction, Provincetown; (508) 487–1750; www.paam.org. A chance to acquire fine works while benefiting the museum.

Early December. Holly Folly, Provincetown; (508) 487–2313 or (888) 933–3023; www.provincetown.com/hollyfolly. "Don we now our gay apparel" takes on a whole new meaning amid a flurry of parties and holiday house tours.

OTHER RECOMMENDED RESTAURANTS AND LODGINGS

East Orleans

Barley Neck Inn, 5 Beach Road; (508) 255–0212 or (800) 281–7505; www.barleyneck.com. Fabulous dinners are the main draw at this spiffily restored captain's house, and an adjoining motel has been transformed into a pampering hideaway. Also on the premises, Joe's Beach Road Bar convenes the liveliest social scene for miles around.

Nauset Beach Club, 222 Main Street; (508) 255–8547. This one-time hunting cabin is now a source of exquisite Northern Italian fare.

Nauset House Inn, 143 Beach Road; (508) 255–2195; www.nausethouseinn. com. Set amid moors a short stroll from Nauset Beach, this 1810 farmhouse has a familial feel, plus a lovely century-old conservatory to soothe the soul.

Parsonage Inn, 202 Main Street; (508) 255–8217. A charming B&B with English innkeepers and all the attendant niceties.

Eastham

Over Look Inn, 3085 Route 6; (508) 255–1886; www.overlookinn.com. This gaudily painted 1869 Queen Anne fairly shouts personality; the colorful rooms and outgoing Scottish innkeepers deliver.

Whalewalk Inn, 220 Bridge Road; (508) 255–0617 or (800) 440–1281; www.whalewalkinn.com. Breezy country decor and gourmet garden breakfasts distinguish this Greek Revival captain's house turned inn.

North Truro

Adrian's, 535 Route 6; (508) 487–4360; www.adriansrestaurant.com. Lavish breakfasts and chic neo-Italian suppers in a handsome dunescape setting with wraparound water view.

Terra Luna, 104 Shore Road; (508) 487–1019. A modest roadhouse serving creative breakfasts and excellent Italian/Pacific cuisine.

Orleans

Land Ho!, 38 Main Street; (508) 255–5165; www.landhoweb.com. Locals love this unpretentious roadhouse for its cheap, good eats.

Morgan's Way, 9 Morgan's Way; (508) 255–0831; www.capecodaccess.com/ morgansway. This stunning contemporary house with pool, tucked away in the woods, has only two guest rooms—plus a cottage that rents weekly—but they're beauties.

Provincetown

The Beaconlight Guesthouse, 12 Winthrop Street; (508) 487–9603 or (800) 595–9603; www.capecod.net/beaconlight. British-inflected bonhomie in an exceptionally stylish and gracious B&B—a true delight.

Bubala's by the Bay, 183-185 Commercial Street; (508) 487–0773; www. bubalas.com. Newfangled comfort foods amid jazzy Picassoesque murals and mustard Naugahyde booths, or on the lively streetside patio.

Cafe Edwige, 33 Commercial Street; (508) 487–2008. An intimate hideaway offering nonpareil natural breakfasts (till 1:00 P.M.), plus romantic dining.

Carpe Diem, 12 Johnson Street; (508) 487–4242 or (800) 487–0132; www. carpediemguesthouse.com. Small and beautifully appointed oasis overseen by a pair of charming hosts who hail from Cologne.

Chester, 404 Commercial Street; (508) 487–8200; www.chesterrestaurant.com. Assertive, uncomplicated presentations of the best in local market ingredi- ents, in a stylish minimalist space carved out of a columned Greek Revival captain's house.

Clem & Ursie's, 85 Shank Painter Road; (508) 487–2333; www.ptownlobster. com. A jazzed-up snack bar serving all the seaside favorites—and more— at populist prices.

The Commons, 386 Commercial Street; (508) 487–7800; www.capecod.net/ commons. Stylish eats (breakfast through dinner) with a prime street-scene view, plus a comfy guest house.

The Crown & Anchor, 247 Commercial Street; (508) 487–1430; www.only atthecrown.com. P-town's signature gay-oriented hotel-restaurant-cabaret complex has risen from the ashes.

Fairbanks Inn, 90 Bradford Street; (508) 487–0386; www.fairbanksinn.com. A 1776 captain's square rigger, plus two neighboring buildings, beautifully restored to traditionalist understatement.

Front Street, 230 Commercial Street; (508) 487–9715; www.capecod.net/ frontstreet. In this intimate brick-walled basement, insiders can count on stimulating company and dazzling New American cuisine.

Gallerani's, 133 Commercial Street; (508) 487–4433. A storefront prized for its congenial booths and rich New/Continental cuisine.

The Inn at Cook Street, 7 Cook Street; (508) 487–3894 or (888) COOK–655; www. innatcookstreet.com. A tasteful and lovingly tended 1836 Greek Revival hideaway in the east end.

Little Fluke Cafe, 401 Commercial Street; (508) 487–4773. From esoteric omelets for breakfast to equally far-out prix-fixe suppers.

Lorraine's, 463 Commercial Street: (508) 487–6074. Weather-worn and water-side, Provincetown's oldest restaurant (Gertrude Stein ate here) is a perfect place to enjoy Lorraine Najar's superlative Latina fare.

Napi's, 7 Freeman Street; (508) 487–1145 or (800) 571–6274; www.napis restaurant.com. An atmospheric restaurant enfolding local arts and cuisines from around the world.

Six Webster Place, 6 Webster Place; (508) 487–2266 or (800) 693–2783; www. sixwebster.com. Classic New England quarters (ca. 1750) with a tasteful gay spin.

Spiritus, 190 Commercial Street: (508) 487–2808; www.spirituspizza.com. More than a pizza joint, it's an assignation point for post-last-call cruisers.

Tropical Joe's, 135 Bradford Street; (508) 487–9941; www.tropicaljoes.com. Tasty nibbles, from reggae rings to Maui crostini, with gay cabaret on the side.

Watermark Inn, 603 Commercial Street; (508) 487–0165 or (800) 734–0165; www.watermark-inn.com. Ten breezy contemporary suites right on the beach, in the peaceful East End.

White Horse Inn, 500 Commercial Street; (508) 487–1790. It may be a bit creaky and cramped, but this eighteenth-century captain's house plus studios is like a living museum of Provincetown's art history.

Truro

Little America AYH-Hostel, Castle and Meetinghouse Roads; (508) 349–3889; www.hiayh.org. Arguably one of the most scenic hostels in the world, housed in a Hopperesque former Coast Guard Station right on Ballston Beach.

Wellfleet

Bayside Lobster Hutt, 91 Commercial Street; (508) 349–6333. Your classic shore dinner, served at an 1857 oyster shack adorned with a rooftop lobsterman.

Cahoon Hollow Bed & Breakfast, 56 Cahoon Hollow Road; (508) 349–6372. A small but stylish B&B within easy biking distance of one of Wellfleet's prettier beaches.

Colony of Wellfleet, 640 Chequessett Neck Road; (508) 349–3761. A ten-acre, ten-cottage Bauhaus preserve built in the fifties, when Marcel Breuer summered hereabouts.

Flying Fish, Briar Lane; (508) 349–3100. A delightful cafe offering three decidedly unsquare meals.

Holden Inn, 140 Commercial Street; (508) 349–3450. Cozy as grandmother's house, and much more relaxed.

FOR MORE INFORMATION

Cape Cod Chamber of Commerce, Routes 6 and 132, Hyannis, MA 02601; (508) 862–0700; www.capecodchamber.org.

Massachusetts Office of Travel & Tourism, 10 Park Plaza, Boston, MA 02116; (617) 973–8500 or (800) 227–MASS; www.massvacation.com.

Provincetown Business Guild, 115 Bradford Street; (508) 487–2313 or (800) 637–8696; www.ptown.org.

Provincetown Chamber of Commerce, 307 Commercial Street, Provincetown, MA 02657; (508) 487–3424; www.ptownchamber. com.

Martha's Vineyard

CELEBRITY PLAYGROUND

2 NIGHTS

*Stars offstage • Candyland cottages • A port for the prosperous
Art in the outback • Breath-taking biking
Ubiquitous beaches • A complete country retreat*

Long before the Clintons showed up as houseguests (following a time-honored island tradition of cadging a free vacation), this sizable island—a tiny continent unto itself—had learned to take stars in stride. Here Jimmy Cagney and John Belushi alike were forgiven for their drunken binges, and Jacqueline Kennedy Onassis at last found peace and quiet. Carly Simon and James Taylor, still the island's First Couple though long divorced, regularly mount concerts to help out their neighbors. In fact all the local notables, from Art Buchwald to Walter Cronkite, contribute to the annual "Possible Dreams" charity auction, a highlight of the summer season.

Self-sufficient enough to sustain a wide socioeconomic spectrum with or without the tourist dollar (though it certainly doesn't hurt), the Vineyard is a very tight-knit community whose fierce sense of independence has helped it withstand some of the tackier temptations of development. What you'll see—and enjoy—today is not all that different from what summerers prized a generation or more ago.

DAY 1

Morning

Get an early start down Route 3 to avoid the weekend crush. After the bridge—the Bourne might be a tiny bit less congested than the Sagamore—

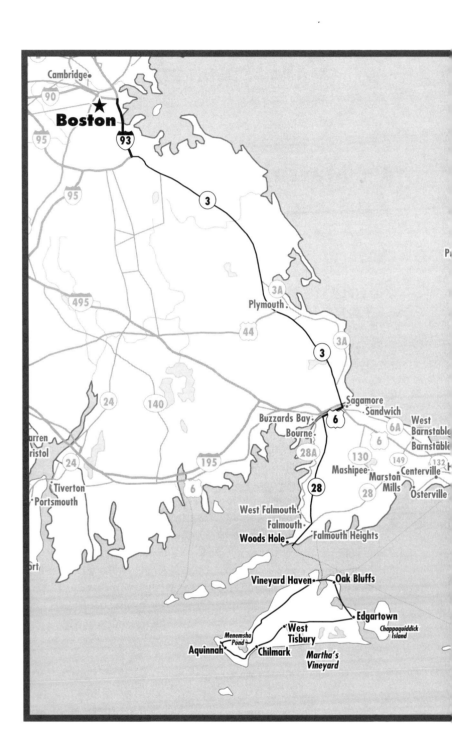

take Route 28 south to Woods Hole and board the ferry to **Vineyard Haven.** The crossing, something of a budget scenic cruise, takes less than an hour. Barring unusual circumstances, spare yourself—and the island—automotive hassle by leaving your car behind in favor of a bike or shuttle buses; the Martha's Vineyard Chamber of Commerce (see For More Information, below) will gladly provide a map and schedule.

Vineyard Haven, the island's workaday commercial center, won't cause any culture shock; it looks a lot like the Cape, with a bustling harbor and Main Street lined with shops. Carly Simon's home-decor store, **Midnight Farm,** at 18 Water-Cromwell Lane (508–693–1997), is worth catching, as is the style-setting **Bramhall & Dunn** at 23 Main (508–693–6437). **Alley Cat** at number 38 (508–693–6970) stocks the necessary clothing for that carefree, post-hippie Vineyard look. Build up your cash reserves at the posh 1905 **Compass Bank** at 75 Main. **C.B. Stark Jewelers** at 126 Main (508–693– 2284 or 888–CB–STARK; www.cbstark.com) features quahog jewelry by singer Kate Taylor, yet another multitalented sibling. The "downtown" area is only a few blocks square; you can cover it all in an hour.

LUNCH: Black Dog Tavern, Beach Street Extension, Vineyard Haven; (508) 693–9223; www.theblackdog.com. This down-home waterfront cafe has, through clever marketing, become something of an international icon. If you're not up for a wait, opt instead for instant neo-Mediterranean gratification at **Cafe Moxie,** 48 Main Street (508–693–1484; www.cafemoxie.com).

Afternoon

Bike or shuttle the 2 miles or so over to **Oak Bluffs,** a vibrant, multicultural town that started out in the mid-1830s as a tent city centered on fiery sermons. A couple of decades later the campers began trading in their musty canvas for cute little carpenter's gothic cottages, which compete to this day in a most unseemly manner for the showiest trim, the flashiest paint combos. It's a treat to meander through tree-shaded **Trinity Park,** comparing favorites. For a glimpse of favored camptown pastimes over the decades, visit the **Cottage Museum** at 1 Trinity Park (508–693–0525; www.mvcma.org), open Monday through Saturday 10:00 A.M. to 4:00 P.M. in-season. Another Oak Bluffs must is a spin aboard the **Flying Horses Carousel** at 33 Circuit Avenue (508–693–9481; www.vineyard.net/org/mvpt/carousel), an 1876 Coney Island import that's said to be the oldest still in operation; it runs daily 10:00 A.M. to 10:00 P.M. in-season, and if you manage to grab the brass ring, you'll score a free ride.

Circuit Avenue is where the interesting shops and eateries tend to concentrate. Midstroll you might want to grab some fresh hand-dipped chocolates from **Hilliard's Kitch-In-Vue** at number 51 (508–693–2191 or 877–MV–CANDY; www.badcandy.com) or a cone from **Mad Martha's** at number 117 (508–693–9151) to fortify yourself for the scenic, shore-hugging 6-mile trek over to **Edgartown**. A bonus for the self-propelled: You can just pull off the bike path for a quick dip in the placid bay.

Edgartown, once a prosperous whaling port, is definitely the island showplace, with its spiffy white captain's mansions clustered along the harbor. You can shop in them, eat in them, sleep in them; they'll invade your dreams. Wander down Main Street—past the fanciest manse, the 1840 **Dr. Daniel Fisher House** at 99 Main—and make a loop along Dock Street and North Water to see what appeals. En route you'll spot the small *On-Time* ferry, which makes a three-minute, 200-yard crossover to Chappy—**Chappaquiddick Island,** home to both the **Wasque Reservation** and **Cape Pogue Wildlife Refuge** (508–693–7662), encompassing over 700 acres of unspoiled barrier beach, and a lovely Japanese garden, **Mytoi** (both 508–627–7689; www.thetrustees.org).

DINNER AND LODGING: The Charlotte Inn, 27 South Summer Street; (508) 627–4151 or (800) 627–4701. A cluster of houses from various eras offers the island's most elegant—and priciest—quarters. In the candlelit conservatory, an enchanting restaurant, **l'etoile** (508–627–4751), serves exquisite nouvelleries.

DAY 2

Morning

BREAKFAST: The Charlotte Inn.

Morning's a good time to learn more about island history, at the various historic-house museums maintained by the **Martha's Vineyard Historical Society** at 59 School Street (508–627–4441; www.vineyard.net/org/mvhs), open Tuesday through Saturday 10:00 A.M. to 5:00 P.M. and occasional Sunday afternoons in-season. Then again, a spectacular day might demand your presence at high-surf **South Beach,** about 4 miles south of town and reachable by trolley. Otherwise the plan is to penetrate the interior—to travel up-island (longitudinally) to visit those spots that day-trippers glimpse only in passing. If you're not sure whether your legs will hold up for a bike trek of roughly 30 miles, you might consider shuttling for chunks of this trip or even renting a car.

The first destination of note is the town of **West Tisbury** about 9 miles west, where, on your left, you'll spot a pasture in which fanciful nudes prance and gambol. These are Tom Maley's sculptures, and more of their kind—plus other interesting local work—can be viewed at the **Field Gallery** just beyond (508–693–5595). Meander up Old County Road, opposite, to visit the **Granary Gallery at the Red Barn Emporium** (508–693–0455 or 800–GRANARY; www.granarygallery.com), another beloved institution that always has something worth viewing. Back in the center of town, pause to sip a cold soda on the porch at **Alley's General Store** (508–693–0088), an 1858 emporium that serves as social matrix.

LUNCH: Farmer's Market, summer Saturdays outside the Old Agricultural Hall, West Tisbury; (508) 693–8989. Arrive by noon and you can feast on exotic homemade treats. Compete for the freshest arugula with semi-incognito media darlings.

Afternoon

Head another 5 miles or so southwest on South Road, with its Celtic vistas of stone-walled pastures and stone-cold sea. Stop in at the 1730 **Allen Farm** (508–645–9064) to see the sheep and perhaps acquire a sweater handknit from their wool. Another mile west is the **Chilmark** crossroads, where perhaps another rest stop is in order. Check out the **Chilmark Flea Market** (508–645–9216), held at the Chilmark Community Church on Menemsha Cross Road Wednesdays and Saturdays in summer from 8:30 A.M. to 2:00 P.M. The 1941 **Chilmark Store** on State Road (508–645–3739) happens to house a dynamite mini-pizzeria, as well as gourmet groceries. A well-earned treat beckons around the next curve, in the form of **Chilmark Chocolates** (508–645–3013).

After another 3 miles west on State Road, veer left onto **Moshup Trail** for the best dune views. Another 3 miles will bring you to the fabled multi-colored clay cliffs of Gay Head, which now go by their original Wampanoag name of Aquinnah (meaning "high land"). They're much more dramatic viewed from below, on **Moshup Beach,** than among the tour buses and trinket-sellers that clutter the summit.

Lighthouse and Lobsterville Roads will take you 4 miles east to the mouth of Menemsha Pond, where, luckily, a **bike ferry** (508–645–3511) awaits to pontoon you across. If Menemsha's weatherworn harbor prompts a bit of déjà vu, you're probably having a *Jaws* flashback. Stop in at **Poole's Fish** on

Dutcher's Dock (508–645–2282) for an on-the-spot seafood cocktail of freshly shucked oysters.

DINNER AND LODGING: Inn at Blueberry Hill, North Road, Chilmark; (508) 645–3322 or (800) 356–3322; www.blueberryinn.com. Everything you could possibly want is right at hand within this well-thought-out eco-resort, including a lap pool and hot tub for soaking away the rigors of the road. There's a Cybex fitness center—though you've probably had a sufficient workout—as well as tennis court, croquet lawn, and walking trails through thousands of acres of conservation land. What you'll probably most appreciate at this point is the stellar restaurant, **Theo's,** which creates true marvels using local delicacies.

DAY 3

Morning

BREAKFAST: Inn at Blueberry Hill. Another chance to enjoy Theo's finesse and soothing ambience.

You could spend the day enjoying the facilities right at hand, or take advantage of the inn's passes to **Lucy Vincent Beach,** easily the island's prettiest. As you head back toward Vineyard Haven (about 7 miles from the inn; they'll be happy to give you a lift), you'll probably find yourself already planning your next visit. Unfortunately, if you're heading back on a Sunday, you'll have more than enough time to envision further trips: The Boston-bound traffic can be brutal. Maybe you'd better stay on the island another day, or two, or three . . .

THERE'S MORE

Aerial tours. Classic Aviators (508–627–7677), which takes sightseers up on a 1941 open-cockpit biplane, and MV Glider Rides (508–627–3833 or 800–762–7464) both operate out of Edgartown Airfield at Herring Creek Road near South Beach.

Arts and crafts. Travis Tuck welds fabulous répoussé copper weathervanes at his studio on State Road in Vineyard Haven (508–693–3914 or 888–693–3914; www.travistuck.com). You might also want to view artisans at work at work at Chilmark Pottery, 145 Field View Lane in West Tisbury (508–693–6476). The Craven Gallery at 459 State Road in West Tisbury (408–693–3535; www.cravengallery.com) mixes stellar new work with that of masters such as Avery, Hopper, and Sargent. Shown by appointment at his studio/gallery at 14 Wisteria Road in Chilmark (508–645–9575), Peter Simon's atmospheric shots, some hand-tinted, really capture the essence of up-island.

Horseback riding. Crow Hollow Farm on Tiah's Cove Road in West Tisbury (508–696–4554; www.crowhollowfarm.com) offers lessons and trail rides for all abilities.

Maritime adventures. See if you can schedule a day-sail aboard the replica revenue cutter *Shenandoah* (508–693–1699; www.coastwisepacket.com) out of Vineyard Haven, or Hugh Taylor's catamaran *Arabella* (508–645–3511) from Menemsha Harbor.

Nature preserves. Ospreys are making a comeback at the 350-acre Felix Neck Wildlife Sanctuary a few miles northwest of Edgartown (508–627–4850; www.massaudubon.org). The Long Point Wildlife Refuge (508–693–3678; www.thetrustees.org) offers access to an unpopulated part of South Beach. The shady Cedar Tree Neck Sanctuary off Indian Hill Road southwest of Vineyard Haven (508–693–5207; www.sheriffsmeadow.org) beckons with water views and a strictly-for-looking stone beach.

Nightlife. Oak Bluffs boasts a number of rocking clubs, including the Ritz Cafe at 4 Circuit Avenue (508–693–9851) and the Atlantic Connection at number 19 (508–693–7129). Lola's, just outside of town on Beach Road (508–693–5007; www.lolassouthernseafood.com), specializes in jazz and blues, with occasional comedy headliners.

Performing arts. The Vineyard Playhouse, housed in an 1833 church at 10 Church Street in Vineyard Haven (508–696–6300; www.mvy.com/play house), is an Equity company with an ambitious mission and the skills to match; they also mount outdoor Shakespeare et al. at the lovely Tisbury amphitheater (bring your bug spray). The Old Whaling Church, a handsome 1843 Greek Revival edifice at 89 Main Street in Edgartown (508–627–4442), now functions as a performing arts center.

Vineyards. The Vineyard actually has a good one, Chicama (508–693–0309; www.chicamavineyards.com), on Stoney Hill Road in West Tisbury; it offers complimentary tastings and tours.

Vintage vehicles. If you're going to rent a car, make it a fun one—a classy chassis from Vineyard Classic Cars in Oak Bluffs and Vineyard Haven (508–693–5551).

Water sports. Wind's Up at 95 Beach Road in Vineyard Haven (508–693–4252; www.windsupmv.com) is windsurfing central; they also rent out canoes, kayaks, and small sailing craft.

SPECIAL EVENTS

Mid-June. A Taste of the Vineyard, Edgartown; (508) 627–4440; www.vineyard.net/org/mvpt. Island restaurateurs show off their specialties to benefit the Martha's Vineyard Preservation Trust.

Early August. Possible Dreams Auction, Edgartown; (508) 693–7900; www.vineyard.net/org/mvcomserv. Local celebs put special privileges on the block to back local charities.

August (date varies). Grand Illumination, Oak Bluffs; (508) 693–0525; www.mvcma.org. The cottage campground glows by Japanese lantern light as voices rise in song.

OTHER RECOMMENDED RESTAURANTS AND LODGINGS

Aquinnah

Duck Inn, State Road; (508) 645–9018. Hippie-quaint, with absolutely glorious views.

Outermost Inn; (508) 645–3511; www.outermostinn.com. Set on a vast bluff overlooking the sea, Hugh and Jean Taylor's house is at once dazzling and homey; you'll get the same staggering view with the fine prix fixe dinners.

Chilmark

Captain R. Flanders House, North Road; (508) 645–3123. This eighteenth-century working farm has a timeless air and a beautiful meadow setting.

The Feast of Chilmark, State Road; (508) 645–3553. A rustic loft space offering extremely sophisticated food.

Edgartown

Among the Flowers Cafe, Mayhew Lane; (508) 627–3233. Brunchy stuff and well-priced dinners outdoors under an awning.

The Arbor Inn, 222 Upper Main Street; (508) 627–8137; www.mvy.com/arborinn. An 1880 farmhouse B&B treated to a dramatic interior makeover.

Colonial Inn, 38 North Water Street; (508) 627–4711 or (800) 627–4701; www.colonialinnmvy.com. A spacious, centrally located 1911 hotel with prettily updated rooms and a pleasant restaurant, Chesca's (508–627–1234).

Harbor View Hotel, 131 North Water Street (508) 627–7000 or (800) 225–6005; www.harbor/view.com. A genuine grand hotel (built in 1891), renovated to the hilt and boasting full resort facilities, plus an imposing restaurant, the Coach House (508–627–3761).

Savoir Faire, 14 Church Street; (508) 627–9864. A stylish open-kitchen bistro featuring robust New American fare infused with Mediterranean brio.

Tuscany Inn, 22 North Water Street; (508) 627–5999; www.mvweb.com/tuscany. A once-derelict captain's house stripped of its Yankee flintiness and turned into a temple of aesthetic delight. Italianate pampering extends to the in-house Tuscan trattoria, La Cucina Ristorante (508–627–8161).

The Winnetu Inn, Katama Road; (508) 627–4747 or (978) 443–1733; www.winnetu.com. The Vineyard's first grand hotel to be built in over a century, the forty-eight-room Winnetu perches near South Beach and seduces nonresidents with a New American restaurant, Opus, accessible from town by water taxi.

Menemsha

The Beach Plum Inn, off North Road; (508) 645–9454; www.beachpluminn.com. A charming farmhouse on the shore, offering lovely rooms and impressive French cuisine.

Home Port, North Road; (508) 645–2679. Classic seafood in a classic setting; also consider take-out lobster for a picnic on the beach.

Menemsha Inn and Cottages, off North Road; (508) 645–2521; www.menemshainn.com. A perfect, low-key retreat on ten waterview acres.

Oak Bluffs

Balance, 57 Circuit Avenue; (508) 696–3000. Talk about star pedigrees: The owner is Harvey Weinstein, who also runs a little enterprise called Miramax, and the genius at the stove is local wonder Ben deForest.

Jimmy Seas Pan Pasta Restaurant, 32 Kennebec Avenue; (508) 696–8550. Creatively loaded pastas, served by the panful in a no-frills luncheonette.

Lola's Southern Seafood, Beach Road; (508) 693–5007; www.lolas southernseafood.com. Feasts with all the fixings—down to the buttermilk biscuits and collard greens—plus a knockout gospel brunch.

The Oak House, Seaview Avenue; (508) 693–4187 or (800) 245–5979; www. vineyardinns.com. Victorian poshness in a former governor's mansion overlooking the sound.

Sea Spray Inn, 2 Nashawena Park; (508) 693–9388. A small artsy inn, drawing a congenial crowd.

Zapotec Cafe, 10 Kennebec Avenue; (508) 693–6800; www.mvy.com/zapotec. Authentic Mexican and Southwestern cuisine, as spicy as you please.

Vineyard Haven

Le Grenier, 96 Main Street; (508) 693–4906; www.tiac.net/users/grenier. Classic French cuisine, skillfully rendered by a native of Lyons.

West Tisbury

Lambert's Cove Country Inn, Lambert's Cove Road; (508) 693–2298; www. lambertscoveinn.com. This former gentleman's farm will appeal to those seeking a respite from the fast lane; the in-house restaurant serves superb New American fare.

FOR MORE INFORMATION

Martha's Vineyard Chamber of Commerce, Beach Road, Vineyard Haven, MA 02568; (508) 693–0085; www.mvy.com.

Massachusetts Office of Travel & Tourism, 10 Park Plaza, Boston, MA 02116; (617) 973–8500 or (800) 227–MASS; www.massvacation.com.

Nantucket

A NATURAL HISTORIC PRESERVE

2 NIGHTS

Quiet delights • Beautiful biking • Wide-open beaches
World-class restaurants • Time to read and roam

If you crave peace and quiet, and thrill to such pursuits as competitive gardening and advanced antiques appreciation (of houses, their contents, even
their occupants), you have come to the right place. Nantucket's 30-mile
"moat" has helped to protect it, so far, from the less pleasant aspects of modern life. Once you board the big old lumbering Steamship Authority ferry—
the most conducive way to time-travel—you can put most contemporary
cares behind you.

Nantucket is much smaller than its off-coast counterpart, Martha's Vineyard. Only 3½ miles wide and 14 long, and never rising much over 100 feet,
it's a breeze to cover by bike—and that's the best way, too, to appreciate the
subtle beauties of multicolored moors, pitch-pine forests, and shimmering
grasslands. And, oh, the beaches—over 100 miles' worth, if you count all the
bays and coves, and welcoming all comers. Summer is of course prime time,
but fall can be fantastic, too, with still-warm waters, barely populated beaches,
and the burnished palette of New England foliage.

DAY 1

Morning

Take Routes 3, 6, and 132 to Hyannis and follow signs for the South Street
dock. Get an early start—sevenish—to catch a morning boat that will deliver

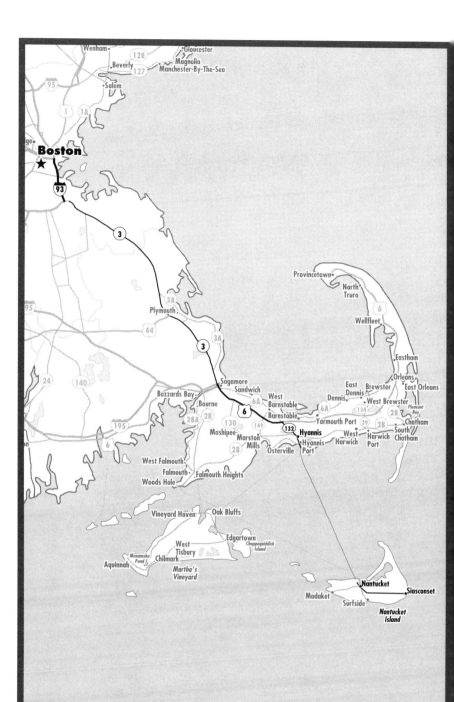

you in time for lunch. The driving distance is only about 70 miles, but two hours should allow you enough time to stow your luggage and ditch your car (Tip: The nearby lawn lots charge far less than the Steamship Authority). For a tanning op en route, claim a portside (east-facing) bench. Be sure to scan the free papers onboard for a rundown of weekend events.

Practically as soon as the mainland fades from sight, you'll spot the "faraway land" (the island's original Algonquian name). It looks much as it might have when the last whaling crews set forth a century ago. It's a bit more populated, to be sure, and the glut of cars "downtown" (both the island and its central village are called Nantucket) somewhat mars the carefully cultivated aura of yesteryear. Still, the cluster of weather-silvered shingled houses, punctuated by the occasional white church spire, remains a magical sight. There's no question you've arrived at a world apart.

Stuff your bags in a locker at the ferry terminal and set out to explore. If you haven't brought your own, you might want to rent bikes for the weekend at **Young's** on Straight Wharf (508–228–1151; www.youngsbicycleshop.com), but that can wait till you've toured the town on foot. On your right, straight ahead, is the **Whaling Museum,** housed in a former spermaceti factory at 13 Broad Street (508–228–1736; www.nha.org). Open daily 10:00 A.M. to 5:00 P.M. in-season, it's a great place to bone up on local history, as are all the properties under the aegis of the Nantucket Historical Association; go ahead and spring for a seasonal pass, which, for a few dollars more than the museum admission, will give you universal entree.

A left on Federal Street will lead you past the town's glorious **Atheneum** (508–228–1110). This 1847 Greek Revival temple to learning serves not only as a library but as a public forum, featuring speakers eager to follow in the tradition of Melville, Thoreau, Audubon, and Douglass; stop in to see what's scheduled. On a less transcendental note, check out the irresistible shops along this tree-shaded street, which will get you warmed up for the emporia of Main Street ahead—a broad expanse of cobblestone ascending toward the 1818 **Pacific National Bank,** from whose roof young local savant (and Atheneum librarian) Maria Mitchell identified a comet, thereby launching an astronomical career that would win her world fame. Again, your sites may tend less to the stars than to the stores. There's something for everyone here, from diehard antiquers to surfer dudes. Take your time, and when you tire, take a lunch break.

LUNCH: Even Keel Cafe, 40 Main Street; (508) 228–1979. Join local cognoscenti for a casual feast. Prices are relatively reasonable, and the international dishes—pastries, too—are superb. In fine weather claim a table in the patio out back.

Afternoon

Before resuming your shopping tour, you might want to detour a few blocks up Main to view a few architectural gems—specifically, the **"Three Bricks"** and **"Two Greeks,"** built in 1840–45 for the offspring of whaling merchant Joseph Starbuck (your historical association pass will get you into one of the Greek Revival manses, the **Hadwen House).** Also peek into the **Coffin School** on Winter Street (508–228–2505), a Greek Revival showplace erected in 1852 to educate the descendants of town founder Tristram Coffin, whose numbers at that point represented half the island's population; look for the paintings of Elizabeth Rebecca Coffin, who studied with Thomas Eakins. Complete the loop with a stopover at the **Macy-Christian House** at 12 Liberty Street, another NHA preserve, which dates back to 1740. Liberty Street will lead you back to the Pacific National Bank and, beside it, the **United Methodist Church** (508–228–1882), a Doric-facaded survivor from 1823. All in all, the National Historic District of downtown Nantucket encompasses some 800 pre-1850 structures, most of them still put to good use.

To your left is **Centre Street**—known during the whaling days as "Petticoat Row" for its cluster of dry-goods shops run by women whose husbands were at sea, some as long as eleven years at a stretch. Centre Street still offers the finest concentration of shops dedicated to the adornment of self and home. Presiding over the far end of the street is the massive three-story **Jared Coffin House** at 29 Broad Street (508–228–2400 or 800–248–2405; www.jaredcoffin house.com), now a hotel and social hub irreverently known as "the JC." Built by a prosperous shipowner in 1845 to please his social-climbing wife, who never deigned to occupy it, the mansion luckily served as a brick barrier during the Great Fire of 1846, which leveled the core of the town. Head about a block beyond the JC to climb the steeple at the **First Congregational Church** at 62 Center Street (508–228–0950) for a stupendous view of village and harbor.

Back on Broad, a downhill stroll leads back to Steamship Wharf, by way of the incomparable **Juice Bar** at 12 Broad (508–228–5799), where you could quaff a healthy carrot juice or, alternately, inhale a homemade hot-fudge sundae before commandeering a bike and heading for the beach. There are lovely little bay beaches—tame Children's, spacious Jetties, and bluff-lined Cliff and Dionis—trailing off to the west, or you could take a 3-mile bike path (Young's will provide a map) leading south to Surfside Beach on the ocean shore, where the waves, and crowds, tend to be a lot livelier. The ultimate sunsets go down at Madaket Beach on the western tip of the island, about a 6-mile bike ride along undulating moors.

DINNER AND LODGING: The White Elephant, 50 Easton Street; (508) 228–2500 or (800) ISLANDS; www.whiteelephant.com. Location, luxe—this decidedly desirable harborfront hotel has everything, including a polished New American restaurant, the **Brant Point Grill** (www.brantpointgrill.com).

DAY 2

Morning

BREAKFAST: The White Elephant. Watch the harbor start to stir.

By now you'll probably have acclimated sufficiently to be primed for a day of pure lazing—whether that takes the form of lugging a novel to the beach or taking a leisurely bike ride around the island. Your destination for the day is the former fishing village of **'Sconset** (short for Siasconset), about 8 miles east of town straight down Milestone Road or its bike path; loop along the Polpis Road bike path if you'd like to extend your mileage while varying the terrain. 'Sconset, which had a brief run as an actors' colony around the turn of the century, is the quintessential seaside village, remarkably unspoiled. Wander its narrow, seashell-lined lanes and marvel at the masses of roses heaped atop each priceless shanty.

Afternoon

LUNCH, DINNER, AND LODGING: The Summer House, 17 Ocean Avenue, Siasconset; (508) 257–4577; www.thesummerhouse.com. Once you've arrived at this picturesque complex of flower-laden 1840s fishing shacks on a bluff overlooking the ocean, you'll have no need to bestir yourself. You can lunch poolside at the inn's grill, surrounded by bountiful kitchen gardens, then traipse across the dunes for a dip in the sea, to be followed, perhaps, by a splash in your marble Jacuzzi . . . The entire restful setting constitutes a set-your-own-pace spa. Adirondack chairs congenially grouped about the shady lawn invite a good read, conversation, a preprandial cocktail, or perhaps all three. The **Summer House Restaurant** (508–257–9976; www.the-summerhouse.com), a summer-chic study in white-on-white, is at once romantic and accomplished, basing its inventive dishes on local bounty. A pianist provides mood music; the moon rising over the water, a veil of enchantment.

MASSACHUSETTS

DAY 3

Morning

BREAKFAST: The Summer House. Help yourself to a gourmet breakfast buffet on the broad porch.

There's little point in rushing back to the mainland to avoid the Boston-bound crowds, since you'll just end up right in the thick of them. You'd do better to linger on-island, swimming the day away or visiting places of interest you'd overlooked, including the more promising lunch and dinner spots (see Other Recommended Restaurants, below). The afternoon ferries are all bound to be mobbed, so you might as well hold out for the very last and make it a moonlight cruise. Be sure to toss a penny over your shoulder as you pass the lighthouse at Brant Point. This ritual, according to island lore, will ensure your return.

THERE'S MORE

Antiques. Nantucket has amassed quite a trove, some of which is on view at such fine shops as Lynda Willauer at 2 India Street (508–228–3631), Nantucket House Antiques at 2 South Beach Street (508–228–4604; www.nantuckethouse.com), and Wayne Pratt Antiques at 28 Main Street (508–228–8788; www.waynepratt.com). In addition, the Rafael Osona auctions, held most in-season Saturdays at the American Legion Hall on Washington Street (508–228–3942), regularly present astonishing hauls.

Arts and crafts. Until recently, Nantucket's art has tended to be on the tame, touristy side. Among the fifty or so galleries now in residence, though, you're apt to find fresh new work at the South Wharf Gallery, 21 Old South Wharf (508–228–0406). For the best traditional entries, check out the Gallery at Four India Street (508–228–8509; www.galleryatfourindia.com) and the Robert Wilson Galleries at 34 Main Street (508–228–2096; www.artnet.com/rwilson). The Golden Basket at 44 Main Street (508–228–4344 or 800–582–8205; www.thegoldenbasket.com), offers the best in handcrafted jewelry. Erica Wilson Needle Works, 27 Main Street (508–228–9881), is an island outpost of the famed Madison Avenue shop, and Claire Murray at 11 South Water Street (508–228–1913 or 800–252–4733; www.clairemurray.com) is the original nexus of a national chain of shops specializing in fabric crafts. Leslie Linsley Nantucket at 0 India Street (508–325–4900) synthesizes the breezy chic of handcrafted, Nantucket-style home decor. Nantucket Looms at 16 Main Street (508–228–1908; www.nantucket looms.com) goes for a more dramatic look, with statementy furniture and luscious woolen throws woven on-site.

Movies. Check out the first-run roster in-season at the roomy Dreamland, a former Quaker meetinghouse at 19 South Water Street (508–228–5356), which sometimes puts on rainy-day matinees. The shoebox-sized Gaslight Theatre at 1 North Union Street (508–228–4435) shows the best new indies and foreign films year-round. The Siasconset Casino, an 1899 tennis club at New Street in 'Sconset (508–257–6661), uses its venerable theater for thrice-weekly summertime showings of new family fare.

Museums and monuments. A Nantucket Historical Association property, the circa 1686 Jethro Coffin House on Sunset Hill Road (508–228–1894; www.nha.org) is not only the island's oldest surviving abode, but the subject of a lovely local Romeo and Juliet legend; docents will fill you in as they show you around. The NHA maintains about a dozen properties in all: others worth visiting include the Old Mill at South Mill Street, built of salvage in 1746 and grinding corn to this day; the cautionary Old Gaol at 15R Vestal Lane, in use from 1805 to 1933; and the Fire Hose Cart House at 8 Gardner Street, which houses a flashy late nineteenth-century fire pumper. The Maria Mitchell Science Center, headquartered at 2 Vestal Street (508–228–0898; www.mmo.org), is a complex of buildings dedicated to the legacy of the native-born nineteenth-century phenom/ astronomer; facilities include a natural history museum, observatory, and science library, and activities such as lectures and nature walks are scheduled throughout the season.

Nature preserves. About one-third of Nantucket's 42 square miles have been placed in some sort of protective custody. The Nantucket Conservation Foundation at 118 Cliff Road (508–228–2884; www.nantucket conservation.com) offers a map outlining its holdings. Among the more noteworthy are the small (seventy-three-acre) but lovely seaview Tuppancy Links, a rehabilitated golf course off Cliff Road; Sanford Farm, Ram Pasture, and the Woods, which together cover over 900 acres of moors and wetlands stretching from Madaket Road to the ocean; the 205-acre Windswept Cranberry Bog off Polpis Road, especially lovely when it turns crimson in the fall; and part of the 1,100-acre Coskata-Coatue Wildlife

Refuge, a spacious barrier beach that sweeps across the harbor beyond Wauwinet. Much of Coatue is owned by the Trustees of Reservations (508–228–6799; www.thetrustees.org).

Nautical jaunts. A number of pleasure boats head out from Straight Wharf, including the Friendship sloop *Endeavor* (508–228–5585; www.endeavor sailing.com); the lobstering/sight-seeing launch *Anna W II* (508–228–1444); and the deep-sea fishing charters *Albacore* (508–228–5074) and *Monomoy* (508–228–6867). To arrange a saltwater fly-fishing expedition, contact Cross Rip Outfitters at 24 Easy Street (508–228–4900; www.crossrip.com).

Nightlife. There isn't much, but what there is rocks. Live-music venues include the Chicken Box at 14 Daves Street (508–228–9717) and the Muse at 44 Atlantic Avenue (508–228–6873; www.museack.com).

Tours. Seventh-generationer Gail Nickerson Johnson has the inside skinny on several centuries worth of juicy gossip; you can catch up during her 1½-hour van tours (508–257–6557; www.nantucket.net/tours/gails). Seeing the streets by horse carriage—courtesy of the Rosewood Carriage Company (508–228–9252)—is a great way to get into the nineteenth-century spirit.

Water sports. Force 5 at 6 Union Street (508–228–0700; www.force5water sports.com) rents out various small craft, from kayaks and sailboards to sailboats; they also offer lessons. To learn to surf on Cisco Beach, call the Nantucket Island Surf School (508–257–9958). Scuba divers, both certified and wanna-bes, will find everything they need at the Sunken Ship at Broad Street (508–228–9226).

SPECIAL EVENTS

Late April. Daffodil Festival; (508) 228–1700; www.nantucketchamber.org. The entire town—including a parade of vintage vehicles—is decked in cheery yellow blossoms.

Mid-June. Nantucket Film Festival; (508) 228–1700; www.nantucketfilm festival.org. Some awesome names of an independent bent show up for an intense week of screenings, readings, and perhaps most important, partying.

Early-December. Christmas Stroll; (508) 228–1700; www.nantucket chamber.org. A last gasp of festivities before the winter hiatus.

MASSACHUSETTS

OTHER RECOMMENDED RESTAURANTS AND LODGINGS

Nantucket

American Seasons, 80 Centre Street; (508) 228–7111; www.americanseasons. com. Sophisticated regional fare in a charming cottage adorned with modern folk art.

Black-Eyed Susan's, 10 India Street; (508) 325–0308. Don't let the drab pine paneling deter you: this former luncheonette counter issues cutting-edge cuisine.

The Brotherhood of Thieves, 23 Broad Street; no phone. A fairly convincing simulacrum of an 1840s whaling bar, where the draw is juicy burgers with a side order of folk/rock.

Cambridge Street, 12 Cambridge Street; (508) 228–7109. A sophisticated bar scene and a little gem of a progressive, world-beat restaurant.

Centre Street Bistro, 29 Centre Street; (508) 228–8470; www.nantucket. net/food/bistro. A tiny dream of a New American restaurant, utterly transporting.

Cioppino's, 20 Broad Street; (508) 228–4622; www.cioppinos.com. Yet another source of skilled New American cuisine. The dining rooms are suitably formal, the garden patio perennially inviting.

Cliffside Beach Club, Jefferson Avenue; (508) 228–0618 or (800) 932–9645; www.cliffsidebeach. com. This luxury/rustic hotel—a former 1920s bathing club located on Jetties Beach—boasts an accomplished New American restaurant, the Galley.

Company of the Cauldron, 5 India Street; (508) 228–4016; www.company ofthecauldron.com. The menu at this intimate restaurant may be limited— to one prix fixe menu per evening—but devotees pack the place for each well-considered repast.

DeMarco, 9 India Street; (508) 228–1836; www.nantucket.net/food/demarco. Killer North Italian, priced accordingly.

India House, 37 India Street; (508) 228–9043. You can still sense the Quaker influence at this pared-down 1803 bed-and-breakfast; dinners at the India House Restaurant are a lot more lavish and modernist.

Jared Coffin House, 29 Broad Street; (508) 228–2400 or (800) 248–2405; www.jaredcoffinhouse.com. The Coffins' grand brick mansion is somewhat stuffy, but lovely in its own way. The same can be said for the formal dining room, Jared's.

Kendrick's, 5 Chestnut Street; (508) 228–9156. Exuberant, big-flavor New American cuisine in a cluster of packed parlors.

Le Languedoc, 24 Broad Street; (508) 228–2552; www.lelanguedoc.com. The romance of Provence meets the provender of Nantucket, with seductive results.

Oran Mor, 2 South Beach Street; (508) 228–8655. Dazzling regional cuisine in a trio of Shaker-spare rooms.

The Pearl, 12 Federal Street; (508) 228–9701. Dazzling decor; astonishing cuisine. If the prices appall, try the adjoining Boarding House (508–228–9622), also provisioned by super-chef Seth Raynor.

The Pineapple Inn, 10 Hussey Street; (508) 228–9992; www.pineappleinn. com. An exemplary B&B.

Rope Walk, Straight Wharf; (508) 228–8886. Contemporary seafood, harborside.

Sfoglia, 130 Pleasant Street; (508) 325–4500. Intriguing New Italian fare.

Ships Inn, 13 Fair Street; (508) 228–0040. An 1831 captain's house doubles as a plain-spun inn and celebratory Californian/French bistro.

Straight Wharf Restaurant, Straight Wharf; (508) 228–4499. Sumptuous regional offerings in a breezy, loftlike space.

Sushi by Yoshi, 2 East Chestnut Street; (508) 228–1801. A tiny restaurant/shop offering the very best way to enjoy Nantucket's fabulous fish.

21 Federal, 21 Federal Street; (508) 228–2121; www.21federal.net. Deft New American dishes in a handsome Greek Revival setting.

The Woodbox, 29 Fair Street; (508) 228–0587; www.woodboxinn.com. New American/Continental dining in an atmospheric 1709 Colonial inn.

Siasconset

Chanticleer Inn, 9 New Street; (508) 257–6231; www.thechanticleerinn.com. Classical French cuisine in an opulent aubergelike setting.

Sconset Cafe, Post Office Square; (508) 257–4008. Tiny but terrific, this village eatery roams the globe for inspiration.

Surfside

Star of the Sea AYH-Hostel, Surfside; (508) 228–0433; www.hiayh.org. A scenic 1874 life-saving station turned youth hostel, right beside the beach.

Wauwinet

The Wauwinet, 120 Wauwinet Road; (508) 228–8768 or (800) 426–8718; www.wauwinet.com. This resplendently updated 1850 resort straddles a "haulover" poised between ocean and bay. Head out by complimentary van or launch for a spectacular regional feast at the in-house restaurant, Topper's.

FOR MORE INFORMATION

Massachusetts Office of Travel & Tourism, 10 Park Plaza, Boston, MA 02116; (617) 973–8500 or (800) 227–MASS; www.massvacation.com.

Nantucket Island Chamber of Commerce, 48 Main Street, Nantucket, MA 02554; (508) 228–1700; www.nantucketchamber.org.

MAINE
ESCAPES

MAINE

The Lower Coast
A COSMOPOLITAN OUTPOST

2 NIGHTS

Vibrant port towns • Historical neighborhoods
Outlet splurges • Antiques to go • A gay resort
Five-star food • World-class art • A seaside retreat

Though Maine certainly has its wild side—the farther Down East you go, or deep into the interior—the southern coast represents a gradual segue from Bostonian sophistication. The gateway towns of Portsmouth, New Hampshire, and Portland, Maine, are easily Boston's equal in terms of cultural energy and interest, if not size. Scattered in between are beach communities ranging from the chichi (Ogunquit) to the kitschy (Old Orchard Beach), strung together by pretty coastal byways.

If you like what you see, all the more incentive to press on. Maine's coast is only 400 miles long end to end, but as broad as the continent if you were to trace every last ripple of shoreline.

DAY 1

Morning

After about an hour on the highway (I-95 north), follow the historic district signs to the center of **Portsmouth,** and pause for a café au lait and authentic French pastry—outdoors, ideally—at **Café Brioche,** 14 Market Square (603–430–9225; www.cafebrioche.com). From here the shops along Market Street beckon like a low-key Newbury analog. After browsing, head southeast to the **Strawbery Banke Museum** on Marcy Street (603–433–1100; www.

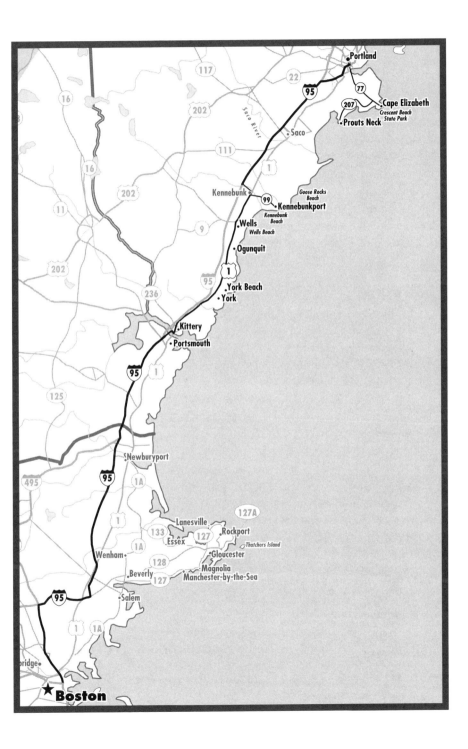

strawberybanke.org). This ten-acre historic preserve, open daily from 10:00 A.M. to 5:00 P.M. May through October (reduced hours off-season), encompasses ten homes dating from 1690 to 1958. By the latter era, this historic shipbuilding community—named for the profusion of wild fruits that the first settlers found here in the 1630s—had fallen on hard times. One half of the Drisco House, for example, embodies the lifestyle of a shipyard worker's family as TV became a focal point of home life; the other half of the 1795 building has been restored to its original function as a dry-goods store. Several abodes, such as the Chase House, a Georgian mansion, and the Federal Bailey House afford a glimpse of the luxuries enjoyed by the merchant class. Though not a living history museum per se, the place is packed with stories.

Cross the Piscataqua River and you've entered Maine. The first town you pass through, **Kittery,** gained fame as the nation's oldest shipyard but is now noted more for its outlets: over one hundred crowd a 1-mile strip of Route 1 (888–KITTERY; www.thekitteryoutlets.com).

In the next town along Route 1, **York,** the focus shifts to antiques—it's a picker's heaven. You can also view antiquities in context by touring some of the seven properties maintained by the **Old York Historical Society** at 207 York Street (207–363–4974; www.oldyork.org), which include John Hancock's wharf and warehouse, plus a 1719 jail. This historic cache, open 10:00 A.M. to 5:00 P.M. Tuesday through Saturday in season, survives largely thanks to the efforts of William Dean Howells and Mark Twain, summering scriveners who also happened to be visionary preservationists. **York Beach** still retains a touch of its Victorian polish, reflected in the **Goldenrod** on Railroad Avenue (207–363–2621; www.thegoldenrod.com), a family restaurant founded in 1896. Enjoy a cool drink at the old-fashioned soda fountain.

The next stop is **Ogunquit**—Abenaki for "beautiful place by the sea." Its charms—including a gorgeous 3-mile beach—have not gone undiscovered: the town has attracted artists and actors since the 1920s and is currently enjoying a new golden age as a gay destination, Maine's answer to Provincetown.

LUNCH: Village Food Market, 141 Main Street, Ogunquit; (207) 646-2122; www.villagefoodmarket.com. Get right into the swim by assembling a splendid outdoor repast.

Afternoon

Laze on the beach or stroll around town, perhaps going so far as to walk the mile-long **Marginal Way** shoreline path to picturesque **Perkins Cove;** you could always catch a tourist trolley back should your feet tire. Be sure to stop in at the **Ogunquit Museum of American Art** on Shore Road (207–646–4909), which showcases locally inspired works, including some by illustrious summerers such as Reginald Marsh. It's open Tuesday through Saturday 10:30 A.M. to 5:00 P.M. and Sunday 2:00 to 5:00 P.M., July through September.

When it suits you, meander further along Route 1 through **Wells,** pausing to visit some of the more enticing antiques stores—**R. Jorgenson** (207–646–9444) is a must—and perhaps to scarf down a homemade Kahlua brownie cone at the classic ice cream stand **Big Daddy's** (207–646–5454).

Pulling into **Kennebunk,** veer east on Route 35 to view the so-called **Wedding Cake House** on Summer Street, an 1826 captain's house lavished with gingerbread trim: legend holds that he gussied it up to compensate for a rushed pre-sail ceremony.

Depending on your pace, you might reach **Kennebunkport** in time to visit the **Brick Store Museum** at 117 Main Street (207–985–4802; www.brickstoremuseum.org), open 10:00 A.M. to 4:30 P.M. Tuesday through Saturday. This 1825 emporium has been retrofitted to showcase fine and decorative arts; the complex also includes the beautiful housewright-built 1803 Taylor-Barry House. The shops of **Dock Square**—including the **Kennebunkport Book Port** in a former gin warehouse at number 10 (207–967–3815)—tend to keep late hours, so stroll away. Wander up Spring Street (Route 9) to Maine Street to view the handsome houses of the historic district and to visit the **Mast Cove Galleries** at Mast Cove Lane (207–967–3453), a gathering of eighty artists who've earned national attention.

DINNER: White Barn Inn, Beach Street, Kennebunkport; (207) 967–2321; www.whitebarninn.com. Count on nouvelle-American bedazzlement within this rustic eatery, Maine's only entry in the ultraprestigious Relais & Chateaux association.

LODGING: Captain Lord Mansion, 6 Pleasant Street, Kennebunkport; (207) 967–3141 or (800) 522–3141; www.captainlord.com. The spiffiest lodgings in a very shipshape town can be found at this imposing 1812 mansion with well-chosen antiques and a cupola offering a knockout view.

DAY 2

Morning

BREAKFAST: Captain Lord Mansion. The breakfasts are justifiably famed.

Kennebunk's signature Wedding Cake House

Poke around Kennebunkport a bit more, perhaps visiting its beaches. To end-run the parking problem, take the **Intown Trolley** (207–967–3686; www.intowntrolley.com) or rent a bike from the **Cape-Able Bike Shop** at 83 Arundel Road (207–967–4382 or 800–220–0907; www.cape-ablebike.com). Whatever your means of transport, be sure to make a scenic loop along Ocean Avenue—site of the Bush compound on **Walkers Point**—before heading back to I–95. Unless you've got children along (in which case, see Kid stuff, below), you can safely skip the rest of the coast—it's pretty honky-tonk for the most part—and head straight for **Portland,** a place that native son Henry Wadsworth Longfellow recalled fondly as "the beautiful town that is seated by the sea."

Thanks to intensive urban renewal, Portland and its trio of Olmsted-designed gardens are quite pretty once again and a pleasure to stroll. In the Old Port area, reclaimed by artists in search of low rents (they're history now!), old Victorian warehouses overflow with inviting restaurants and shops. Crafts are a big draw: check out generalist **Gallery 7** at 49 Exchange Street (207–761–7007; www.galleryseven.com) and **Fibula** at 50 Exchange (207-761-4432) for Maine-fashioned jewelry. Breezy contemporary fashion can be found in boutiques such as **Amaryllis** at 41 Exchange (207–772–4439); **Portmanteau,** 191 Middle Street (207–774–7276), creates coats and carryalls in handsome fabrics, including hemp. Home accessories are another forte—they range from antique to futuristic at **Decorum,** 231 Commercial Street (207–775–3346 or 800– 288–3346)—and you might turn up some serious furniture at the multidealer **Portland Antiques Center** at 382 Commercial Street (207–773–7052 or 888–950–2226; www.portlandantiques.com).

LUNCH: Head uphill to cruise the **Portland Public Market** at 25 Preble Street (207–228–2000; www.portlandmarket.com). The vast, timber-framed food hall, built in 1998 and philanthropically funded, hosts a panoply of purveyors, as well as a Maine-showcase restaurant, Commissary (207–228–2057).

Afternoon

Housed in an I.M. Pei brick box topped with playful Palladian arches, the **Portland Museum of Art** at 7 Congress Square (207–773–ARTS or 800–639–4067; www.portlandmuseum.org) is excuse enough for a jaunt to Portland. The in-depth American holdings are particularly rich in such local phenomena as Winslow Homer and Andrew Wyeth, and the addition of Joan Whitney Payson's astute Impressionist collection jacks up the collection to world-class. Ordinarily open 10:00 A.M. to 5:00 P.M., the museum stays open till 9:00 on Thursdays and Fridays. There's usually some contemporary work on display; to spot local up-and-comers, meander down increasingly artsy Congress Street to visit the **Institute of Contemporary Art** at the **Maine College of Art,** number 522 (207–879–5742; www.meca.edu/ica), a department store turned gallery.

End your tour of Portland with a panoramic view from the 1807 **Portland Observatory** at 138 Congress Street in the eastern end of town (207–774–5561; www.portlandlandmarks.org/observatory/htm), open 10:00 A.M. to 5:00 P.M. daily in-season. The view extends from the hundreds of islands dotting Casco Bay to the White Mountains looming in the west.

DINNER AND LODGING: Inn by the Sea, 40 Bowery Beach Road, Cape Elizabeth; (207) 799–3134 or (800) 888–4287; www.innbythesea.com. Ten minutes from downtown Portland, Cape Elizabeth beckons with pretty **Crescent Beach,** a pristine state park connected by private boardwalk to this neotraditional luxurious all-suite hotel with heated pool, two lighted tennis courts, a croquet lawn, and an accomplished New American restaurant, the **Audubon Room** (207–767–0888).

Evening

Between Portland's 1929 **State Theater** at 609 Congress Street (207–773–3331), a one-time vaudeville venue now booking touring musicians, and a dozen other interesting performance spaces, nightlife options abound. For current listings, consult a local paper such as the *Casco Bay Weekly.*

DAY 3

Morning

BREAKFAST/BRUNCH: Inn by the Sea. Enjoy a lavish spread in the Audubon Room; you might even want to sleep in to await the sumptuous buffet brunch.

After enjoying the grounds, you could backtrack a bit to visit **The Museum at Portland Head Light** at 1000 Shore Road in Fort Williams Park (207–799–2661; www.portlandheadlight.com), open daily in-season 10:00 A.M. to 4:00 P.M. Though decommissioned, Maine's oldest lighthouse remains nonetheless scenic, and the keeper's house has been converted into a spiffy museum covering lighthouses throughout history. Or you could continue southwest along the coast to visit **Prouts Neck,** immortalized by Winslow Homer, whose studio—a shed attached to a private house—stands untouched, as if he'd just stepped out to lunch. Visitors are welcome daily in-season from 10:00 A.M. to 4:00 P.M.: ask for directions at the **Black Point Inn Resort** at 510 Black Point Road (207–883–2500 or 800–258–0003; www.blackpoint inn. com), a grand 1878 summer hotel that serves a bountiful poolside buffet, should you need shoring up.

Afternoon

Pick your favorite beach, of all you've visited, and peacefully bide your time till dinner. You can afford to linger: It's only about an hour from Maine's border to Boston, and the longer you hang around, the less traffic you'll have to contend with. Besides, this wait will be worth it.

DINNER: Arrows, Berwick Road off Route 1, Ogunquit; (207–361–1100; www.arrows.com). Many cognoscenti happily drive up from Boston just to visit this exquisite restaurant, a 1765 farmhouse decorated in comfy-luxurious

English country style. The emphasis is on regional delicacies—many grown right on the spot—and the approach is exotic and invariably brilliant.

THERE'S MORE

Boat excursions. In Portsmouth, the Isles of Shoals Steamship Company at 315 Market Street (603–431–5500 or 800–441–4620; www.isleofshoals.com) offers glimpses of the islands favored first by pirates, then Impressionist painters. Twenty miles off the Maine coast is Jeffreys Ledge, a whale feeding ground; Cape Arundel Cruises' *Nautilus* out of Kennebunkport (207–967–0707 or 800–933–0707; www.cacruises.com) will take you there. Portland's Casco Bay Lines ferries (207–774–7871; www.cascobaylines.com) offer a terrific opportunity for island-hopping.

Historic houses. The Society for the Preservation of New England Antiquities (603–436–3205; www.spnea.org) maintains three beauties in Portsmouth: the 1664 Jackson House at 76 Northwest Street, the oldest surviving wood-frame house in the region; the 1784 Governor John Langdon House at 143 Pleasant Street, noted for its decorative carvings and perennial gardens; and the Rundlet-May House at 364 Middle Street, an 1807 Federal mansion full of fine Portsmouth furniture. Portland is home to the 1785 Wadsworth-Longfellow House at 485 Congress Street (207–774–1822; www.mainehistory.org), built by the famous poet's grandfather, and the 1858 Morse-Libby House—a.k.a. Victoria Mansion—at 109 Danforth Street (207–772–4841), an elaborate Italianate villa.

Kid stuff. Funtown/Splashtown U.S.A on Route 1 in Saco (207–284–5139 or 800–878–2900; www.funtownsplashtownusa.com) is a combination amusement/water park with a wholesome atmosphere. Maine's largest water slide sits on the 7-mile beach near the venerable—if somewhat seedy— Palace Playland in Old Orchard Beach (207–934–2001; www.palace playland.com). For educational fun, try the highly interactive Children's Museum of Maine at 142 Free Street in Portland (207–797–5483; www. childrensmuseumofme.org).

Nature preserves. Within the 332-acre Odiorne Point State Park off Route 1 in Rye, New Hampshire (603–436–7406; www.nhparks.state.nh.us/parks/ odiorne), the New Hampshire Audubon Society maintains the Seacoast Science Center with its giant tide pool touch tank (603–436–8043; www. seactr.org). In Maine the Wells National Estuarine Reserve at Laudholm

Farm Road (207–646–1555; www.wellsreserve.org) offers 1,600 more acres to explore, including seven miles of walking paths fanning out from a beautiful Victorian farmhouse. Wells also harbors the 7,435-acre Rachel Carson Refuge off Route 9 (207–646–9226; www.sirius.com/~fitch/wells/carson/ carson). The 3,000-acre Scarborough Marsh Nature Center (207–781–2330; www.maineaudubon.org) protects the largest salt marsh in the state, tourable by canoe.

Performing arts. Portsmouth's Seacoast Repertory Theater at 125 Bow Street (603–433–4472 or 800–639–7650; www.seacoastrep.org) keeps up with the cosmopolitan competition year-round, and The Music Hall at 28 Chestnut Street (603–436–2400; www.themusichall.org) imports nationally known musicians, comedians, and more. Touring TV stars tend to head the roster at the Ogunquit Playhouse (207–646–5511; www.ogunquit playhouse.org), a straw-hat theatre founded in the thirties. The distinguished Portland Stage Company performs at 25A Forest Avenue (207–774–0465, www.portlandstage.com). The Portland Symphony Orchestra and touring at big-name acts are booked into Merrill Auditorium, 389 Congress Street (www.portlandevents.com).

Specialty museums. At the Port of Portsmouth Maritime Museum/Albacore Park at 600 Market Street (603–436–3680; www.portsmouth.com/ visitors/albacore), you can clamber about a grounded 1952 submarine. The University of Southern Maine maintains the fascinating Osher Map Library at a former baked-goods factory at the corner of Forest Avenue and Bedford Street (207–780–4850; www.usm.maine.edu/~maps), as well as the Southworth Planetarium at 96 Falmouth Street (207–780–4249; www.usm.maine.edu/~planet).

SPECIAL EVENTS

Late June to late August. Prescott Park Arts Festival, Portsmouth; (603) 436–2848; www.artfest.org. A full roster of concerts, theater, dance, arts, and food fests on the waterfront.

Mid-August. Kennebunkport Riverfest; (207) 967–0857. A craft fair plus water-craft races including the category "whatever floats."

December 31. First Night, Portsmouth; (603) 431–5388; www.proportsmouth. org/firstnight. Citywide festivities feature local performers.

New Year's Portland; (207) 772–9012 or (800) 639–4212; www.main-earts.org. A multi-performance extravaganza.

OTHER RECOMMENDED RESTAURANTS AND LODGINGS

Cape Elizabeth

Two Lights Lobster Shack, 225 Two Lights Road off Route 77; (207) 799–1677. A 1920s landmark serving lobster in the rough.

Kennebunkport

The Beach House, 211 Beach Avenue; (207) 967–3850; www.beachhseinn.com. A breezy, stylish B&B overlooking Gooch's Beach.

Bufflehead Cove, Bufflehead Cove Road; (207) 967–3879; www.bufflehead cove.com. A Victorian Dutch Colonial with lovely, peaceful riverside rooms.

Cape Arundel Inn, Ocean Avenue; (207) 967–2125; www.capearundelinn. com. An 1895 summer cottage with ocean-view rooms and an adventurous menu.

Colony Hotel, 140 Ocean Avenue; (207) 967–3331 or (800) 678–8946; www. thecolonyhotel.com. A 1914 grand hotel with all the traditional amenities—a modern-day treasure.

Grissini Trattoria, 27 Western Avenue; (207) 967–2211; www.restaurantgrissini. com. A snappy, northern Italian offshoot of the White Barn Inn.

Maine Stay Inn and Cottages, 34 Maine Street; (207) 967–2117 or (800) 950–2117; www.mainestayinn.com. An agreeable B&B with a festive feel and terrific breakfasts.

Old Fort Inn, 8 Old Fort Avenue; (207) 967–5353 or (800) 826–3678; www. oldfortinn.com. Country panache—complete with heated pool and tennis court—in a stylishly converted barn and brick carriage house.

On the Marsh, 46 Western Avenue; (207) 967–2299. A farmhouse and barn turned stylish repository for buyable arts and antiques, as well as savory New American cuisine.

Salt Marsh Tavern, 46 Western Avenue (Route 9); (207) 967–4500. City-polish New American cuisine in a beamed farmhouse.

Seascapes, 77 Pier Road; (207) 967–8500; www.seascapesrestaurant.com. Fabulous Maine fusion at the tip of a Cape Porpoise peninsula.

Windows on the Water, 12 Chase Hill Road; (207) 967–3313 or (800) 773–3313; www.windowsonthewater.com. A contemporary restaurant known for its inventive ways with lobster.

Ogunquit

Anchorage by the Sea, 55 Shore Road; (207) 646–9384; www.anchorage bythesea.com. A large (220-room) modern waterside resort with classic touches such as gazebos and a boardwalk.

Hurricane, Perkins Cove; (207) 646–6348 or (800) 649–6348; www.hurricane restaurant.com. Trendy eats—Maine/Asian fusion—with a lofty water view.

Portland

Cafe Uffa, 190 State Street; (207) 775–3380. Well-priced multi-influenced fare.

The Danforth, 163 Danforth Street; (207) 879–8755 or (800) 991–6557; www. danforthmaine.com. A grand 1881 brick Federal with luxurious rooms.

Fore Street, 288 Fore Street; (207) 775–2717. Wood-grilling rules at this cousin of Street & Company.

Hugo's Portland Bistro, 88 Middle Street; (207) 774–8538; www.hugos.net. A prime contender among Portland's favorite "first name" restaurants.

Katahdin, 106 High Street; (207) 774–1740. Eclectic decor; lively atmosphere and cuisine.

Natasha's, 40 Portland Street; (207) 774–4004. Straightforward, well-priced New American fare in a pared-down, neo-industrial setting.

Perfetto, 28 Exchange Street; (207) 828–0001. Low-key Mediterranean perfection.

Pomegranate Inn, 49 Neal Street; (207) 772–1006 or (800) 356–0408; www. pomegranateinn.com. An artful B&B in the residential West End.

Portland Regency, 20 Milk Street; (207) 774–4200 or (800) 727–3436; www. theregency.com. A nineteenth-century armory transformed into a contemporary hotel, in the heart of the old port.

Rachel's Wood Grill, 90 Exchange Street; (207) 774–1192. A polished and personable trattoria.

Street & Company, 33 Wharf Street; (207) 775–0887. Seafood every which way, in a setting of studied rusticity.

Walter's, 15 Exchange Street; (207) 871–9258; www.walterscafe.com. A winning international bistro.

Portsmouth, New Hampshire

Anthony Alberto's Ristorante Italiano, 59 Penhallow Street; (603) 436–4000; www.anthonyalbertos.com. Stellar renditions, in a sexy stone cellar.

Blue Mermaid World Grill, 409 The Hill; (603) 427–2583; www.blue mermaid.com. A jazzy boite serving spicy southern-clime cuisine.

Bow Street Inn, 121 Bow Street; (603) 431–7760; www.bowstreetinn.com. River-view rooms in a former brewery.

The Library Restaurant at the Rockingham House, 401 State Street; (603) 431–5202; www.libraryrestaurant.com. International cuisine in the mahogany-paneled library of a 1785 manse.

Lindbergh's Crossing Bistro and Wine Bar, 29 Ceres Street; (603) 431–0887; www.lindberghscrossing.com. An atmospheric tavern offering adventurous, mostly Mediterranean cuisine.

Martin Hill Inn, 404 Islington Street; (603) 436–2287; www.portsmouthinn.com/martinhillinn. An 1820 B&B with period furnishings and gourmet breakfasts.

Roxanne's, 105 Daniel Street; (603) 431–1948. A comfy, creative cafe beloved for its breakfasts.

York Harbor

Dockside Guest Quarters, Harris Island Road; (207) 363–2868 or (800) 270–1977; www.docksidegq.com. Cottages flank a classic seacoast inn on seven acres; the seafood specialties are available in both traditional and New American preparations.

FOR MORE INFORMATION

Convention & Visitor's Bureau of Greater Portland, 305 Commercial Street, Portland, ME 04101; (207) 772–5800 or (877) 833–1374; www.visit portland.com.

Greater Portsmouth Chamber of Commerce, 500 Market Street, PO Box 239, Portsmouth, NH 03802-0239; (603) 436–1118; www.portcity.org.

Kennebunk–Kennbunkport Chamber of Commerce, 17 Western Avenue, Kennebunk, ME 04043; (207) 967–0857 or (800) 982–4421; www.kkcc. maine.org.

Maine Office of Tourism, 33 Stone Street, Augusta, ME 04330; (207) 287–5711 or (888) MAINE45; www.visitmaine.com.

MAINE

The Midcoast

TREASURE HUNTING

ALONG THE SHORE

---

2 NIGHTS

Underwater mountains • Schooner adventures
Alluring islands • The Wyeths' world • Recreational shopping

From Portland to Rockland, the coastline goes haywire where eons ago, melting glaciers created a now-drowned mountain range. The result is a wild zigzag of inlets and peninsulas. It's fun to poke around, because you never know what the next vista will bring: a protected cove dotted with sailboats, perhaps, or a meadow flecked with wildflowers. Although this region is pretty well touristed, and has been for some time, you'll still catch glimpses of rugged Maine beauty.

Each town along this stretch has a distinctive personality. Freeport is outlet central superimposed upon a classic New England town. The result is a mega-mall that feels like a village (or perhaps vice versa, depending on your viewpoint). Brunswick is a congenial college town (the site of Bowdoin College since 1794), and Bath a shipbuilding center with emerging elements of hipness. Wiscasset, with its handsome Federal houses, is the beauty of the bunch. Rockland is experiencing artful stirrings, and in Rockport and Camden, favored by artists and socialites alike since the turn of the century, there's still plenty of picturesqueness to go around.

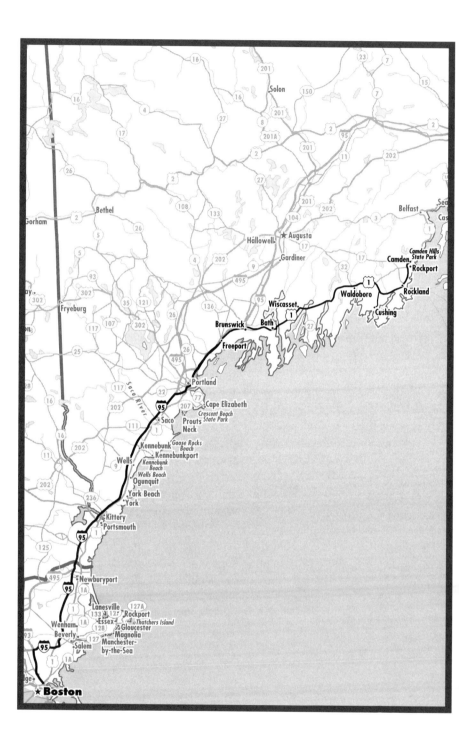

ESCAPE TWO

MAINE

DAY 1

Morning

Take I–95 (the Maine Turnpike) straight to **Brunswick,** saving your Freeport shopping spree for Sunday, when the crowds are sparser. Pull right up to **Cabot Mill Antiques,** housed in an 1820s brick mill building at 14 Maine Street (207–725–2855; www.cabotiques.com); this spacious collective emporium offers superior inventory at relatively modest prices. Visit Bowdoin's verdant campus (Hawthorne and Longfellow went here), stopping off at the **Bowdoin College Museum of Art** in the Walker Art Building (207–725–3275; www.academic.bowdoin.edu/artmuseum), open Tuesday through Saturday 10:00 A.M. to 5:00 P.M. and Sunday 2:00 to 5:00 P.M. The holdings—including Stuart and Copley portraits—are limited but priceless.

Press on to **Bath** to the **Maine Maritime Museum & Shipyard** at 243 Washington Street south of Route 1 (207–443–1316; www.bathmaine.com), open daily 9:30 A.M. to 5:00 P.M. You don't have to be boat-crazy to enjoy the exhibits, which range from elaborate models to an actual schooner. Watch wooden boats being made from scratch, or take a barge tour to get a water-side view of the Bath shipyards. Afterward you might want to stroll through town, checking out the antiques shops along Front Street.

LUNCH: Kristina's, 160 Center Street, Bath; (207) 442–8577. This stylish cafe carved out of a pair of nineteenth-century houses serves the freshest, most imaginative fare in the area.

Afternoon

As you pull into **Wiscasset,** accurately touted as Maine's prettiest village, make a brief stop at the **Musical Wonder House,** 18 High Street (207–882–6373 or 800–336–3725; www.musicalwonderhouse.com), an 1852 mansion harboring over 400 music boxes. Forgo the full house tour; there's plenty to see, for free, in the gift shop. As you meander down Main Street toward the Sheepscot River, you'll pass the beautifully proportioned 1808 **Nickels-Sortwell House** at Federal Street, a Society for the Preservation of New England Antiquities property (207–882–6218; www.spnea.org); tours begin hourly Wednesday through Sunday from 11:00 A.M. to 4:00 P.M. in-season. Head north on Federal Street to visit the rather forbidding **Old Lincoln County Jail** (207–882–6817; www.mainemuseums.org), a dank, granite-walled fortress in use from 1811 to 1913; it's open 11:00 A.M. to 4:00 P.M.

Tuesday through Sunday in-season. Then take a westerly route to view what's up at the **Maine Art Gallery,** housed in a handsome 1807 academy on Warren Street (207– 882–7511). Pick up a map that lists further galleries and antiques shops, mostly centered back on Main Street, where you can nab a zingy homemade gingersnap at **Treats** (207–882–6192) before strolling out onto the bridge to admire the river view.

DINNER AND LODGING: Squire Tarbox Inn, Route 144, Wiscasset; (207) 882–7693; www.squiretarboxinn.com. At this late eighteenth-century inn, about 8½ miles south of Route 1, you can snack on fresh-made flavored chèvres before enjoying an elegant four-course prix fixe dinner. Guests are welcome to visit the resident goats, or go rowing on a saltwater inlet, before bedding down in any of eleven country-comfort rooms.

DAY 2

Morning

BREAKFAST: Squire Tarbox Inn. You can count on a farm-fresh breakfast here. But should you need a subsequent coffee boost, with an optional slice of cream pie on the side, make a pit stop on Route 1 in **Waldoboro** at **Moody's Diner** (207–832–7468; www.moodysdiner.com), a 1927 classic awash in turquoise Formica and appreciative locals.

About 10 miles down the road, follow southward signs to **Cushing,** where you're in for a sight: the field and house featured in Andrew Wyeth's famous painting *Christina's World.* Open Wednesday through Sunday 11:00 A.M. to 4:00 P.M. in-season, the **Olson House** on Hathron Point Road is now an outpost of the **Farnsworth Art Museum** (207–596–6457; www.farnsworthmuseum. org), a few miles further along Route 1 at 352 Main Street in **Rockland.** This extraordinary facility—open 9:00 A.M. to 5:00 P.M. (Wednesday until 7:00 P.M.) daily in-season, less off—holds an outstanding cache of American art, including the output of three generations of Wyeths (N.C., Andrew, and Jamie) as well as sculptor Louise Nevelson, who spent her childhood knocking about a Rockland lumberyard. The increasing cachet of the museum, plus the moneyed tastes of itinerant windjammers, has brought a certain panache to this once-plain fishing town.

The neighboring town of **Rockport,** north along Penobscot Bay, is the site of the **Maine Photographic Workshops,** whose students roam in the streets in search of appropriate subjects for study. Its gallery, at 2 Central Street

The Victory Chimes, *a classic coastal windjammer*

(207–236–8581 or 800–227–1541; www.meworkshops.com), warrants a visit, as does the **Maine Coast Artists Gallery** in a former firehouse at 162 Russell Avenue (207–236–2875).

Camden was a popular tourist spot long before Edna St. Vincent Millay, employed as a chambermaid at the still-thriving **Whitehall Inn,** lauded its beauties in her 1912 poem "Renascence" (her reading to gathered guests earned her a Vassar College scholarship). To get a good view of the "three long mountains" that distinguish the shoreline (Ragged Mountain even sports a tiny downhill ski area, the Camden Snow Bowl), you might want to take a short cruise on one of the picturesque windjammers that line the town dock; the largest daysailer, at 86 feet, is the *Appledore* (207–236–8353), a veteran of several world tours. Concomitantly, to gaze out over the "three islands in a bay," consider hiking Mount Megunticook within 6,500-acre **Camden Hills State Park** (207–236–3109; www.state.me.us/doc/prkslnds/camden.htm). Or you can cheat a bit and drive up Mount Battie. Most visitors just meander about town, and that can be fun, too, so rich is the mix of shops and eateries.

LUNCH: Atlantica, 1 Bay View Landing; (207) 236–6011 or 888–507–8514; www.atlanticarestaurant.com. Glorious new-style seafood, indoors or on the deck.

Afternoon

Continue poking about Camden, venture onto one of the peninsulas you passed up en route, or head straight to **Freeport** to rest up for tomorrow's shopathon.

DINNER AND LODGING: Harraseeket Inn, 162 Main Street, Freeport; (207) 865–9377 or (800) 342–6423; www.stayfreeport.com. This modernized hotel in the traditionalist mode offers a luxurious oasis amid the off-price fray. Enjoy a superb New American meal, showcasing local provender. For bedtime reading, as well as campaign planning, pick up a store map published by the Freeport Merchants Association (207–865–1212 or 800–865–1994; www. freeportusa.com). And if you just can't wait, hit up the mega-emporium **L. L. Bean** at 95 Main Street (800–341–4341; www.llbean.com): it's open twenty-four hours. Savvy shoppers, though, will wait to check out the deep discounts at Bean's factory store on Depot Street.

DAY 3

Morning

BREAKFAST: Harraseeket Inn. The breakfast is bounteous.

Having mapped out your hit list, you're all set for the siege, starting at 10:00 A.M. sharp. By the time the other shoppers show up, postnoon, you'll have done your plundering and have turned your thoughts to lunch and home.

LUNCH: Harraseeket Lunch & Lobster Company, Town Wharf off Main Street, South Freeport; (207) 865–4888. Consume a farewell lobster on the spot and perhaps grab a couple of live ones to go.

THERE'S MORE

Arts and antiques. Rockland is fast becoming a collectors' mecca: the Harbor Square Gallery, housed in a handsome 1912 bank at 374 Main Street

(207–594–8700 or 877–594–8700; www.harborsquaregallery.com) shows fine arts and crafts; Gamage Antiques at 467 Main Street (207–594–4963) stocks precious primitives. ABCD Books at 23 Bayview Street in Camden (207–236–3903; www.abcdbooks.com) is a honey os a old-books trove.

Beaches. Few people come this far north to swim, but you might want to put in some sunning time at historically significant Popham Beach State Park, a pretty 3-mile stretch near the end of Route 209 in Phippsburg (207–389–1335; www.state.me.us/doc/prkslnds/popham.htm), the site of a short-lived 1607 colony.

Island detours. Consider tacking an extra day (or more) onto your trip to explore some islands. On Eagle Island, accessed from South Freeport via Atlantic Seal Cruises (207–865–6112), Admiral Peary's summer house remains much as it might have looked in 1909 when he was the first to reach the North Pole. Monhegan, served by ferries from Boothbay Harbor (207–633–2284 or 800–298–2284; www.balmydayscruises.com), New Harbor (207–677–2026 or 800–2–PUFFIN; www.hardyboat.com), and Port Clyde (207–372–8848; www.monheganboat.com), is a craggy wonder, beloved of painters such as Jamie Wyeth. Rockland ferries serve Vinalhaven (207–863–4421) and North Haven (207–867–4441), old-money redoubts ideal for biking. Isleboro, a short ferry ride from Lincolnville (207–789–5611), is another great place to hike or bike. For a map and schedules, check the Maine State Ferry Service Web site (www.state.me.us/mdot/opt/ferry/ferry.htm).

Nature spots. Wolfe's Neck Woods State Park at 106 Wolf Neck Road in Freeport (207–865–4465) offers 244 shoreline acres to wander. Specializing in indigenous plants, the sixty-six-acre Merryspring Horticultural Nature Park and Learning Center on Conway Road in Camden (207–236–2239) includes an arboretum and outstanding perennial gardens.

Performing arts. The Maine State Music Theater (207–725–8769; www.msmt.org), housed at Bowdoin College in Brunswick, has been mounting professional summer productions since 1950. The Chocolate Church Arts Center at 804 Washington Street in Bath (207–442–8455; www.chocolatechurcharts.org)—a Greek Revival building painted dark brown—hosts plays, concerts, gallery shows, and other events year-round. Round Top Center for the Arts on Route 1 in Damariscotta (207–563–1507; www.lincoln.midcoast.com/~nrtca) offers a varied lineup, including some festive outdoor events.

Sea excursions. H2Outfitters, based on Orrs Island south of Brunswick (207–833–5257 or 800–20KAYAK; www.h2outfitters.com), offers sea-kayak rentals, instruction, and tours. For an interesting "Rail & Sail" combo—a jaunt aboard a lobster boat plus a scenic coastal train ride—contact the Maine Coast Railroad in Wiscasset (207–882–8000 or 800–795–5404). To inquire about long- and short-term windjammer cruises out of Rockland, contact the Maine Windjammer Association (207–374–2993 or 800–807–WIND; www.sailmainecoast.com). The *Shantih II,* a classic wooden sailboat, takes small groups (six or fewer) for lobster lunch and gourmet sunset cruises out of Rockport Harbor (800–599–8605; www.midcoast.com/~shantih). When not ferrying to Monhegan, the *Hardy III* out of New Harbor (see Island detours, above) sets off in search of puffins and seals. Maine Sport Outfitters on Route 1 south of Camden (207–236–7120 or 888–236–8797; www.mainesport.com) rents all sorts of water craft and leads excursions around the harbor and bay.

Specialty museums. At the Colonial Pemaquid State Historic Site off Route 130 in Bristol (207–677–2423; www.mainemuseums.org), an on-site museum documents the ongoing excavation of this early seventeenth-century settlement. Farther down Route 130, the keeper's house for the 1824 Pemaquid Point Lighthouse (207–677–2494; www.lighthouse.cc/pemaquid) contains a museum dedicated to Maine's fishing history. The Owls Head Transportation Museum at Knox County Airport on Route 73 in Owls Head (207–594–4418; www.ohtm.org) harbors all sorts of vintage vehicles, from bicycles to biplanes.

SPECIAL EVENTS

Late June. Ultimate Sidewalk Sale, Freeport; (207) 865–1212 or (800) 865–1994; www.freeportusa.com. The discount outlets take to the streets, with even steeper markdowns.

Late June through August. Bowdoin Summer Music Festival, Brunswick; (207) 725–3322; www.summermusic.org. A roster of international as well as local talent.

Early August. Maine Festival, Brunswick; (207) 772–9012 or (800) 639–4212; www.mainearts.org. International performers and local arts, crafts, and products combine in a carnival on Thomas Point Beach.

Maine Lobster Festival, Rockland; (207) 596–0376 or 800–LOB–CLAW; www.mainelobsterfestival.com. A half-century-old tradition of feasting, lobster crate racing, and the crowning of the Maine Sea Goddess.

OTHER RECOMMENDED RESTAURANTS AND LODGINGS

Bath

The Inn at Bath, 969 Washington Street; (207) 443–4294 or 800–423–0934; www.innatbath.com. A strikingly decorated 1830 inn on Bath's showpiece street.

Boothbay Harbor

Spruce Point Inn and Lodges, Grandview Avenue; (207) 633–4152 or (800) 553–0289; www.sprucepointinn.com. This turn-of-the-century inn on its own manicured fifteen-acre peninsula has charmed successive generations with rustic decor and plentiful meals, of late quite sophisticated.

Camden

The Belmont, 6 Belmont Avenue; (207) 236–8053 or 800–238–0853; www.thebelmontinn.com. A prettily decorated 1896 Victorian with a commendable New American dining room, Marquis (www.marquisatthe belmont.com.

Frogwater Café, 31 Elm Street; (207) 236–8998. A dream bistro offering innovative comfort foods—try the Spanish onion rings—and delectable desserts.

Hartstone Inn, 41 Elm Street; (207) 236–5629 or (800) 788–4823; www.hartstoneinn.com. An 1835 Second Empire house offering luxury lodging and award-worthy prix fixe dinners.

Hawthorn Inn, 9 High Street; (207) 236–8842; www.camdeninn.com. A fanciful Victorian graced with harbor views and delectable teas.

A Little Dream, 66 High Street; (207) 236–8742 or 800–217–0109; www.littledream.com. A pampering 1888 Victorian with English country decor.

The Maine Stay, 22 High Street; (207) 236–9636; www.mainestay.com. A Greek Revival beauty with cheery rooms.

Norumbega, 61 High Street; (207) 236–4646 or 877–363–4646; www. norumbegainn.com. A Victorian stone castle perfect for romantic retreats.

East Boothbay

Five Gables Inn, Murray Hill Road; (207) 633–4551 or (800) 451–5048; www.fivegablesinn.com. Every bedroom in this 1865 guest house boasts a bay view and country-opulent decor.

Linekin Bay Resort, Route 96; (207) 633–2494; www.linekinbayresort.com. Sailing is the raison d'être of this weathered resort; lessons and rentals are included in the modest room rates.

Friendship

The Outsiders' Inn, Routes 97 and 200; (207) 832–5197. An 1830 house in the town that spawned the Friendship sloop. The innkeepers can help get you on one, the *Gladiator;* they also guide kayak trips in nearby Muscongous Bay.

Georgetown Island

Grey Havens Inn, Seguinland Road; (207) 371–2616 or 800–431–2316; www. grayhavens.com. A classic 1904 Shingle-style inn overlooking Sheepscot Bay.

Robinhood Free Meetinghouse, Robinhood Road off Route 127; (207) 371–2188; www.robinhood-meetinghouse.com. This 1855 Greek Revival hall harbors an ambitious multicultural restaurant.

Harpswell

Captain's Watch B&B, 2467 Cundy's Harbor Road; (207) 725–0979; www. gwi.net/~cwatch. A splendid four-square 1862 house overlooking a harbor where the inn's own charter sailboat, the *Symbion,* is moored.

Isleboro

Dark Harbor House, Main Road; (207) 734–6669; www.darkharborhouse. com. A grand 1896 Georgian summer cottage offering elegant lodgings and dinner.

Monhegan

The Island Inn; (207) 596–0371; www.islandinnmonhegan.com. A 1900 inn with forty-five rooms notable mostly for their views, and a three-meal-a-day dining room.

Newcastle

Newcastle Inn, 60 River Road; (207) 563–5685 or (800) 323–8669; www.newcastleinn.com. A romantic riverview inn with extraordinary prix-fixe dinners.

New Harbor

The Bradley Inn, 3063 Bristol Road; (207) 677–2105 and (800) 942–5560; www.bradleyinn.com. Pretty rooms, lovely gardens, and astounding New American dinners.

Nobleboro

Mill Pond Inn, 50 Main Street; (207) 563–8014; www.millpondinn.com. A 1780 clapboard overlooking a peaceful mill pond, ready to be explored by canoe or antique launch—or just dive in off the swimming dock.

Phippsburg

Popham Beach Bed & Breakfast; (207) 389–2409; www.pophambeachbandb. com. An 1883 Coast Guard station retrofitted as a charming waterside B&B.

Rockland

Primo, 2 South Main Street; (207) 596–0770; www.primorestaurant.com. Superchef Melissa Kelly delivers knockout Mediterranean fare in a prettily rehabbed Victorian.

Thomaston

Thomaston Café & Bakery, 88 Main Street; (207) 354–8589; www.midcoast maine.net/thomastoncafe. Homemade standards plus innovations such as wild mushroom hash.

Vinalhaven

The Haven, 245 Main Street; (207) 863–4969. A tiny restaurant serving basic breakfasts and blowout dinners.

Payne Homestead at the Moses Webster House, Atlantic Avenue: (207) 863–9963 or (888) 863–9963; www.paynehomestead.com. A glorious Gothic manse surrounded by gardens.

Waldoboro

Pine Cone Café, 13 Friendship Street; (207) 832–6337. A rural cafe capable of fulfilling big-city dreams.

Wiscasset

Le Garage, Water Street; (207) 822–5409; www.legarageme.com. A 1920s garage makes a good seafood restaurant overlooking the river.

Sarah's Café, Route 1 and Water Street; (207) 882–7504; www.sarahscafe.com. River views plus fabulous homemade soups, pizzas, lobster dishes, and desserts—especially desserts.

FOR MORE INFORMATION

Camden-Rockport-Lincolnville Chamber of Commerce, PO Box 919, Camden, ME 04843; (207) 236–4404 or 800–223–5459; www.camdenme.org.

Chamber of Commerce of the Bath-Brunswick Region, 45 Front Street, Bath, ME 04530; (207) 443–9751; www.midcoastmaine.com.

Maine Office of Tourism, 33 Stone Street, Augusta, ME 04430; (207) 287–5711 or (888) MAINE45; www.visitmaine.com.

Penobscot Bay

THE QUIET COAST

---
2 NIGHTS
---

*Antiquing Central • A tidy Tory holdout • World-class crafts
Islands off islands • A musical oasis*

In wandering off Route 1 to explore Deer Isle and Castine and Blue Hill, the venerable towns that flank it, you'll be following a less-trodden trail, one where Maine's rugged, rural beauty survives relatively intact. It's a landscape of utmost simplicity: prim whitewashed villages, meandering meadows limned by stone walls, pines profiled against sparkling sea.

There isn't a whole lot to do here, so bring a book or sketchpad, and by all means, leave your laptop home. This is your chance to be borne aloft on salt-laden breezes and to forget what century it is.

DAY 1

Morning

Belfast, an all-American town whose main claim to fame—until Fred Wiseman's 1999 documentary—was serving as the setting for the movie *Peyton Place,* is about a four-hour drive from Boston: take I–95 (the Maine Turnpike) to Augusta, then Route 3 east. Lately the town has begun to catch some artsy spillover from its more cosmopolitan neighbor, Camden, so you'll find a strollable brick-building Main Street with appealing galleries, shops, and cafes.

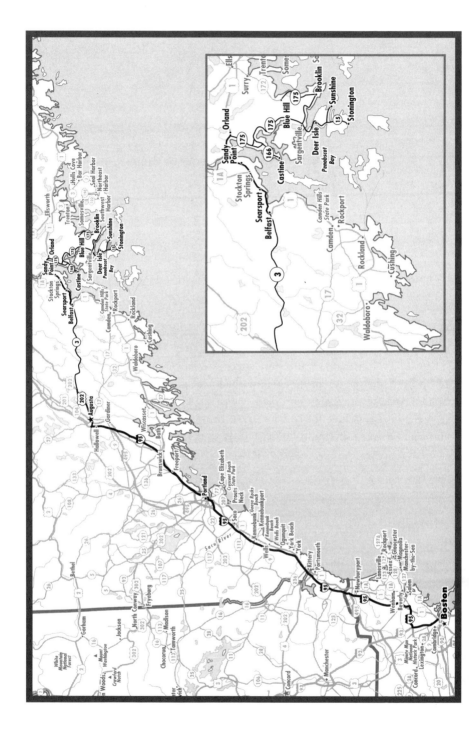

LUNCH: Bay Wrap, 20 Beaver Street, Belfast; (207) 338–9757; www.belfast maine.com/baywrap. Pick up a tasty multicultural sandwich-to-go.

Afternoon

Searsport, the next town down Route 1, is lined with impressive captains' houses, many of which have been converted into inns and antiques stores. So active was the China trade in this region that a great many treasures are still circulating: the town bills itself as Maine's "antiques capital." Seek out the multi-dealer **Searsport Antique Mall** at 149 East Main Street (207–548–2640) and the open-air flea market. The 1845 town hall on Church Street off Route 1 plus seven other historic buildings house the **Penobscot Marine Museum** (207–548–2529; www.penobscotmarinemuseum.org), which documents the town's primacy as a nineteenth-century shipbuilding center; it's open in-season Monday through Saturday 10:00 A.M. to 5:00 P.M. and Sunday noon to 5:00 P.M.

Heading farther Down East, pause 1 mile north of Stockton Springs for a refreshing dip—or perhaps just a token splash, given the frigid waters—at **Sandy Point Beach.** Continue along Route 1 through Bucksport, to **Orland,** where the nonprofit **H.O.M.E. Co-op** (207–469–7961; www.homecoop.net) operates a farmstand and crafts village with ongoing demos. From here follow Routes 175 and 166A south to **Castine,** a Pilgrim trading post that remains one of Maine's most pristine towns.

Owned in turn by the French, Dutch, and British (Tory sympathizers welcomed a British invasion in 1779, and the town was again occupied for the better part of 1812), Castine now attracts high-profile yachts as it once did moneyed summer rusticators. Meander down elm-lined Main Street to see who's in port. One likely bet is the *Laurie Ellen* steamboat (207–326–9045; www.castinesteamboat.com), a wood-fired anachronism that offers one-hour harbor tours. Landlubbers might prefer to view curiosities ranging from Native American artifacts to old farm tools at the **Wilson Museum** on Perkins Street (207–326–8545), open in-season Tuesday through Sunday from 2:00 to 5:00 P.M.

DINNER AND LODGING: Castine Inn, Main Street, Castine; (207) 326–4365; www.castineinn.com. Many rooms in this lovingly refurbished 1898 summer hotel offer harbor vistas, and you can enjoy beautifully rendered local provender—innkeeper Tom Gutow cooked at Bouley in New York—in a pretty garden-view dining room.

DAY 2

Morning

BREAKFAST: Castine Inn. Enjoy a lovely breakfast perfumed by the inn's out-standing perennial gardens.

Today's destination is **Blue Hill,** another venerable summer colony, by way of a long detour through peaceful **Deer Isle.** Follow routes 166 and 199 to regain Route 175, which leads southward to Sargentville; from here Route 15 runs through Little Deer Isle onto Deer Isle itself. In **Deer Isle Village,** a few miles south of the suspension bridge, stop in at the **Blue Heron Gallery** (207–348–6051; http://w5.downeast.net/blueheron), which features work by the faculty of the world-renowned **Haystack Mountain School of Crafts** (207–348–2306; www.haystack-mtn.org), located about 7 miles east in Sunshine; you might want to drive by the dazzling campus, tucked into a spruce-covered bluff overlooking Jericho Bay. En route, at 598 Sunshine Road, you'll run into **Nervous Nellie's** (207–348–6182 or 800–777–6845; www.nervous nellies.com), a rural jam kitchen with a whimsical café and sculpture garden.

Eventually all roads lead to **Stonington,** a rugged port on the southernmost tip where a couple of interesting curio shops—including the ultrasophisticated **Eastern Bay Gallery** on Main Street (207–367–6368)—have cropped up to cater to the summer crowd. As you wander about town, look for the charming miniature version built by resident Everett Knowlton years ago and now dis-played in its own little garden. Time and energy permitting, you might want to get even further away from it all by hopping an hour-long mailboat 8 miles south to **Isle au Haut** (207–367–5193; www. isleauhaut. com), where 2,800 acres of National Park Service nature trails await hikers.

LUNCH: Penobscot Bay Provisions, West Main Street, Stonington; (207) 367–5177. Pack a salami-and-chevre sandwich—or some other rarefied combo—to go.

Afternoon

Head back to the mainland, and circuitously northeast along Route 175, which follows the coast through rural **Brooklin**—longtime home to E. B. White and, more recently, the **Wooden Boat School** (207–359–4651; www.woodenboat.com), where his son Joel often taught—to **Blue Hill,** an enduring magnet for artists and visionaries. The **Parson Fisher House,** a half-mile south of town on Route 15/176 (207–374–2459), is the 1814 abode of one early resident genius, a Harvard grad whose intense interests ranged from education to art (some of his extraordinary primitive oeuvre can be seen at Rockland's Farnsworth Museum); tours are offered in-season Monday through Saturday from 2:00 to 5:00 P.M. For a further glimpse of Blue Hill creativity, peruse the arts and crafts galleries scattered throughout town. For news of local doings, tune into **WERU**—for "We Are You"—at 89.9 FM (207–469–6600; www.weru.org), the community radio station founded by resident Noel Paul Stookey, the "Paul" of Peter, Paul & Mary.

DINNER AND LODGING: Captain Merrill Inn, One Union Street, Blue Hill; (207) 374–2555 or (877) 374–2555; www.captainmerrillinn.com. The captain's great-granddaughter turned this 1830 house into an elegant inn where the dining is locally derived.

DAY 3
Morning

BREAKFAST: Captain Merrill Inn. The inn provides a beauty.

Boston is now about five hours distant. You could loll about town (the Maine Turnpike can be a bear, so depart on the late side if you can get away with it), or break up your trip with a stop along the coast, among the choices described in previous chapters.

THERE'S MORE

Performing arts. Strung across the summer weekends, the Kneisel Hall Chamber Music Festival (207–374–2811; www.kneisel.org) serves as a showcase for this venerable summer institute in Blue Hill. The Surry Opera Company (207–667–9551), founded by local Zen master/musician Walter Nowick, draws international performers to its Concert Barn.

Sea excursions. Check the schedule for the Pinky schooner *Summertime* (800–562–8839; www.schoonersummertime.com), which embarks on day sails from various Penobscot Bay ports. Or play marine biologist aboard the Marine Environmental Research Institute's eco-cruiser *R/V Meri* out of Brooklin (207–374–2135; www.meriresearch.org). Would-be sea kayakers can set out from the Phoenix Center on Route 175 in Blue Hill Falls (207–374–2113).

The light at Eggemoggin Reach

SPECIAL EVENTS

Mid-July. Downeast Antiques Fair, Blue Hill; (207) 866–2241; www. downeast.
net/nonprof/antiqbsa. An indoor/outdoor extravaganza at the Blue Hill
Fairgrounds.

Early September. Blue Hill Fair; (207) 374–3701; Labor Day brings a classic harvest festival, with livestock and comestible competitions.

OTHER RECOMMENDED RESTAURANTS AND LODGINGS

Blue Hill

Arborvine, Main Street; (207) 374–2119; www.arborvine.com. This restful
Mediterranean restaurant in a 1823 Cape also harbors the Moveable Feasts
Delicatessen (207–374–2441).

The Blue Hill Inn, Union Street; (207) 374–2844 or (800) 826–7415. Circa 1830s elegance—candlelit dinner included—in the center of a lovely village.

Jonathan's, Main Street; (207) 374–5226. A congenial restaurant serving generous portions of internationally influenced fare.

Brooklin

The Lookout, Flye Point; (207) 359–2188; www.acadia.net/lookout. The fine food at this century-old hotel comes accompanied by exceptional views of Mount Desert.

Castine

Dennett's Wharf, Sea Street; (207) 326–9045; www.dennettswharf.com. A perfect harborside perch for enjoying the freshest possible seafood.

The Pentagoet Inn, Main Street; (207) 326–8616 or (800) 845–1701; www.pentagoet.com. A turreted 1894 Victorian offering quaint rooms and appealing prix fixe dinners.

Deer Isle

The Inn at Ferry Landing, Old Ferry Road; (207) 348–7760; www.ferrylanding.com. An 1840s farmhouse featuring glorious views of Eggemoggin Reach.

Pilgrim's Inn, Main Street; (207) 348–6615 or 888–778–7505; www.pilgrimsinn.com. This 1793 house harbors a luxury B&B and a barn serving sophisticated home-grown prix fixe dinners.

Isle au Haut

Keeper's House, Lighthouse Road; (207) 367–2261; www.keepershouse.com. The lighthouse keeper's quarters make for a peaceful, if remote, inn, where overnighters are served a candlelit dinner (there's no electricity).

Little Deer Isle

Eaton's Lobster Pool, Blastow's Cove Road; (207) 348–2383. A classic waterside restaurant where the lobsters come straight from the boat.

Stonington

Bayview Restaurant, Seabreeze Avenue; (207) 367–2274. Local seafood in various guises.

Fisherman's Friend Restaurant, School Street; (207) 367–2442. Super seafood, especially the homemade chowders, plus delectable pies.

Inn on the Harbor, Main Street; (207) 367–2420 or (800) 942–2420; www. innontheharbor.com. Rooms perched right on the water.

Sunset

Goose Cove Lodge; (207) 348–2508 or (800) 728–1963; www.goosecovelodge. com. A secluded, family-friendly compound on twenty-one seaside acres; the food is bountiful and good.

FOR MORE INFORMATION

Belfast Area Chamber of Commerce, PO Box 58, Belfast, ME 04915; (207) 338–5900; www.belfastmaine.org.

Blue Hill Peninsula Chamber of Commerce, PO Box 520, Blue Hill, ME 04614; (207) 374–3242; www.bluehillmaine.com.

Deer Isle-Stonington Chamber of Commerce, PO Box 459, Stonington, ME 04681; (207) 348–6124; www.deerislemaine.com.

Maine Office of Tourism, 33 Stone Street, Augusta, ME 04330; (207) 287–5711 or (888) MAINE45; www.visitmaine.com.

Mount Desert Island

A NATIONAL TREASURE

2 NIGHTS

Incredible "cottages" • *Carriage-trade adventures*
Yachting havens • *Whales and seals* • *Blue-ribbon gardens*

Once the backwoods playground of the ultrarich and old-money famous, Mount Desert has come down in the world since the turn of the century, and especially since 1947, when an indiscriminate, month-long fire destroyed scores of opulent "cottages" (outsize summer homes). In recent decades the proles have pretty much taken over. The 46,000-acre Acadia National Park, patched together by foresighted philanthropists in 1919, is now the second most popular in the country, attracting millions of visitors yearly. Yet there remain plenty of byways where you can evade the masses—including John D. Rockefeller Jr.'s 57-mile network of once-private bridle paths, now yours for the strolling, mountain biking, or, in winter, cross-country skiing.

It's a lovely chunk of land, this strange place where stony mountains poke straight up from the vast blue sea—a sight that inspired explorer Samuel de Champlain to name the 13-by-16-mile land mass *"l'isle des Monts-deserts."* The largest of these bare peaks, 1,530-foot Cadillac Mountain, is the highest point on the East Coast. Another unusual geographical feature is the East Coast's only natural fjord, Somes Sound, which nearly splits the island in two.

The eastern half tends to be splashier (it's here that Martha Stewart plunked down several million for Edsel B. Ford's former estate), whereas the western lobe cleaves to the rugged Maine mystique. A weekend is too brief to provide much more than a superficial overview but will probably leave you yearning to return.

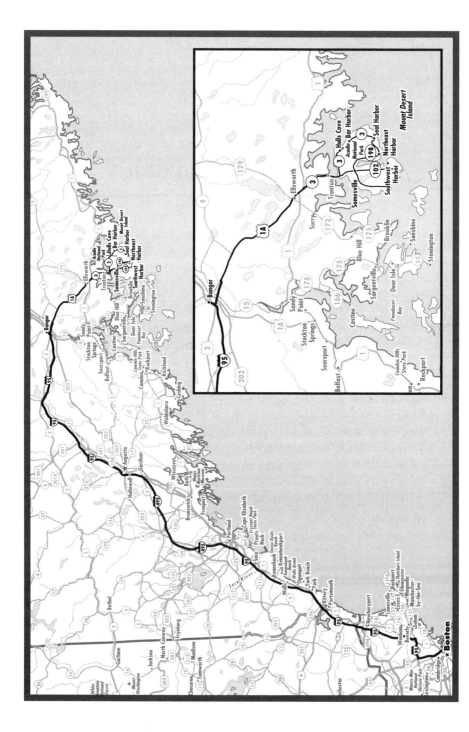

MAINE

DAY 1

Morning

Figure on a roughly six-hour drive. It's about 240 miles from Boston to Bangor via the Maine Turnpike (I–95), then about 30 miles on Route 1A to rather tacky, congested Ellsworth, and another 20 on Route 3 to **Bar Harbor.**

LUNCH: Oak Point Lobster Pound, Oak Point Road, Trenton; (207) 667–6998. Just before the bridge, head 4 miles southwest on Route 230 to enjoy an alfresco seafood feast with spectacular views.

Afternoon

You've probably had quite enough driving for the day, so put off till tomorrow the obligatory 27-mile drive through **Acadia National Park.** At most get oriented at the Visitors Center on Route 3 in Hulls Cove (207–288–3338; www.nps.gov/acad), open daily from 8:00 A.M. to 6:00 P.M. in-season. Here you can watch an introductory film, check the listings of ranger-led activities, and pick up a free map for planning tomorrow's itinerary.

For now you might just want to poke around Bar Harbor to find, amid the tourist-directed dreck, such interesting shops as **Island Artisans,** an outstanding crafts co-op at 99 Main Street (207–288–4214; www.islandartisans.com), and **J. H. Butterfield** at 152 Main (207–288–3386), purveyors to the cottage trade since 1887. Sneak a piece of tea cake, or go all out and head over to **Ben & Bill's Chocolate Emporium** at 66 Main (207–288–3281; www.benandbills.com) to check out the lobster ice cream—truly. If you're feeling energetic and it happens to be low tide, consider walking out along the exposed bar that gave the harbor its name. At the very least stroll along mile-long **Shore Path,** where the cottages are laid out like so many architectural jewels.

DINNER: Thrumcap, 123 Cottage Street, Bar Harbor; (207) 288–3884. At this study in buttoned-down, yacht-club nattiness (named for an island in Frenchman's Bay), quaff a fresh-fruit daiquiri at the antique oak bar before enjoying an assortment of small plates embodying "Maine global fusion" cuisine.

LODGING: Inn at Canoe Point, Eden Street, Hulls Cove; (207) 288–9511; www.innatcanoepoint.com. You can't beat this secluded, cliff-hanging Tudor aerie for lovely views and runaway romanticism.

Evening

Almost every summer weekend brings some special event, if only a band concert on the village green. Do some more strolling around (the shops stay open late in-season), or catch a live performance or first-run flick at the 1932 art deco **Criterion Theatre** on Cottage Street (207–288–3441; www.criterion theatre.com). Live it up and sit in one of the semiprivate loges.

DAY 2

Morning

BREAKFAST: Inn at Canoe Point. Enjoy a hearty repast on the deck or in the dramatic Ocean Room, with its grand piano, granite fireplace, and 180-degree view.

Get an early start—eightish—to try to keep one step ahead of the motoring throngs that clog Acadia's Park Loop Drive, a one-way toll road with a modest fee. Enter near the Visitors Center and select your stopping points judiciously. The most popular spot, **Thunder Hole,** where waves create a noisy, 30-foot "geyser," is not all that exciting when you factor in the inevitable crowds. Far more thrilling is the chance, at **Schooner Head,** to venture under overhanging cliffs and find tide pools subtly awave with sea anemones. Similarly forgo the overrun stretch of sand at **Seal Harbor** in favor of a less visited hideaway such as the rocky beach at **Otter Point.** Ask nicely, and some kindhearted native might steer you to other such undersung wonders.

Even the hiking trails—120 miles' worth, not even counting the carriage roads—can sometimes clog up, but they offer the very best way to experience the countryside. The challenge level ranges from easy (the virtually horizontal 3⅓-mile **Jordan Pond Loop**) to exhausting (the 1½-mile **Precipice Trail** seems to head straight up). Perhaps the most scenic is the century-old **Ladder Trail** on the east side of **Dorr Mountain,** where a thousand stone steps yield ever more dramatic vistas. Those not up to the rigors of backwoods hiking might enjoy a two-hour carriage tour conducted from the **Wildwood Stables** (207–276–3622; www.acadia.net/wildwood) near Jordan Pond.

LUNCH: Jordan Pond House, Seal Harbor, Acadia National Park; (207) 276–3316; www.jordanpond.com. If you end up tarrying in the woods past lunch time, don't worry because tea here is every bit as delectable; in fact, it's a century-old tradition. Opt for an outdoor table, where you can slather strawberry jam on fresh, hot popovers with abandon.

Hiking the spine of Maine's "desert mountain"

Afternoon

A drive up **Cadillac Mountain** is perhaps de rigueur, for the 360-degree view of blue seas speckled with islands and what look like toy boats. But if you've filled your scenery quota while still on the trail, you could exit Park Loop Drive at Seal Harbor and head directly to **Northeast Harbor** along Route 3, saving another full loop.

This yachting haven has plenty of scenery of its own to offer, starting with the spectacular **Thuya Gardens** off Route 3 (207–276–5130), a semiformal perennial array set amid a 215-acre hilltop park linked to the harbor by zigzagging rustic pathways. It's open from 7:00 A.M. to 7:00 P.M. daily in season, and you can drive up if you're all hiked out. Farther down Route 3, near the junction of Route 198, are the small (two-and-a-half-acre) but exquisite **Asticou Azalea Gardens,** where twenty multicolored varieties peak in late June. With its Japanese elements, including a sand garden, it's a refreshing spot throughout the summer.

Pulling into the town proper, you'll find a seemingly modest Main Street lined with posh shops, such as **Local Color** at number 147 (207–276–5544), a temple to wearable art, and **Shaw Contemporary Jewelry** at number 100 (207–276–5000; www.shawjewelry.com), featuring beach stones set in 22-karat gold.

DINNER AND LODGING: Asticou Inn, Route 3, Northeast Harbor; (207) 276–3344 or (800) 258–3373; www.asticou.com. This 1883 holdover from Bar Harbor's heyday is the perfect place to observe the eternal summertime verities of porch sitting at sunset and dressing up to enjoy stalwart Yankee/Continental standards.

DAY 3

Morning

BREAKFAST: Asticou Inn. This one comes with a harbor view.

Enjoy the inn's formal gardens, tennis courts, and heated swimming pool, before heading out along mansion-lined Sargent Drive to cross over to the "quiet side" via Route 198. On Route 102 two miles west of Somesville, stop at the National Park Outdoor Recreation Center concession at the northern end of **Long Pond** (207–244–5854 or 877–378–6907; www.nporc.com), where you can rent a canoe or kayak, and get out on the water for a while.

LUNCH: The Claremont Hotel, Claremont Road, Southwest Harbor; (207) 244–5036 or (800) 244–5036; www.theclaremonthotel.com. This is the island's other grand dame of a summer hotel, built in 1884. Lunch, with a few sub-dued modernist touches, is served at the Boat House, on the water.

Afternoon

If you wish to linger a while before joining the homeward-bound mobs, take some time to wander along the shoreline at the Nature Conservancy's 110-hundred-acre **Blagden Preserve** on Indian Point Road off Route 198 north of Somesville, where seal sightings are virtually guaranteed.

THERE'S MORE

Museums. The College of the Atlantic's Natural History Museum on Route 3 outside Bar Harbor (207–288–5015; www.coamuseum.org) features interactive exhibits on local flora and fauna. Founded in 1928, the Abbe

Museum at Sieur de Monts Spring off the Park Loop Road (207–288–3519; www.abbemuseum.org), showcases Native American artifacts through the summer; a snazzy 2001 satellite in Bar Harbor is open year-round. The Mount Desert Oceanarium at 172 Clark Point Road in South Harbor (207–244–7330) is a small and appealingly rough-hewn hands-on learning center.

Outdoor adventures. Acadia Bike & Canoe Company at 48 Cottage Street in Bar Harbor (207–288–9605 or 800–526–8615; www.acadiabike.com), which also rents out kayaks, provides both means and maps. If you've always wanted to learn to rock climb, there's no better place. Sign on with the Atlantic Climbing School at Cadillac Mountain Sports, 24 Cottage Street (207–288–2521; www.acsclimb.com). The Bar Harbor Whale Watch Company's catamaran, the *Friendship V* (207–288–2386 or 800–WHALES–4; www.whalesrus.com) also seeks out seals and puffins.

Sight-seeing. Island Soaring Glider Rides (207–667–SOAR) offer quiet, air-borne views, and Acadia Air (207–667–5534; www.acadiaair.com) sets out to sight whales. Both operate out of the Hancock County-Bar Harbor Airport on Route 3 in Trenton.

SPECIAL EVENTS

Early July to early August. Bar Harbor Music Festival; (207) 288–5744. Classical, pops, and jazz concerts.

Mid-July to mid-August. Mount Desert Festival of Chamber Music, Northeast Harbor; (207) 288–4144. A brief but shining season, once graced by Paderewski.

OTHER RECOMMENDED RESTAURANTS AND LODGINGS

Bar Harbor

Balance Rock Inn, 7 Albert Meadow; (207) 288–2610 or (800) 753–0494; www.barhorborvacations.com. A 1903 seaside mansion featuring every conceivable amenity, including a fitness center and heated pool.

Bar Harbor Tides, 119 West Street; (207) 288–4968; www.barharbortides.com. A richly accoutered 1887 Georgian-style inn; the breakfast veranda overlooks a vast lawn that slopes to the bay.

Chiltern Inn, 3 Cromwell Harbor Road; (207) 288–0114; www.chilterninn. com. This 1906 carriage house has been rendered a luxurious haven with a heated indoor lap pool and a cathedral-ceilinged great room.

Cove Farm Inn, Crooked Road; (207) 288–5355 or (800) 291–0952; www. covefarm.com. A postcard-pretty farmhouse B&B, where families will feel welcome.

George's Restaurant, 7 Stephens Lane; (207) 288–4505; www.georgesbar harbor.com. A summery house serving elegant, mostly Mediterranean fare.

The Inn at Bay Ledge, 1385 Sand Point Road; (207) 288–4204 or 800–848– 6885; www.innatbayledge.com. A cliffside spa with it own heated pool and pebble beach.

Nannau Seaside B&B, Lower Main Street; (207) 288–5575; www.nannau. com. A 1904 Shingle-style summer cottage—luxuriantly updated—over-looking Compass Harbor.

Southwest Harbor

Beal's Lobster Pier, Clark Point Road; (207) 244–7178 or (800) 245–7178; www.bealslobster.com. A no-frills lobster shack that ships nationwide.

Fiddlers' Green, 411 Main Street; (207) 244–9416. Inspired New Americanisms, with a dash of fusion.

Inn at Southwest, 371 Main Street; (207) 244–3835; www.innatsouthwest. com. A grand Victorian (1884) base for exploring the "quiet side."

Preble Grille, 14 Clark Point Road; (207) 244–3034. Regional cuisine—fish, especially—warmed with Mediterranean touches.

The Yellow Aster, 53 Clark Point Road; (207) 244–4422 or (800) 724–7228; www.acadia.net/yellowaster. A fresh and pretty B&B serving hearty gourmet organic breakfasts.

FOR MORE INFORMATION

Bar Harbor Chamber of Commerce, 93 Cottage Street, Bar Harbor, ME 04609; (207) 288–5103 or (800) 288–5103; www.barharbormaine.com.

Maine Office of Tourism, 33 Stone Street, Augusta, ME 04330; (207) 287– 5711 or (888) MAINE45; www.visitmaine.com.

The Interior

THRILLS AND CHILLS

2 NIGHTS

A white-water blast • Prospecting for jewels
A venerable spa • Peculiar museums • Beach-hopping via canoe

Maine's woodlands are somehow more awe-inspiring than New Hampshire's or Vermont's. It's their very vastness: in the northern half of the state, the roads all but vanish, giving way to a mosaic of lakes and streams.

This trip will only take you to the fringes of this forest primeval, in deep just enough to get an introductory peek. If you like what you see, you can come back and forage further. Meanwhile rest assured that you'll find plenty of creature comforts in this neck of the woods.

DAY 1

Morning

Tonight's goal is **The Forks,** a staging area for a white-water rafting adventure through **Kennebec Gorge.** It's a five- to six-hour drive, best broken up with diversionary detours.

LUNCH: A-1 Diner, 3 Bridge Street, Gardiner; (207) 582–4804; www. a1diner. com. Pull off the Maine Turnpike (I–95) in Gardiner to chow down on trendy neo-diner treats at this wood-trimmed 1946 Worcester original.

Afternoon

A few miles north on Route 201 is the well-preserved nineteenth-century town of **Hallowell,** where antiquers strolling Water Street will find themselves

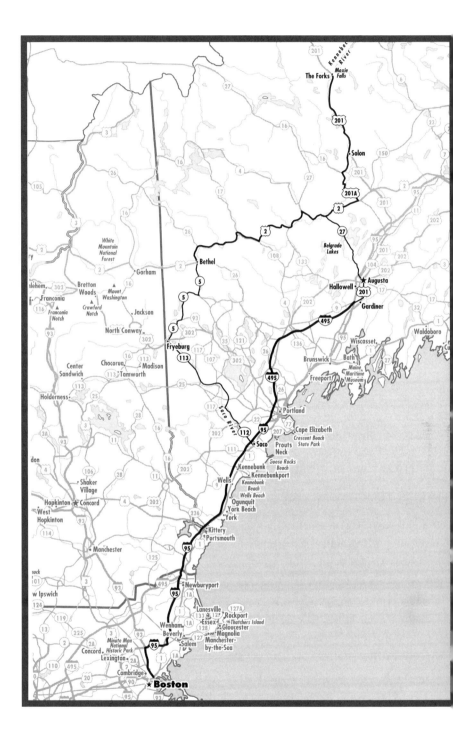

in secondhand heaven. The state capital of **Augusta,** a few miles farther north, is worth visiting to view the Bulfinch-designed 1832 **State House** on State Street and, within the same complex, the free and fascinating **Maine State Museum** (207–287–2301; www.state.me.us/museum), open Monday through Friday 9:00 A.M. to 5:00 P.M., Saturday 10:00 A.M. to 4:00 P.M., and Sunday 1:00 to 4:00 P.M.

Resuming the northward journey, choose scenic Route 27, which passes through Belgrade Lakes, a rusticators' haven. Head east when you reach Route 2, then north on 201A, which hugs the Kennebec River, merging with 201 at Solon. From here it's another 30 miles to The Forks. To refresh and reward yourself after the long journey, stop short of the bridge and follow Moxie Road to the trailhead where a ⅔-mile hike will lead you to **Moxie Falls**—a swimming hole fed by a 90-foot cascade.

DINNER AND LODGING: Northern Outdoors, Route 201, The Forks; (207) 663–2244 or (800) 765–RAFT; www.northernoutdoors.com. Of the dozen or so outfitters offering rafting trips along the Kennebec, this one has by far the fanciest facilities: a landscaped compound encompassing campsites, cabins, and "logdominiums"; a pool, hot tub, and private lake; and a platform tennis court, plus a spacious beamed lodge with bar and restaurant. You'll find everything you might possibly need right here—including reassurance that you'll do just fine when it's time to face down that roiling river.

DAY 2

Morning

BREAKFAST: Northern Outdoors. Breakfast in the restaurant is followed by a briefing.

Northern Outdoors' rafting program is among the best available, partly because it gave rise to all the rest. Founder Wayne Hochmeyer was the first daredevil kayaker to ride the waters released by the Harris Hydroelectric Station back in 1976; now some 800 thrill-seekers ride these rapids daily in-season (late spring to mid-October), cushioned in fat rubber rafts. In honor of his exploit, Northern Outdoors' boats get to go first, which means that you get to enjoy the dramatic gorge in all its pristine glory.

Perhaps the most trying aspect of the ordeal is slipping on a slimy wetsuit for the half-hour schoolbus shuttle to the dam. This is no placid cruise, however. With 10-foot drops and whirlpools that go by names such as Maytag,

Rafters tackle the Kennebec's "Magic Hole."

you'll be paddling for dear life. But it's doable, even for the nonathletically inclined, and offers an unparalleled adrenaline rush. After the first few miles, the river settles down into relative calm and you can venture out in "duckies"—inflatable kayaks—and even solo, where it's not too shallow. The sensation is a bit like floating in space—cold, cold space.

LUNCH: About halfway down, the Northern Outdoor boats pull over onto a rocky beach for a steak barbecue. With appetites whetted by the wetness, it'll be about the best you ever tasted.

Afternoon

You can expect to be dry and mobile by late afternoon, and ready to make the roughly 2½-hour (130-mile) drive along Routes 201/201A and 2 to **Bethel,** near the New Hampshire border.

DINNER AND LODGING: Bethel Inn & Country Club, 1 Broad Street; (207) 824–2175 or (800) 654–0125; www.bethelinn.com. The first thing you might want to do upon checking into this 1913 rambling yellow clapboard hotel overlooking the prim Village Common is to head straight for the outdoor heated pool and hot tub. This pampering hideaway got its start as a spa, after all, and was so attractive to frazzled academics that it earned the sobriquet "the resting place of Harvard." It's questionable how much rest you'll get, given facilities that include a health club, eighteen-hole golf course (turned cross-country center in the winter), tennis courts, and a pond for boating and swimming; however, you're guaranteed plenty of recreation, as well as excellent New American cuisine.

DAY 3

Morning

BREAKFAST: Bethel Inn & Country Club. A hearty breakfast is served in the spacious, mountain-view dining room.

Having explored all the entertainment options on-site at the inn, take a stroll through town to plunder some of the interesting shops. Several, such as **Far East Antiques** (207–824–2997) and **True North Adventureware** (207–824–2201), are clustered in the **Philbrook Place** complex at 162 Main Street. **Mountain Mann Jewelers** at 57 Main Street (207–824–3030) specializes in Maine-mined gems. At **Perham's of West Paris** (207–674–2341 or 800–371–GEMS), about 20 miles northeast along Route 26, you can either ogle the native jewels in stock—amethyst, tourmaline, topaz, and more—or buy a rock hammer and head for the hills to pick out your own. They'll give you a map to a handful of local quarries where you just might strike it semiprecious rich. You could even prospect for gold: the first strike in this country, pre–Gold Rush, occurred along the Swift River in Byron to the north, and these rugged hills continue to yield the occasional flake and nugget.

Alternately, you might paddle down a lazy river—the shallow, gentle **Saco River,** whose many sandbars double as semiprivate beaches. **Saco River Canoe and Kayak** on Route 5 in Fryeburg (207–935–2369 or 888–772–6573; www.sacorivercanoe.com), about 15 miles southwest, will suggest an itinerary, outfit you, and shuttle you to and fro. You can regain I–95 in the town of Saco; Boston is only about 1½ hours away.

THERE'S MORE

Airborne adventures. Lake Region Air in Rangeley (207–864–5307) and Bethel Air Service (207–824–4321) offer scenic flights.

Antiquing. Lyons' Den Antiques on Route 2 in Hanover (207–364–8634) is a picturesque barn where you might unearth some appealing primitive furniture. The Wales and Hamblen Antique Center at 134 Main Street in Bridgton (207–647–3840) is a multidealer emporium housed in a nicely restored 1882 building.

Art museums. The Jones Museum of Glass and Ceramics at 35 Douglas Mountain Road off Route 107 in Sebago (207–787–3370) showcases works ranging from ancient Egyptian to contemporary. The Colby College Museum of Art at 5600 Mayflower Hill Drive in Waterville (207–872–3228; www.colby.edu/museum) contains a sampling by such Maine luminaries as Winslow Homer, Louise Nevelson, and Andrew Wyeth.

Historic houses. The Old Fort Western Museum at 16 Coney Street in Augusta (207–626–2385; www.oldfortwestern.org) is a 1754 garrison, preserved intact. The Bethel Historical Society's Moses Mason House at 14 Broad Street on the Common (207–824–2908) is an 1813 Federal beauty graced with a mural by famous itinerant artist Rufus Porter.

Mountain biking/skiing. The area is rife with old logging roads. Should you desire a vertical assist, both Sugarloaf (207–237–2000 or 800–THE– LOAF; www.sugarloaf.com) and Sunday River (207–824–3000 or 800– 543–2SKI; www.sundayriver.com) transform from ski area to biking park—with rentals and instruction—in the summer.

Mushing/canoeing. Mahoosuc Mountain Adventures at 1513 Bear River Road in Newry (207–824–2073; www.mahoosuc.com) offers on-site dog-sledding or, in summer, guided canoe trips.

Oddities. One of Maine's lesser-known repositories is the L. C. Bates Museum on Route 201 in Hinckley (207–453–4894; www.gwh.org/museum), a grand 1903 Romanesque edifice housing a hodgepodge ranging from pre-Columbian art to a mounted caribou head with three antlers. Housed in a 1903 Georgian schoolhouse, the Stanley Museum on School Street in Kingfield (207–265–2729; www.stanleymuseum.org) commemorates the twin inventors of the Stanley Steamer car, as well as their sister Chansonetta, a remarkable rural photographer. The Wilhelm

Reich Museum on Dodge Pond Road off Route 4 in Rangeley (207–864–3443; www.somtel.com/~wreich) is where the beleaguered psychoanalyst holed up in the wilderness to try to quantify and capture a hypothetical "universal life force."

Performing arts. Strawhat enterprises include the Theater at Monmouth (207–933–2952; www.theateratmonmouth.org), housed in the grandiose 1900 Cumston Hall; the Waterville Summer Music Theater in the Waterville Opera House (207–873–7000; www.operahouse.com); and the Deer-Trees Theater in Harrison (207–583–6747; www.deertreestheatre.org), built in 1936 by Clark Gable's sister-in-law. The Celebration Barn Theater in South Paris (207–743–8452; www.celebrationbarn.com) is a hotbed of the "New Vaudeville."

Rural preserves. The Sabbathday Lake Shaker Community and Museum on Route 26 in New Gloucester (207‑926–4597; www.shakerworkshop.com/sdl.htm) is the only remaining Shaker community with an active membership; visitors may take guided tours, purchase herbs and crafts in the shop, or attend Sunday-morning services. The Norlands Living History Center at 290 Norlands Road off Route 108 northeast of Livermore (207–897–4366; www.norlands.org) is a 450-acre complex dedicated to preserving the traditions of farm life circa 1870, which you can view during a two-hour tour or experience firsthand in the course of a live-in weekend. Geared more to tourists, Willowbrook at Newfield, off Route 11 on Elm Street (207–793–2784; www.willowbrookmuseum.org), is a re-created nineteenth-century village with several dozen buildings full of period furnishings, including an 1894 carousel.

Swimming. With this many lakes and streams, it would be quite a feat not to get wet. Worth seeking out, though, are the carved-rock swimming holes of Coos Canyon in Byron, where the river runs parallel to Route 17.

SPECIAL EVENTS

January. Bethel Winter Festival; (207) 824–2282; www.bethelmaine.com. Fireworks, moonlight skiing and sleigh rides, a snowshoe romp, and more.

Early April. April Fool's Pole, Paddle, and Paw Race, Bethel; (207) 824–2410; www.sundayriverinn.com. The Sunday River Cross Country Ski Center puts on a skiing/canoeing/snowshoeing triathlon—all in good fun, with crazy costumes, too.

Early July. Moxie Festival, Lisbon Falls; (207) 783–2249; www.androscoggin county.com. A parade and more to celebrate Maine's inimitable 1895 contribution to the soft-drink industry.

Mid-July. Maine International Film Festival, Waterville; (207) 861–8138; www. miff.org. A cinematic convocation at the Railroad Square Cinema.

Late August. Rangeley Lakes Blueberry Festival; (207) 864–5364 or 800–MT–LAKES; www.rangeley.maine.com. Featuring pies, muffins, jams, and crafts.

Late September. Common Ground Country Fair, Unity; (207) 568–4142; www.mofga.org. This harvest fair, sponsored by the Maine Organic Farmers and Gardeners Association, is something of a perennial Woodstock.

Early December. Chester Greenwood Days, Farmington; (207) 778–4215; www.farmingtonchamber.org. A parade and "polar dip" honor the inventor of earmuffs.

OTHER RECOMMENDED RESTAURANTS AND LODGINGS

Bethel

Cafe Di Cocoa, 125 Main Street; (207) 824–JAVA. From morning jump starts to gourmet trail food.

Great Grizzly, Sunday River Road; (207) 824–6271. A neo-rustic barn with real food smarts.

Sunday River Inn, 23 Skiway Road, Newry; (207) 824–2410; www.sunday riverinn.com. A handsome ski dorm with its own cross-country center.

Telemark Inn; (207) 836–2703; www.telemarkinn.com. Llama treks set out from this remote backwoods manse, a 1900 multimillionaire's hideaway; in winter, the sport of choice is "ski-joring" (cross-country with an assist from sled dogs).

Bingham

Harrison's Pierce Pond Sporting Camps; (207) 672–3625. Seclusion (off a 15-mile dirt road) and fine home cooking.

Thompson's Restaurant, Main Street; (207) 672–3245. A 1939 lunchroom retaining its wooden booths and homemade doughnuts.

Carrabassett Valley

Hugs, Route 27; (207) 237–2392. A delightful little trattoria serving classic Italian dishes.

Center Lovell

Quisisana; (207) 925–3500; www.quisisanaresort.com. This classic lodge-plus-cabins on Lake Kezar, founded in 1917, has a little something extra: a performing musical staff.

Fryeburg

Admiral Peary House, 9 Elm Street; (207) 935–3365 or (800) 237–8080; www.mountwashingtonvalley.com/admiralpearyhouse. The Arctic explorer lived here in the late 1870s; the hot tub and clay tennis court are rather more recent.

Oxford House Inn, 105 Main Street; (207) 935–3442 or (800) 261–7206; www.oxfordhouseinn.com. A 1913 B&B with a popular continental restaurant.

Hallowell

Maple Hill Farm, Outlet Road; (207) 622–2708 or 800–622–2708; www.maplebb.com. A sixty-two-acre country retreat with a varied menagerie and spring-fed swimming hole.

Slate's, 169 Water Street; (207) 622–9575. An expansive tin-ceilinged coffee-house with a daring menu.

Harrison

Greenwood Manor Inn, Tolman Road; (207) 583–4445 or (866) 583–4445; www.greenwoodmanorinn.com. An 1870 carriage house turned inn, on 108 acres near Long Lake.

Kingfield

The Herbert Hotel, Main Street; (207) 265–2000 or (800) THE–HERB; www.mainemountaininn.com. Built for summer rusticators in 1918, this "palace in the wilderness" has modest rooms but a grand paneled lobby and an appealing, eclectic dining room.

Longfellow's, Main Street; (207) 265–4394. A well-priced riverside cafe with international fare.

One Stanley Avenue and Three Stanley Avenue; (207) 265–5541. Regional delicacies, artfully rendered and elegantly presented throughout ski season; next door is a cozy B&B.

Rangeley

Grant's Kennebago Camps, Kennebago Lake, off Route 16; (207) 864–3608; www.grantscamps.com. A century-old lakeside compound with spacious cabins.

The Rangeley Inn, Main Street; (207) 864–3341 or (800) MOMENTS; www.rangeleyinn.com. A 1907 relic, pleasantly updated, with a fairly formal dining room.

Richmond

Richmond Sauna and Bed and Breakfast, Dingley Road (off Route 197); (207) 737–4752 or (800) 400–5751. Guests at this rural Federal (1831) home enjoy complimentary use of the sauna, hot tub, and pool housed in the barn.

South Hiram

Wadsworth Blanchard Farm Hostel, 174 Tripptown Road (207) 625–7509; www.hiayh.org. Dorm accommodations in an eighteenth-century farmstead convenient to canoeing sites.

Waterford

Lake House, Routes 35 and 37; (207) 583–4182 or 800–223–4182; www.lake houseinn.com. This former stagecoach inn, also a former "hygienic institute for ladies," is now a charming B&B with a very accomplished dining room.

Waterville

Kafe Kino, 13 Railroad Square; (207) 873–5900; www.railroadcinema.com/ kafekino. This offbeat cafe serves as anteroom to the independently minded Railroad Cinema.

ESCAPE FIVE

MAINE

FOR MORE INFORMATION

Bethel Area Chamber of Commerce, 30 Cross Street, PO Box 1247, Bethel, ME 04217; (207) 824–2282 or (800) 442–5826; www.bethelmaine.com.

Maine Office of Tourism, 33 Stone Street, Augusta, ME 04330; (207) 287–5711 or (888) MAINE45; www.visitmaine.com.

Rangeley Lakes Region Chamber of Commerce, Main Street, Rangeley, MA 04970; (207) 864–5571 or (800) MT-LAKES, www.rangeleymaine.com.

NEW HAMPSHIRE

ESCAPES

NEW HAMPSHIRE

The Quiet Corner

INVIGORATING LEISURE

2 NIGHTS

Post-Industrial pleasures • Ample antiquing
Bucolic hiking and biking • A monumental mountain

"It's restful just to think of New Hampshire," Robert Frost once wrote. It's still pretty peaceful, in places. In fact, an hour's drive is all it takes to flee creeping exurbia and encounter timeless country beauty.

New Hampshire's quiet corner—the southwestern quadrant—numbers among New England's lovelier and, so far, less appreciated treasures. Here small hamlets abandoned in the wake of the Industrial Revolution appear to have enjoyed an enchanted sleep. Not for this region the drama of towering peaks—though there is one, the singular Mount Monadnock—or spacious lakes all too attractive to carousing crowds. If it's a respite you seek, the opportunity to wander aimlessly through the woods or tuck into a novel on a shady porch, you have come to just the right place.

DAY 1

Morning

Head northwest on Routes 2, 2A, 225, and 119 successively; the last will lead you, within an hour and a half, over the border and into pretty **Fitzwilliam,** where you can peruse several centuries' worth of antiques within a dozen shops. You might also want to stock up on neglected classics at **Bequaert Old Books** (603–585–3448; wwwbeqbooks.com).

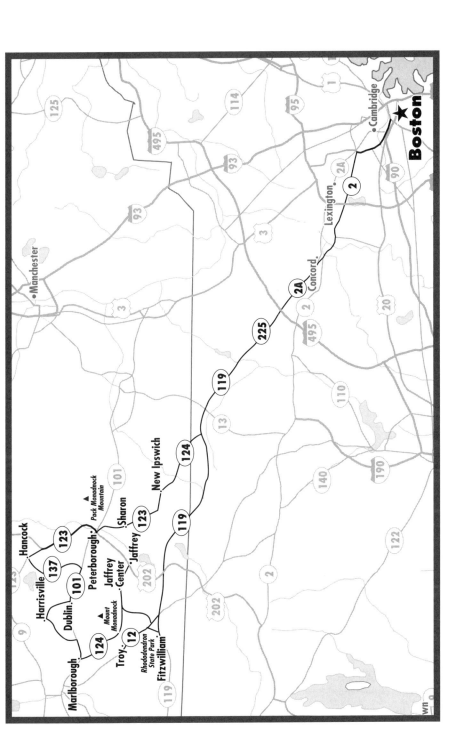

LUNCH: Fitzwilliam Inn, Route 119; (603) 585–9000. The fare is hearty, as befits old-fashioned road food. (The inn has been a stagecoach stop for two centuries.) Be sure to poke around the charming parlors and try to decode the rebus over the hearth.

Afternoon

Enjoy a pleasant stroll through **Rhododendron State Park** off Route 119 a few miles west of Fitzwilliam (603–239–8153; www.nhparks.state.nh.us. parkops/parks/rhododen), where sixteen acres of multicolored shrubs—some 30 feet high—peak in mid-July. Or if you're feeling energetic, tackle 3,165-foot **Mount Monadnock** (603–532–8862), whose Native American name translates roughly as "stands alone." Rangers at the Monadnock State Park headquarters off Route 124 west of Jaffrey Center (603–532–8862; www.nhparks.state.us/ parkops/parks/monadnock) can suggest an ascent suited to your ability. (The shorter ascents, though they might look enticing on the map, tend to be much steeper.) The 360-degree views from the bare rock summit more than warrant the effort: in clear weather, you'll see Boston and the sea beyond.

DINNER AND LODGING: The Grand View Inn & Resort, 580 Mountain Road, Jaffrey; (603) 532–9880; www.thegrandviewinn.com. An early nineteenth-century brick mansion on 330 acres is now a destination inn, spa, and equestrian center, with quite the most rarefied regional dining ever to be seen—or tasted—in these parts.

DAY 2

Morning

BREAKFAST: The Grand View Inn. Enjoy a continental breakfast while contemplating your itinerary.

The day shapes up as a backroads ramble. A dozen or so miles northwest along Route 124, in **Marlborough,** stop in at **Woodward Antiques** (603–876–3360) and the **Homestead Bookshop** (603–876–4213 or 800–834–3618), both on Route 101, to peruse, respectively, substantial country antiques and 50,000-odd old tomes. A few miles east of Marlborough, take the turnoff to tiny Chesham, and from there head northeast to **Harrisville,** a nineteenth-century mill town seemingly preserved in amber. A far cry from the "dark satanic mills" that arose later during the Industrial Revolution, this village of tidy brick buildings suggests a work ethic laced with idealism and pleasing

Summertime in Jaffrey

aesthetics. The work continues, in a more creative bent, within the 1850 brick storehouse that now serves as the **Harrisville Designs Weaving Center** (603–827–3996; www.harrisville.com), a mecca for serious artisans as well as neophyte hobbyists. You can observe works in progress, perhaps purchase a few finished products. Be sure, also, to pick up a brochure mapping out a self-guided walking tour. The cemetery bordering the mill pond is a particularly peaceful spot.

LUNCH: A few miles southeast of Harrisville is the picture-postcard-perfect town of **Dublin,** home base to *Yankee* magazine. You can patch together a picnic at the **Dublin General Store,** about a half-mile east along Route 101 (603–563–8401).

Afternoon

Two more antiques stores on Route 101 demand a look: **Peter Pap Oriental Rugs** (603–563–8717; www.peterpap.citysearch.com) for museum-quality exemplars in a gallerylike setting, and **Seaver & McLellan Antiques** (603–563–7144), where the stock tends to statementy Continental and Oriental.

Heading 7 miles north on Route 137, seek out the simple life on the grounds of the **Harris Center for Conservation Education** at 83 King's Highway in **Hancock** (603–525–3394; www.harriscenter.org), a 4,500-acre nature preserve crisscrossed by 7 miles of hiking trails. There's usually some sort of interesting educational activity under way, such as hawk walks and mushroom hunts, so call ahead for a schedule.

DINNER AND LODGING: John Hancock Inn, 33 Main Street, Hancock; (603) 525–3318 or (800) 525–1789; www.hancockinn.com. Enjoy New American fare such as a Shaker-derived cranberry pot roast before bedding down in a canopied four-poster at this 1789 beauty whose pillared facade presides over a classic Main Street. One of the bedrooms boasts an 1820s mural by famed itinerant painter Rufus Porter.

DAY 3

Morning

BREAKFAST: John Hancock Inn. The inn will send you on your way well fed.

You could start the day with a bracing plunge into **Norway Pond,** a short stroll down Main Street. Directly across from the inn, the **Barn of Hancock Village** (603–525–3529), offers a trove of charming antiques and compatible home accessories.

Eight miles south of Hancock on Route 123 is **Peterborough,** the inspiration for Thornton Wilder's *Our Town;* he envisioned his archetypal Grover's Corners while ensconced at the MacDowell Colony, the immensely productive artists' retreat founded in 1907. The constant presence of practicing intelligentsia perhaps accounts for Peterborough's air of thoughtful industriousness. The shops along Main Street and School Street—such as **Joseph's Coat** at 10 School Street (603–924–6683)—invite contemplative browsing, as do the galleries of the **Sharon Arts Center** at Depot Square and Grove Street (603–924– 7676, www.sharonarts.org). In your wanderings, also check out the **Unitarian Church** on Summer Street, designed by Boston's preeminent architect Charles Bulfinch.

LUNCH: Twelve Pine, Depot Square; (603) 924–6140. Pick up some superlative takeout; the great outdoors beckons.

Afternoon

If you passed up Mount Monadnock but wouldn't mind a drive-by approximation of the view, head up 2,290-foot **Pack Monadnock Mountain** in Miller State Park (603–924–3672; www.nhparks.state.nh.us/parkops/parks/miller) on Route 101 three miles east of Peterborough. Then return to Route 123 to head south through **Sharon,** where the working core of the Sharon Arts Center (603–924–7256; www.sharonarts.org) offers all sorts of workshops, demonstrations, exhibits, lectures, and concerts.

Six miles southeast, back on Route 124, is the pretty village of **New Ipswich,** where the Society for the Preservation of New England Antiquities maintains the circa 1800 **Barrett House** (603–878–2517; www.spnea.org): you might recognize this grand Federal manse with its Gothic Revival gazebo as the setting for the Merchant-Ivory film *The Europeans.* Hour-long tours are offered from 11:00 A.M. to 5:00 P.M. Saturday and Sunday in-season. This glimpse of a quieter, calmer life is the perfect capper for a weekend spent where the pleasures of the past live on.

DINNER AND LODGING: But if you can't bear to head home quite yet, follow Route 124 into Massachusetts and then take Route 113 past I–93 to Tyngsboro, where you can splurge on a rarefied French Provincial dinner at **Silks** within the ultra-luxe **Stonehedge Inn** at 160 Pawtucket Boulevard (978–649–4400 or 800–648–7070; www.stonehedgeinn.com). Boston is so close—go all out and spend the night.

THERE'S MORE

Antiquing. The Colony Mill Marketplace at 222 West Street in Keene (603–357–1240; www.colonymill.com) is an 1838 woolen mill smartly restored as a shopping emporium; the second floor is given over to a 200-dealer antiques center (603–358–6343).

Kid stuff. The Monadnock Children's Museum at 147 Washington Street in Keene (603–357–5161) occupies an 1840s house with appealing hands-on exhibits. The Friendly Farm on Route 101 in Dublin (603–563–8444; www.friendlyfarm.com) is a seven-acre petting zoo irresistible to children. They might also enjoy a tour—with complimentary frozen yogurt tastings—of the Stonyfield Farm factory at 10 Burton Drive in Londonderry (800–PRO–COWS; www.stonyfield.com). And anyone carting kids along absolutely owes them a summertime detour to Canobie Lake Park in Salem (603–893–3506; www. canobie.com), a spiffy, family-oriented 1902 amusement park with all the latest thrill rides.

Memorials. The Cathedral of the Pines on Cathedral Road off Route 119 in Rindge (603–899–3300; www.cathedralpines.com), an outdoor monument built in 1945 to commemorate the American war dead, features four bronze bas-reliefs designed by Norman Rockwell.

Museums. The Amos J. Blake House in Fitzwilliam (603–585–7742) is a small historical museum with a charming shop. Keene harbors the historic Wyman Tavern at 339 Main Street (603–352–1895), where a contingent of New Hampshire Minutemen gathered, and Keene State College has the small but interesting Thorne-Sagendorph Art Gallery at 229 Main Street (603–358–2720; www.keene.edu/tsag). The Peterborough Historical Society and Museum at 19 Grove Street (603–924–3235; www.townof peterborough.com/htm/histsoc) mounts exhibits elucidating the town's industrial past; the complex includes a restored mill boardinghouse. Art lovers will want to venture into Manchester to visit the small but exciting Currier Gallery of Art at 201 Myrtle Way (603–669–6144; www.currier. org); the museum's holdings range from medieval to contemporary, with a fine showing of French and American Impressionism. The Currier also maintains the nearby Frank Lloyd Wright–designed Zimmerman House, tourable by reservation.

Performing arts. The Apple Hill Center for Chamber Music on Apple Hill Road in East Sullivan (603–847–3371 or 800–472–6677; www.applehill. org) puts on concerts and workshops. Cultural events are regularly scheduled at Keene State College's Redfern Arts Center on Brickyard Pond, at 299 Main Street (603–358–2168; www.keene.edu/racbp), as well as at the grand old Colonial Theatre at 95 Main Street (603–352–2033; www.the colonial.org). The Peterborough Players at 55 Hadley Road in Peterborough (603–924–7585; www.peterboroughplayers.com), a professional company founded in 1934, mounts an ambitious summer season in a faux-rustic barn. With theatres in Milford and Nashua, the American Stage Festival (603–673–7515; www.americanstagefestival.org) is New Hampshire's largest professional theater, and the Milford Drive-in Theatre (603–673–4090) upholds an endangered tradition. Manchester's Palace Theatre at 80 Hanover Street (603–668–5588; www.palacetheatre.org), a restored 1915 behemoth, supports local theater, opera, and ballet, while showcasing touring productions.

SPECIAL EVENTS

Mid-July to late August. Monadnock Music, various towns; (603) 924–7610 or (800) 868–9613; www.monmusic.org. Outstanding concerts—free and for-a-fee—performed throughout the region.

Mid-August. Arts Festival/MacDowell Day, Peterborough; (603) 924–3886; wwwmacdowellcolony.org. Visitors are welcome to tour the ordinarily reclusive artists' colony, and the exhibits and performances spill into town.

Late October. Pumpkin Festival, Keene; (603) 358–5344; www.pumpkin festival.com. A Guinness record array of jack-o'-lanterns.

December 31. First Night, Keene; (603) 357–3906. Creative celebrations take to the streets.

OTHER RECOMMENDED RESTAURANTS AND LODGINGS

Chesterfield

Chesterfield Inn, Route 9; (603) 256–3211 or (800) 365–5515; www.chester fieldinn.com. A Federal-era tavern turned twentieth-century showplace with luxurious touches, including ambitious dinners.

Dublin

Del Rossi's Trattoria, Route 137; (603) 563–7195; www.delrossi.com. Delicious dinners centered on homemade pasta, with occasional folk music.

Fitzwilliam

Amos A. Parker House, Route 119; (603) 585–6540; www.nhlodging.org/amosparkerhouse. A formal eighteenth-century home with lovely gardens and gourmet breakfasts.

Hannah Davis House, Route 119; (603) 585–3344; www/nhlodging.org/hannadavishouse. A circa 1800 inn with pond views.

Francestown

Inn at Crotched Mountain, 534 Mountain Road; (603) 588–6840; www.inn book.com/crotched. An 1822 inn with lovely views, a pool, two clay tennis courts, and a restaurant where Indonesia meets New England.

Henniker

Colby Hill Inn, The Oaks; (603) 428–3281 or (800) 531–0330; www.colby hillinn.com. A 1789 country inn offering fine New American dinners and charming rooms.

Jaffrey Center

The Inn at Jaffrey Center, 379 Main Street; (603) 532–7900 or (877) 510–7019; www.theinnatjaffreycenter.com. Reward yourself, as hikers have for the past century, with a hearty country repast—now with international accents—and a cozy room.

Keene

Nicola's Trattoria, 39 Central Square; (603) 355–5242. Rome's loss is Keene's gain, when Nicola Bencivenga dishes out Italian classics in a homey storefront.

Manchester

Cafe Pavone, 75 Arms Park Drive; (603) 622–5488. Tasteful Italian, in a renovated mill building.

Red Arrow Lunch, 61 Lowell Street; (603) 626–1118. A 1903 survivor, open twenty-four hours.

Mason

Parker's Maple Barn, 1316 Brookline Road; (603) 878–2308; www.parkersmaplebarn.com. A nineteenth-century barn serving homemade pancakes with home-collected syrup and other American standards.

Pickity Place, Nutting Hill Road; (603) 878–1151; www.visit-newhampshire.com/pickityplace. Summer luncheons fresh from the garden.

Milford

The Ram in the Thicket, 24 Maple Street; (603) 654–6540; www.jlc.net. A stylish farmhouse inn, with a restaurant to match.

Peterborough

Acqua Bistro, 9 School Street; (603) 924–9905. A city-bistro setting for luscious Mediterranean fare.

Aesop's Tables, 12 Depot Square; (603) 924–1612. A great place to grab a quick, casual bite, amid an A&P-turned bookstore.

Apple Gate B&B, 199 Upland Farm Road; (603) 924–6543; www.apple gatenh.mv.com. A nicely restored 1830s farmhouse adjoining a pick-your-own apple orchard.

Peterboro Diner, 10 Depot Square; (603) 924-6202. A circa 1940 original, serving all the staples.

Temple

The Birchwood Inn, Route 45; (603) 878–3285. An 1800 brick inn decorated with Rufus Porter murals; Thoreau once dined here.

Troy

Gap Mountain Breads, 31 Gap Square (Route 12); (603) 242–3284. Wholesome country breads and cafe offerings.

Walpole

Inn at Valley Farms, Wentworth Road; (603) 756–2855 or (877) 327–2855; www.innatvalleyfarms.com. A beautifully updated 1774 colonial plus cottages, encircled by 105 acres of organic gardens.

FOR MORE INFORMATION

Monadnock Travel Council, 8 Central Square, Keene, NH 03431; (603) 924–7234 or (800) HEART–NH; www.monadnocktravel.com.

New Hampshire Division of Travel & Tourism Development, Box 1856, Concord, NH 03302, (603) 271–2343 or (800) FUN–IN–NH; www.visitnh.gov.

The Western Lakes

INTELLIGENT LUXURY

2 NIGHTS

Civilized college towns • An amazing mine • Shaker legacies
Canoeing the Connecticut

Sprawling Lake Winnipesaukee on the eastern side of central New Hampshire tends to draw the bulk of midstate tourists; you can check it out en route to the White Mountains (see New Hampshire Escape Three). To the west, however, are many smaller lakes, just as lovely and much less developed, as well as the broad Connecticut River, placid enough for rafting and canoeing.

Rusticators of an artistic bent have favored this neck of the woods for well over a century. It does not hurt that Dartmouth College, in Hanover, serves as something of a cultural beacon, bringing to the outback all sorts of stimulating sights and events. You can dine and dally splendidly here, all the while surrounded by gentle vistas of verdant hills.

DAY 1

Morning

Take I–93 about one hour northwest to the state capital of **Concord,** where you might want to view the 1819 **State House** on North Main Street and bone up a bit at the **Museum of New Hampshire History** at 6 Eagle Square (603–226–3189; www.nhhistory.org), open Tuesday through Saturday 9:30 A.M. to 5:00 P.M. (till 8:30 on Thursday) and Sunday noon to 5:00 P.M. Set beside the **Eagle Hotel,** which in its long reign housed movers and shakers such as Andrew Jackson and Eleanor Roosevelt (it's now a marketplace),

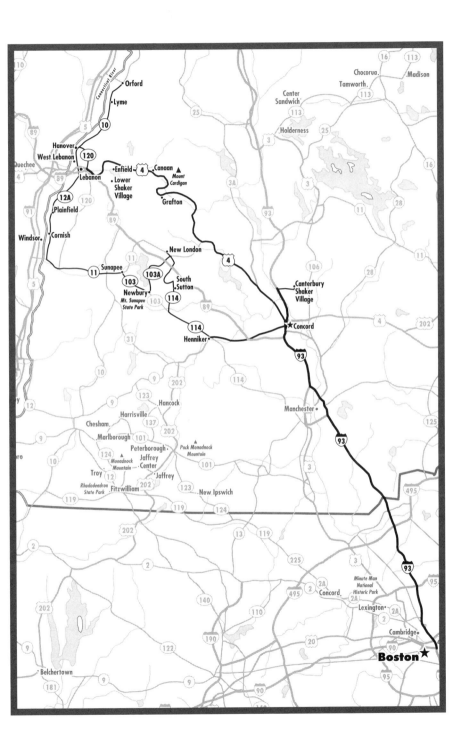

this stone warehouse bears witness to various state feats, such as the nineteenth-century manufacture of the Concord Coach, the vehicle largely responsible for expanding the Western frontier.

Next, follow Route 4 out of town for a scenic back-roads ramble. In **Grafton,** about 40 miles northwest, follow signs to the **Ruggles Mine** (603–523–4275; www.rugglesmine.com), a mountaintop pit mine in operation from 1803 to 1959. Its main product was—and is—mica, still found in great sheaves underfoot. However, rock hounds have made other interesting finds (including gold) amid the carved-out chambers of this pocked peak, and the view of **Mount Cardigan** is enhanced by the prospect of chance score. The mine is open daily from 9:00 A.M. to 6:00 P.M. in July and August, with reduced hours in the shoulder seasons. Bring a hammer and be prepared to clamber about.

Continue along Route 4 about another 10 miles to **Canaan,** where the National Register-acknowledged **Canaan Street** presents an idyllic image of nineteenth-century town life. About 10 miles further, past **Enfield,** veer southwest along Route 4A to reach the **Enfield Shaker Museum** at 24 Caleb Dyer Lane (603–632–4346; www.shakermuseum.org), open Monday through Saturday from 10:00 A.M. to 5:00 P.M. and Sunday noon to 5:00 P.M. in season (weekends only, off season). This religious community, founded in 1793, once comprised 200 buildings spanning 3,000 acres; its centerpiece, the Great Stone Dwelling, has been converted into **The Shaker Inn** (603–632–7810 or 888–707–4257; www.theshakerinn.com), featuring period furnishings produced on-site by **Dana Robes Wood Craftsmen** (603–632–5385 or 800–722–5036; www. danarobes.com).

Regaining Route 4, follow it to **Lebanon,** where you can view contemporary artistic output at the **Alliance for the Visual Arts Gallery and Art Center** at 11 Bank Street (603–448–3117; www.avagallery.org), open Tuesday through Saturday from 11:00 A.M. to 5:00 P.M. Then take Route 120 north into **Hanover,** home of **Dartmouth College,** which Eleazer Wheelock founded in 1769 "for the education of the Youth of Indian Tribes." Despite its reputation for conservatism, Dartmouth still has a vital Native American studies program, and on the north side of the green, in the lower reading room of **Baker Library** (603–646–2560; www.dartmouth.edu/~library)—a neo-Georgian monument modeled on Philadelphia's Independence Hall—you'll find an intentionally unsettling 1932–34 mural, *The Epic of American Civilization,* executed by visiting Mexican painting instructor Jose Clemente Orozco. Also seek out the library's Treasure Room to view a first-edition *Birds of America,* as well as numerous Shakespeare folios and a 1439 Bible. The green's east side—a.k.a. "Dartmouth Row"—is a Greek Revival repository that housed the entire college up to 1845.

LUNCH: Lou's, 30 South Main Street; (603) 643–3321. The community's favorite greasy spoon (and I mean that in the most complimentary way), Lou's has been a popular student hangout since 1947.

Afternoon

South Main is lined with an assortment of shops catering to a sophisticated student body. At 13 Lebanon Street the **League of New Hampshire Craftsmen** (603–643–5050; www.nhcrafts.org) showcases the best the state has to offer. Nearby, on the south side of the green at 5 Wheelock Street, is the college's **Hood Museum of Art** (603–646–2808; www.dartmouth.edu/~hood). Ten galleries house a collection of some 60,000 items, spanning the centuries and continents: Nelson Rockefeller (class of 1930) donated Picasso's *Guitar on the Table.* Admission is free and the hours are Tuesday through Saturday 10:00 A.M. to 5:00 P.M. (till 9:00 P.M. on Wednesdays), and Sunday noon to 5:00 P.M.

DINNER: Hanover Inn, Main and Wheelock Streets, Hanover; (603) 643–4300 or (800) 443–7024; www.hanoverinn.com. Enjoy a robust New American repast in the formal **Daniel Webster Room** or the more casual **Zins.**

LODGING: Breakfast on the Connecticut, 651 River Road, Lyme; (603) 363–4444 or (888) 353–4440; www.breakfastonthect.com. The most luxurious quarters at this custom-built inn on twenty-three riverview acres, a dozen or so miles northwest on Route 10, are located in the Shaker-style round barn.

DAY 2

Morning

BREAKFAST: Breakfast on the Connecticut. After a fine country breakfast you might want to take one of the inn's canoes or kayaks out for a spin on the lakelike river.

When you're ready to decamp, continue north along River Road toward **Orford,** a small town noted for its "Ridge Houses," a row of seven exemplary Federal dwellings based on Bulfinch protégé Asher Benjamin's pattern book, *The Country Builder's Assistant.* Circle back south along Route 10, through Hanover, and follow Route 12A to the **Powerhouse Mall** in West Lebanon

(603–298–5236). The old mill complex now sports several dozen stylish shops, including the **Anichini Outlet Store** (603–298–8656; www.anichini.com), a source of exquisite linens and other sensual delights.

LUNCH: Lui, Lui, Powerhouse Mall; (603) 298–7070; www.blueskyrestau rants.com/luilui. A casual Italian trattoria in the mill's former boiler house.

Afternoon

Maxfield Parrish lived in **Plainfield,** about 10 miles south along Route 12A, in the early twentieth century, and his 1916 stage-set mural of the local landscape survives in the 1798 town hall. Further work is viewable a few miles south at the **Cornish Colony Gallery and Museum** on Route 12A in **Cornish** (603–675–6000; www.almagilbert.com). Cornish is a must-visit, in any case, for the **Saint-Gaudens National Historic Site** (603–675–2175; www.sghs.org). Here, from 1885 to 1907, the monumental sculptor Augustus Saint-Gaudens—whose works include the Robert Gould Shaw Memorial opposite Boston's State House—lived and worked amid a community of apprentices and fellow artists; he and his wife, painter Augusta Saint-Gaudens, turned an abandoned 1800 tavern into a modest home full of light and liveliness. His studio houses studies for many of his more famous works, as well as changing exhibits by contemporary artists. The grounds, graced with Italian gardens, are particularly lovely, and the site of summertime Sunday concerts. The Saint-Gaudens site is open daily from 9:00 A.M. to 4:30 P.M. late May through October. To fall in love with the landscape that captivated these artists, consider a river paddle past the 1886 Cornish-Windsor wooden covered bridge (the country's longest, in use to this day): **North Star Canoe** rentals (603–542–5802; www.kayak-canoe.com) can set you up.

DINNER AND LODGING: Home Hill Inn, River Road, Plainfield; (603) 675–6165; www.homehillinn.com. You'll think you've died and gone to Provence when you enter this 1818 manse on twenty-five riverside acres, where chef-owner Victoria du Roure, who trained at the Ritz-Escoffier Culinary School in Paris, creates exquisite regional fare à la Provençale. The rooms are dreamy, too.

DAY 3

Morning

BREAKFAST: The continental breakfast should keep you going a while, but play it safe and request a *pique-nique* to go.

Reluctantly taking your leave, head east along Routes 103 and 11 for about 15 miles to **Sunapee,** a summer hotspot since the mid-nineteenth century, when the coming of the railroad meant the arrival of the sweltering gentry. Old photographs on display at the **Sunapee Historical Society Museum,** housed in a former livery stable in Sunapee Harbor (603–763–2245: hours are limited), attest to the lake's preeminence as a Gilded Age getaway. Its water-centric attractions endure. If you passed up canoeing on the Connecticut, splash around a bit here, with rental craft—including sailboards—available at the small sandy beach maintained by **Mount Sunapee State Park** at the southern end of the lake (603–763–5561; www.nhparks.state.nh.us/parkops/parks/mtsunapee). Or you could hop on a chair lift to the 2,700-foot summit of Mount Sunapee (603–763–2356 or 800–MT–SUNAPEE; www.mtsunapee.com), which offers a prime view of the 10-mile-long lake, along with various Green and White Mountains. The lift runs daily from 10:00 A.M. to 5:00 P.M. in July and August, and on weekends in the shoulder season; it's fun to ride up and bound down.

Continue circling the eastern side of the lake along Route 103A. In **Newbury** you might want to wander the grounds of the **Fells Historic Site at the John Hay National Wildlife Refuge** (603–763–4789; www.thefells.org), enjoying the alpine garden that extends from the forty-two-room mansion—once home to Lincoln's private secretary—down to the shoreline. At **Blodgetts Landing**, north along the lakefront, look for the gingerbread cottages that grew out of the Sunapee Lake Spiritualist Camp Meeting Association tents of the 1890s.

I–89 awaits just a few miles farther. If you're still loath to join the homebound throngs, take time out to visit the **Christa McAuliffe Planetarium** at 3 Institute Drive off I-393 in eastern Concord (603–271–STAR; www.starhop.com), a state-of-the-art, interactive facility commemorating the beloved local schoolteacher who was aboard the ill-fated *Challenger.* It's open Tuesday through Sunday, and you'll need to call ahead for show times and reservations.

If Enfield whetted your appetite for all things Shaker, consider a detour about 10 miles north of Concord to **Canterbury Shaker Village** at 288 Shaker Road off I–93's exit 18 (603–783–9511 or 800–982–9511; www.shakers.org). Open daily from 10:00 A.M. to 5:00 P.M. May through October, and weekends during the shoulder seasons, this twenty-four-building complex has been respectfully preserved. Guided tours help elucidate the Shakers' willfully "simple" way of life, and candlelight dinners (by reservation) attest to its tangible rewards. Maybe some of their purposeful peace will follow you home.

THERE'S MORE

Antiquing. A visit to Prospect Hill Antiques on Prospect Hill Road in Georges Mills (603–763–9676; www.prospecthillantiques.com) will reward you with a barn's worth of browsables.

Cruises. Short of a private craft, the best way to view Lake Sunapee is aboard a 1½-hour-long narrated tour on the M/V *Mount Sunapee II* or the M/V *Kearsarge*; the latter, a replica of the nineteenth-century steamers that once plied the lake, offers a dinner cruise. Both depart from Sunapee Harbor (603–763–4030, www.sunapeecruises.com).

Hiking. The area boasts two scenic peaks in addition to Mount Sunapee. The bald-topped, 2,937-foot Mount Kearsarge is an easy half-mile ascent from Rollins State Park off Route 103 north of Warner (603–456–3808; www.nhparks.state.nh.us/parkops/parks/rollins) or 1 mile from the auto road in Winslow State Park off Route 11 south of Wilmot (603–526–6168; www.nhparks.state.nh.us/parkops/parks/winslow). The 3,121-foot Mount Cardigan contains 50 miles of trails, all part of Mount Cardigan State Park (603–547–3373; www.nhparks.state.nh.us/parkops/parks/cardigan) off Routes 4 and 118 east of Canaan.

Museums. At the Mount Kearsarge Indian Museum on Kearsarge Mountain Road in Warner (603–456–2600; www.indianmusem.org), Native American artifacts from across the country are presented in a respectful context, and a two-acre self-guided walk introduces medicinal plants. The Fort at No. 4 on Route 11 in Charlestown (603–826–5700 or 888–367–8284; www.fort at4.com) is a living history museum that re-creates a frontier settlement of the 1740s, when the region was in the throes of the French and Indian War.

Performing arts. The Capitol Center for the Arts at 46 South Main Street in Concord (603–225–1111; www.ccanh.com) is a restored vaudeville theater offering popular entertainment. In Hanover, Dartmouth's Hopkins Center for the Arts (603–646–2422; www.hop.dartmouth.edu), a precursor to Lincoln Center designed by Wallace Harrison, hosts scores of live performances and hundreds of films yearly. The region is also rich in turn-of-the-century auditoriums, all still going strong: these include the Lebanon Opera House (603–448–0400; www.lebanonoperahouse.org), the Claremont Opera House (603–542–4433), and the Newport Opera House (603–863–2412; www.newportoperahouse.com). The New London Barn

Playhouse on Main Street (603–526–6710; www.nlrec.com/orgs/nlbarn) has been offering summer fare since 1934.

Skiing. Mount Sunapee (603–763–2356 or 800–MTSUNAPEE; www.mt sunapee.com) is a good-sized area—1,510 vertical feet—with few frills, but no inflated prices either. For details on smaller downhill areas in the region, contact Ski New Hampshire (603–887–5464 or 800–88–SKI–NH; www.skinh.com). These include the family-oriented, 900-foot-high Dartmouth Skiway in Lyme Center (603–795–2143; www.dartmouth.edu/~skiway), where New England skiing got its start. New London is home to one of the larger cross-country facilities in New England: Norsk on Route 11 (603–526–6040 or 800–42–NORSK; www.skinorsk.com) has a trail system running to 70 kilometers.

SPECIAL EVENTS

Mid–February. Dartmouth Winter Carnival, Hanover; (603) 643–3115; www.hanoverchamber.org. Classic frolics including sporting events and awesome ice sculptures.

Early August. Craftsmen's Fair, Mount Sunapee; (603) 224–3375; www.nhcrafts.org. For nine action-packed days, members of the venerable League of New Hampshire Craftsmen not only display their wares but demonstrate their techniques, to the accompaniment of various entertainers.

Early October. Shaker Village Harvest Day, Canterbury; (603) 783–9511 or (800) 982–9511; www.shakers.org. Hayrides, fresh-pressed cider, and crafts.

OTHER RECOMMENDED RESTAURANTS AND LODGINGS

Alexandria

Cardigan Mountain Lodge; (603) 744–8011; www.outdoors.org. For a modest fee the Appalachian Mountain Club provides a bunk and three squares, high on a mountainside.

Bradford

Mountain Lake Inn, 2871 Route 114; (603) 938–2136 or (800) 662–6005; www.mountainlakeinn.com. Pastoral peace at a 1760 inn on 168 acres, including a private beach.

Rosewood Country Inn, Pleasant View Road; (603) 938–5253 or (800) 938–5273; www.rosewoodcountryinn.com. A hit with the early Hollywood crowd (Pickford, Gish, Chaplin, et al.), this spacious Victorian inn offers lavishly decorated rooms in a spectrum of styles, from rustic to frilly.

Claremont

Goddard Mansion, 25 Hillstead Road; (603) 543–0603 or (800) 736–0603; www.goddardmansion.com. That rarity, an elegant summer home-turned-B&B that actively welcomes families.

Etna

Moose Mountain Lodge, Moose Mountain Highway; (603) 643–3529 www.moosemountainlodge.com. Dazzling mountain views and hearty dinners distinguish this classic 1938 lodge, favored by hikers.

Hanover

Cafe Buon Gustaio, 72 South Main Street; (603) 643–5711. Featuring evolved Italian delicacies.

Molly's Restaurant, 43 South Main Street; (603) 643–2570; www.mollys restaurant.com. A festive casual eatery.

Henniker

Colby Hill Inn; (603) 428-3281 or (800) 531-0330; www.colbyhillinn.com. A rambling two-century-old inn with a pool and tennis court, plus a dining room known for rich, neo-Continental cuisine.

Meeting House Inn and Restaurant, Flanders Road; (603) 428–3228; www.conknet.com/meetinghouse. A late eighteenth-century farmhouse with pleasant quarters and a barn turned restaurant.

Lebanon

Monsoon, 18 Centerra Parkway; (603) 643–9227. Pacific Rim excitement invades academia.

Lyme

Alden Country Inn, On the Common; (603) 795–2222 or 800–794–2296; www.aldencountryinn.com. Offering lodgings as well as sophisticated dinner fare, this 1809 tavern is the social hub of a timeless town.

The Dowds' Country Inn, On The Common; (603) 795–4712 or (800) 482–4712; www.dowdscountryinn.com. A 1780 house and barn, nicely updated.

Loch Lyme Lodge and Cottages, Route 10; (603) 795–2141 or (800) 423–2141; www.communityinfo.com/lochlyme. A family-friendly lakefront complex little changed since 1917.

New London

Colonial Farm Inn, Route 11; (603) 526–6121 or (800) 805–8504; www.colonialfarminn.com. A prettily renovated 1836 house turned small inn serving dinner.

Hide-Away Inn, Twin Lakes Villa Road; (603) 526–4861 or (800) 457–0589; www.hideawayinn.net. A country house and restaurant overlooking Little Lake Sunapee.

Inn at Pleasant Lake, Pleasant Street; (603) 526–6271 or (800) 626–4907; www.innatpleasantlake.com. A 1790 inn on five pastoral lakeside acres with a private beach; distinguished New American dinners.

Millstone Restaurant, Newport Road; (603) 526–4201. A cheery eatery strong on local ingredients.

North Sutton

Follansbee Inn, Route 114; (603) 927–4221 or (800) 626–4221; www.follansbeeinn.com. A comfortable 1840 inn set amid 500 wooded acres alongside Kezar Lake.

Orford

White Goose Inn, Route 10; (603) 353–4812 or (800) 358–4267; www.whitegooseinn.com. A sweet country inn with unexpected style and hearty Germanic breakfasts.

Sunapee

The Anchorage, 17 Garnet Street; (603) 763–3334. Neo-American nibbles—
e.g., "North Country Rasta Pasta"—overlooking the harbor.

Dexter's Inn and Tennis Club, Stage Coach Road; (603) 763–5571 and (800)
232–5571; www.bbhost.com/dextersinn. This cheery 1801 country house
comes equipped with three all-weather courts, plus a pool and lakeview
dining room.

The Inn at Sunapee, Burkehaven Hill Road; (603) 763–4444 or (800) 327–
2466; www.innatsunapee.com. An 1875 farmhouse set on ten lakeview
acres, with pool, tennis court, and restaurant.

FOR MORE INFORMATION

Hanover Area Chamber of Commerce, 216 Nugget Building, Main Street;
Hanover, NH 03755; (603) 643–3115; www.hanoverchamber.org.

New Hampshire Division of Travel & Tourism Development, Box 1856,
Concord, NH 03302, (603) 271–2343 or (800) FUN–IN–NH; www.
visitnh.gov.

New London-Lake Sunapee Region Chamber of Commerce, PO Box 532,
New London, NH 03257; (603) 526–6565 or (877) 526–6575; www.lake
sunapeenh.org.

The White Mountains

A PEAK-SEEKER'S PARADISE

2 NIGHTS

Rapture of the steep • Happy trails • Million-dollar vistas
Off-price shops galore • Quiet hideaways

On the map the 768,000-acre White Mountain National Forest, presciently founded in 1911, is a big green blob that engulfs most of northern New Hampshire. Up close it's a great big gulp of fresh air—succeeding scrims of violet-tinted mountaintops that seem to go on forever, interlaced with some 1,200 miles of forest trails. If you want to have a primal encounter with nature here, it's not hard. Then again, if you just want to dabble while enjoying less strenuous tourist pastimes such as marathon outlet shopping, that's easy, too.

The Victorian gentry managed to vacation here quite nicely for months at a time, dragging along their entourages and wardrobes by the railroad-car-load. You can stuff some essentials in a backpack, hop in the car, and plunge deep within the woods in a matter of hours.

DAY 1

Morning

Drive straight up I–93 for about 1½ hours to exit 24, where Route 25 east leads to the **Squam Lakes Natural Science Center** off Route 113 in **Holderness** (603–968–7194; www.nhnature.org). At this 200-acre refuge for injured native animals unable to survive in the wild, you'll be able to see, close up, just whom you'll be sharing the woods with. It's open May through October 9:30 A.M. to 4:30 P.M. daily.

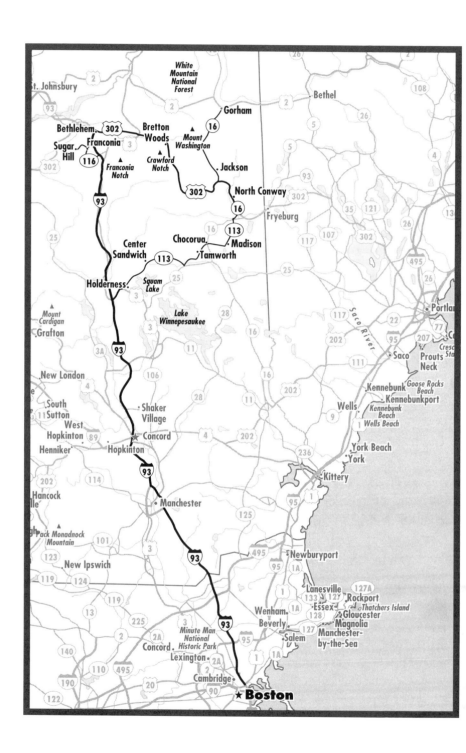

Route 113 skirts peaceful **Squam Lake,** ending up a dozen miles later at postcard-prim **Center Sandwich,** where you can poke around the **Sandwich Historical Society Museum** at 4 Maple Street (603–284–6269; www. sandwichnh.com/historg), open Tuesday through Saturday 11:00 A.M. to 5:00 P.M. in season, and various antiques and craft shops, including the **League of New Hampshire Craftmen** shop on Main Street, (603–284–6831; www. nhcrafts. org), which started out in the 1920s as Sandwich Home Industries.

LUNCH: Corner House Inn, 22 Main Street, Center Sandwich; (603) 284–6219. This 1849 guest house has a handful of tiny bedrooms upstairs and as many cozy dining rooms down. The lobster-and-mushroom bisque is a must-order, as is—given the setting, named for a buddy of the region's royal governor—a gourmet sandwich.

Afternoon

From here Route 113 leads through the pretty towns of **Tamworth, Chocorua,** and **Madison.** Less than a mile past the junction of Routes 113 and 16, the scenic **Kancamagus Highway** (named for a Native American chieftain known as "The Fearless One") proffers a number of relatively easy hikes—such as **Sabbaday Falls**—for those eager to stretch their legs. Get your bearings, and an array of options, from the **White Mountains National Forest Saco Ranger Station** at the intersection (603–447–5448; www.fs.us/r9/white).

Northward Route 16 funnels, laboriously, through the outlet gauntlet that is **North Conway.** It's hard to hit all 200-plus gloriously tax-free stores, but we always brake for **L. L. Bean** (603–356–2100; www.llbean.com) at the very least. Incidentally, if you want to skip the commercial maw, take West Side Road out of Conway. It passes the trailhead to **Diana's Baths,** a lovely cascade well worth the half-mile hike.

Either way, about 10 miles farther north, a picturesque covered bridge leads to the relatively calm hamlet of **Jackson,** the center of a vast network of hiking/cross-country trails. Walk uphill from the grandly restored **Wentworth Hotel** to cool your toes, and perhaps a bit more, at **Jackson Falls,** a pothole-pocked cascade that has inspired painters since the mid-nineteenth century. Or hold out for a soothing soak at the outdoor hot tub that awaits at your hotel.

DINNER AND LODGING: Inn at Thorn Hill, Thorn Hill Road, Jackson; (603) 383–4242 or (800) 289–8990; www.innatthornhill.com. Designed as a summer home by Stanford White in 1895, this is the kind of gracious country house that inspires visions of bracing walks and cozy evenings, enhanced by

fine dining—all of which you'll find here, along with prime Mount Washington views.

DAY 2

Morning

BREAKFAST: Inn at Thorn Hill.

There are several ways to tackle **Mount Washington,** at 6,288 feet the highest peak in the Northeast. If you're hardy enough, you could hike it. The ascent takes four to five hours. At the **Pinkham Notch Visitors Center** on Route 16 in Gorham (603–466–2725; www.outdoors.org), the Appalachian Mountain Club provides crucial pointers, maps, and even gear for this climb, as well as others not quite so strenuous. Ascents along the western flank tend to be less precipitous; in fact, from Bretton Woods, off Route 302, you could take a slow and somewhat scary ride up the **Mount Washington Cog Railway** (603–846–5404 or 800–922–8825; www.thecog.com), an 1869 steam-powered locomotive that climbs 3½ miles at grades of up to 37.5 percent. Or, sticking to the east, you could drive up the winding 8-mile **Mount Washington Auto Road** off Route 16 in Gorham (603–466–3988; www.mt washington.com). Once up top, unglue your eyes from the view long enough to take in the fascinating flora/fauna exhibits at the **Mount Washington Observatory Museum** (603–356–8345; www.mountwashington.org), and also poke around the **Tip Top House,** a tiny, roughhewn 1853 hotel restored as a curiosity. On the way down be sure to heed the warnings about pulling over to cool your brakes; you'll find they come in handy.

For a view *of* Mount Washington, rather than from it, consider hopping a **Wildcat Mountain** gondola, opposite the visitors center on Route 16 (603–466–3326 or 800–255–6439; www.skiwildcat.com), an experience ordinarily reserved for skiers. In the spring you may spot an antlike procession heading up **Tuckerman Ravine** (www.tuckerman.org), directly opposite: it's New England's ultimate *au naturel*—as in liftless—ski challenge.

LUNCH: Thompson House Eatery, Routes 16A and 16, Jackson; (603) 383–9341; www.thompsonhouse-eatery.com. A nineteenth-century barn makes an atmospheric setting for inventive dishes; it's especially refreshing when the patio is in bloom.

Afternoon

The drive through **Crawford Notch,** on the western side of the Presidential range, via Route 302, is easily one of the most scenic in New England. You might want to de-car at the southern entrance of the park for a 1½-mile hike to **Arethusa Falls,** at 176 feet New Hampshire's highest cascade. North on 302, past cliffs where you can usually spot rock climbers making their arduous way, the vista suddenly opens up to reveal the fabulous **Mt. Washington Resort** in Bretton Woods (603–278–1000 or 800–258–0330; www.mt washington.com), a 1902 behemoth that is the largest surviving grand hotel in these parts. Now owned by local entrepreneurs, it's looking grander than ever and affords fascinating glimpses of the good life, past and present tense. Meander through the hotel's pillared lobby and pause to catch the breezes, as well as a phenomenal view, from a porch rocker. You can tour the grounds on horseback or cross-country skis from the stable adjoining the **Bretton Arms Inn,** an 1896 satellite.

Bethlehem, about 15 miles west on Route 302, was embraced by the sniveling masses around the turn of the century for its supposedly pollen-free air. Dozens of grand hotels once lined these sleepy streets, and you'll see vestiges here and there, such as the **Maplewood Country Club's** grand Shingle-style casino; the eighteen holes are open to the public (603–869–3335 or 800–869–3335; www.maplewoodgolfresort.com). Sundry legacies of the era are tucked away in the antiques shops along Main Street.

DINNER AND LODGING: Adair, 80 Guider Lane off Route 302, Bethlehem; (603) 444–2600 or (888) 444–2600; www.adairinn.com. A 1927 Georgian Colonial Revival manse set on 200 acres with extensive Olmstead-designed gardens provides an idyllic country retreat. The in-house New American restaurant, **Tim-Bir Alley,** is by far the most accomplished in the area.

DAY 3

Morning

BREAKFAST: Adair. A hearty country breakfast makes a rousing prelude to a wake-up nature walk.

Wander the hiking trails that surround the inn, or explore **The Rocks,** a model nineteenth-century farmstead maintained by the Society for the Protection of New Hampshire Forests (603–444–6228; www.spnhf.org), which also sees to the pleasantly tousled terrace gardens. Continue along Route 302 to I–93 south, which you'll follow for 6 miles before exiting at **Franconia.** From here it's a couple of uphill miles along Route 117 to pretty **Sugar Hill,**

Scenic Franconia Notch and Echo Lake

where downhill skiing got its start in the East; a plaque marks the spot. You can learn more about this charming village at the **Sugar Hill Historical Museum** on the green (603–823–5336), open Thursday, Saturday, and Sunday from 1:00 to 4:00 P.M.

LUNCH: Polly's Pancake Parlor, Route 117; (603) 823–5575; www.pollys pancakeparlor.com. Open mid-May through foliage, Polly's has been dishing up maple-drenched pancakes since 1938.

Returning to Franconia, head south on Route 116 and look for the R. FROST mailbox on Ridge Road at your right. The "R" stands for Robert, who occupied this weathered farmhouse from 1915 to 1920. At the **Frost Place** (603–823–5510; www.frostplace.com)—open 1:00 to 5:00 P.M. daily July to mid-October weekends in the spring—you'll find interesting memorabilia, occasional readings, and a half-mile nature trail where poems serve as signage.

Return to Route 93 for a dazzling drive through **Franconia Notch.** At the foot of the **Cannon Mountain Aerial Tramway** (603–823–8800; www.cannonmt.com), a fun and easy view-enhancer, you'll come upon the **New England Ski Museum** (603–823–7177 or 800–639–4181; www.nesm.org), open daily late May to mid-October from noon to 5:00 P.M., and Thursday through Tuesday in ski season; admission is free. Fashion howlers aside, you've got to hand it to the mid-twentieth-century pioneers who braved not only the elements but awfully crude equipment.

For one last foray into the woods before joining the Boston-bound, stop at **The Basin** and look for the trailhead to **Cascade Brook** and **Kinsman Falls,** where you'll find plenty of rocks to climb, caves to explore, and pools to chill out in.

THERE'S MORE

Excursions. The M/S *Mount Washington* (603–366–4837 or 888–THE–MOUNT; www.cruisenh.com) plies Lake Winnipesaukee between Weirs Beach and Wolfeboro. The 75 miles of hiking trails that interlace the 5,200-acre grounds of the Castle in the Clouds, a grandiose 1920 estate off Route 171 in Moltonborough (603–476–2352 or 800–729–2468; www.castlesprings.com), are also open for Western-style trail rides. Operating out of an 1874 station in North Conway, the Conway Scenic Railroad (603–356–5251 or 800–232–5251; www.conwayscenic.com) runs antique trains—including a vintage dining car—over 11 miles of mountainside track. The Stables at the Farm by the River B&B, at 2555 West Side Road in North Conway (603–356–4855; www.farmbytheriver.com), offer fall wagon and winter sleigh rides as well as horseback riding year-round. Northern Forest Moose Tours track the humongous deer relatives in relative comfort, from Gorham (603–752–6060 or 800–992–7480).

Kid stuff. Weirs Beach features the kinds of tacky attractions kids favor, including the Surf Coaster USA water park—with corkscrew slides plus a wave pool—on Route 11B (603–366–4991; www.surfcoasterusa.com). A cherished dinosaur, the Weirs Drive-In Theatre on Route 3 (603–366–4723) features first-run movies; you might want to follow up with an ice cream sundae smorgasbord at the nearby Kellerhaus (603–366–4466 or 888–KLR–HAUS; www.kellerhaus.com.) For an educational, interactive look at Mount Washington's record-shattering weather, visit the Weather Discovery Center at 2936 White Mountain Highway (Route 16) in North

Conway (603–356–2137; www.mountwashington.org). Story Land on Route 16 in Glen (603–383–4293; www.storylandnh.com) is a small-scale, family-run amusement park that little kids will love.

Outfitters. Saco Bound/Downeast on Route 302 in Center Conway (603–447–2177; www.sacobound.com) sets up canoe, kayak, and rafting trips throughout the region. White Mountain Cyclists at Main Street in Lincoln (603–745–6466) can equip you for a scenic downhill ride along the 6-mile Franconia Notch Bike Path.

Performing arts. The Lakes Region Summer Theatre on Route 25 in Meredith (603–279–9933) does an all-Broadway summer stock season, plus children's matinees. The Barnstormers in Tamworth (603–323–8500; www.barnstormers.theatre.com) has been producing straw-hat theatre since 1931. The Papermill Theatre on Route 112 in Lincoln (603–745–2141; www.papermilltheatre.org) mounts popular summer shows for all ages. The New Hampshire Shakespeare Festival (www.nhsf.org) appears at various venues in summer, as does a classical orchestra, the North Country Chamber Players (603–444–0309; www.newww.com/org).

Skiing. The sport got its start in the United States here in the 1870s, thanks to Scandinavian loggers. Sizable peaks include—in roughly descending size, measured in vertical feet—Cannon (603–823–8880; www.cannonmt.com), Wildcat (603–466–3326 or 800–255–6439; www.skiwildcat.com) and Loon (603–745–8111 or 800–229–5666; www.loonmtn.com), Attitash (603–374–2368 or 800–223–7669; www.attitash.com), Waterville Valley (603–236–8311 or 800–GO–VALLEY; www.waterville.com), Bretton Woods (603–278–1000 or 800–232–2972; www.brettonwoods.com), and Mount Cranmore (603–356–5544 or 800–SUN–N–SKI; www.cranmore.com). The Jackson Ski Touring Foundation (603–383–9355 or 800–XCSNOWS; www.jacksonxc.com) maintains New England's most extensive trail network, covering over 150 kilometers and linking dozens of restaurants and inns. Another good base is Great Glen Trails on Route 16 in Pinkham Notch, opposite the Mount Washington Auto Road (603–466–3988, www. mt-washington.com), where you might want to hop a Sno-Cat shuttle to the summit.

NEW HAMPSHIRE

SPECIAL EVENTS

Late February. Mt. Washington Valley Chocolate Festival; (603) 356–5701 or (800) 367–3334; www.mtwashingtonvalley.org. Ski—or drive—inn to inn for treats.

Mid-June. Fields of Lupine Festival, Sugar Hill; (603) 823–5661 or (800) 237–9007; www.franconianotch.org. The inns put on teas and garden tours, and celebrants don their summer whites for gourmet picnics amid the purple spires.

Late August. Mount Washington Bicycle Hillclimb, Gorham; (603) 447–6991; www.tinmtn.org/hillclimb. This straight-up thigh-burner attracts big-name racers, as well as the merely masochistic.

OTHER RECOMMENDED RESTAURANTS AND LODGINGS

Bethlehem

Mulburn Inn, 2370 Main Street; (603) 869–3389 or (800) 457–9440; www.mulburn.com. Sylvanus D. Morgan, architect for the Mount Washington Hotel, built this Tudor manor for a Woolworth heiress in 1908.

Center Harbor

Red Hill Inn, Route 25B and College Road; (603) 279–7001 or (800) 5-REDHILL; www.redhillinn.com. This brick hilltop Victorian was built for the heir of the inventor of the soda fountain; the restaurant favors new-fangled New England fare.

Chocorua

Riverbend Inn, Route 16; (603) 323–7440 or (800) 628–6944. A colonial estate on fourteen riverside acres.

Conway

Chinook Café, 66 Main Street; (603) 447–6300. From great nibbles to seriously wonderful casual dinners.

Darby Field Inn, Bald Hill Road; (603) 447–2181 or (800) 426–4147; www. darbfield.com. Mountain views encircle this comfortable 1826 country inn, named for the first colonist to climb Mount Washington and famed for its dinners.

Dixville Notch

The Balsams Grand Resort Hotel; (603) 255–3400; www.thebalsams.com. Located *way* north (about 70 miles beyond Bethlehem), this huge, old-fashioned 1866–1918 resort set on 15,000 unspoiled acres is a world unto itself.

Eaton Center

The Inn at Crystal Lake, Route 153; (603) 447–2120 or (800) 343–7336; www. innatcrystallake.com. This Greek Revival beauty presides over a peaceful, swimmable lake.

Franconia

Bungay Jar, Easton Valley Road; (603) 823–7775 or (800) 421-0701; www. bungayjar. com. A stylishly retrofitted eighteenth-century barn turned B&B, with enviable mountain views.

Franconia Inn, Route 116; (603) 823–5542 or (800) 473–5299; www.fran coniainn.com. A pleasantly appointed mid-nineteenth-century inn offering interesting New American dining.

Glen

Bernerhof, Route 302; (603) 383–4414 or (800) 548–8007; www.bernerhof inn.com. A glorious Victorian enfolding spacious rooms plus a Swiss-influenced brewpub and restaurant, Prince Place (www.princeplace.com).

Red Parka Pub, Route 302; (603) 383–4344; www.redparkapub.com. A memorabilia-packed ski tavern/steakhouse.

Gorham

Pinkham Notch Visitors Center, Route 16; (603) 466–2725; www.outdoors. org. The Appalachian Mountain Club maintains two rather spiffy dorms (the other one's in Crawford Notch), plus eight high-mountain "huts," all offering budget lodging, hearty food, and hikerly camaraderie.

Hart's Location

The Notchland Inn, Route 302; (603) 374–6131 or (800) 866–6131; www.notchland.com. Gustav Stickley designed the parlor of this imposing 1862 granite manor near Crawford Notch; the five-course dinners, open to the public, pack surprising sophistication.

Holderness

The Manor on Golden Pond, Route 3; (603) 968–3348 or (800) 545–2141; www.manorongoldenpond.com. This imposing thirteen-acre 1907 lakeside estate encompasses a sumptuous New American dining room, a clay tennis court, and a sizable swimming pool.

Intervale

New England Inn, Route 16A; (603) 356–5541 or (800) 826–3466; www. newenglandinn.com. An 1809 inn surrounded by outbuildings (including an "adults only" timber lodge). The dining room serves continental fare; Tuckerman's Tavern, pub grub.

Jackson

Carter Notch Inn, Carter Notch Road; (603) 383–9630 or (800) 794–9434; www.carternotchinn.com. A hillside honey with spectacular views.

Eagle Mountain House, Carter Notch Road; (603) 383–9111 or (800) 966–5779; www. eaglemt.com. A nicely renovated 1879 grand hotel with a wraparound porch and a proficient dining room, Highfields.

Wentworth Resort Hotel, Route 16A; (603) 383–9700 or (800) 637–0013; www.thewentworth.com. This 1869 grand hotel comes encircled by an eighteen-hole golf course and tasteful condos. The elegant dining room serves exciting New American cuisine.

Whitneys' Inn, Route 16B; (603) 383–6886 or (800) 252–5622; www. whitneysinn.com. Boasting a congenial barn-turned-pub and an excellent restaurant, this comfy inn sits right at the foot of Black Mountain, a family-scale ski area.

Wildcat Inn & Tavern, Route 16A; (603) 383–4245 or (800) 228–4245; www. wildcatinnandtavern.com. The tavern is tops in terms of Jackson nightlife, and the restaurant more than satisfies; smallish rooms and suites are nicely priced.

Meredith

The Inns at Mill Falls and Bay Point, Route 3 and 25; (603) 279–7006 or (800) 622–6455; www.millfalls.com. A trio of handsomely rehabbed buildings flanking Meredith Falls Marketplace.

North Conway

Cranmore Mountain Lodge, Kearsarge Road; (603) 356–2044 or (800) 356–3596; www.cranmoremtlodge.com. Sporting types and families appreciate this rambling complex, where accommodations range from a private townhouse to bunkroom dorms and the heated pool is open year-round.

Horsefeathers, Main Street; (603) 356–6862; www.horsefeathers.com. A contemporary pub with an adventurous menu.

The 1785 Inn, Route 16; (603) 356–9025 or (800) 421–1785; www.the1785inn.com. Cozy rooms and romantic continental dining backed by mountain views.

Stonehurst Manor, Route 16; (603) 356–3113 or (800) 525–9100; www. stonehurstmanor.com. A turn-of-the-century summer estate with modernized lodgings, outdoor pool, hot tub, and tennis court; the dining bridges candlelit continental cuisine and stone-hearth pizzas.

North Woodstock

Woodstock Inn, Main Street; (603) 745–3951 or (800) 321–3985; www.wood stockinnnh.com. A scattering of B&B rooms, plus a continental restaurant, the Clement Room, and a lively brewpub, Woodstock Station.

Shelburne

Philbrook Farm Inn, 881 North Road; (603) 466–3831; www.nettx. com/philbrook. Hosted by the same family since 1861, this rambling farmhouse on 1,000 wooded acres near the Maine border is a precious and timeless retreat.

Snowville

Snowvillage Inn, 92 Stuart Road; (603) 447–2818 or (800) 447–4345; www. snowvillageinn.com. A 1912 summer house turned inn with a winning restaurant, high on a forested hillside.

Sugar Hill

Foxglove, Route 117; (603) 823–8840 or 888–343–2220; www.foxgloveinn. com. An intensively renovated summer manse serving champagne hors-d'oeuvres, in addition to a lavish breakfast.

Sugar Hill Inn, Route 117; (603) 823–5621 or (800) 548–4748; www.sugarhill inn.com. A rambling eighteenth-century country inn, where hominess— in decor and dining—still reigns.

Sunset Hill House, Sunset Hill Road; (603) 823–5522 or (800) 786–4455. A mere vestige of the grand hotels that once ringed town (it was actually the servants' quarters), this thirty-room inn boasts ridgetop views, an ambitious dining room, and its own nine-hole golf course.

Tamworth

The Tamworth Inn, Main Street; (603) 323–7721 or (800) 642–7352; www. tamworth.com. Updated with an outdoor pool, this 1833 inn-plus-restaurant serves as centerpiece to a classic New England village.

Wolfeboro

Back Bay Club, Back Bay off Mill Street; (603) 569–9200. This lakeside restaurant's country club-style decor belies its unstuffy cuisine.

The Bittersweet, Route 28; (603) 569–3636. An 1820s barn packed with rustic artifacts and specializing in regional cuisine (e.g., cider pie).

Bread & Roses Bakery, 57 Mill Street; (603) 569–4449. The perfect place to pick up a delectable breakfast or lunch on the run.

Wolfeboro Inn, 90 North Main Street; (603) 569–3016 or (800) 451–2389; www.wolfeboroinn.com. The core of this lakeside inn dates to 1812, but

constant updating has kept the complex luxurious; guests are offered a complimentary paddleboat excursion.

FOR MORE INFORMATION

Mount Washington Valley Chamber of Commerce, PO Box 2300, North Conway, NH 03860; (603) 356–5701 or (800) 367–3364; www.mt washingtonvalley.org.

New Hampshire Office of Travel & Tourism, PO Box 1856, Concord, NH 03302-1856; (603) 271–2666 or (800) FUN–IN–NH; www.visitnh.gov.

CANADA
ESCAPE

CANADA

Quebec City

EUROPE NEXT DOOR

2 NIGHTS

The pentimento of centuries • Extreme seasons
The best auberges • Dazzling dining

Of all the escapes in this book, Quebec is the least quick (it's about a 6½-hour drive), but by far the most escapist. Wrapped in our smug Yankee solipsism, we tend to forget there's a radically different culture just over the border, with a history as rich as, yet distinct from, our own—easily accessible and effusively welcoming.

Unlike their Old Country counterparts, Quebecois hoteliers and shop-keepers will actually applaud your attempts to dredge up your rusty French (the population is 95 percent Francophone). For a true immersion experience, opt for an off-season excursion, when the tourist presence is at a low ebb. Lovely as it is abloom in summer, Quebec is starkly beautiful in winter. The architecture, nearly four centuries' worth, stands out in sharp relief, and the broad St. Lawrence River is a shifting mosaic of ice floes. *En hiver,* the atmosphere is intimate and convivial, as if to fend off the fierce reality of subzero temperatures (bundle up). In summer Quebec blossoms into one big cosmopolitan block party. Try several seasons to see which suits you.

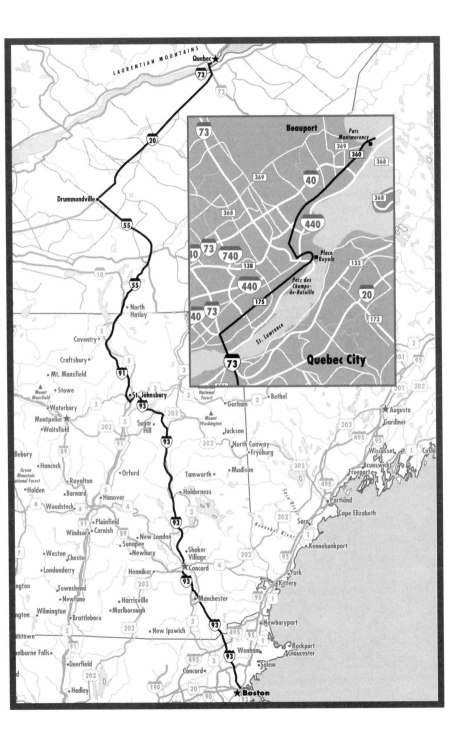

CANADA

DAY 1

Morning

A three-hour straight shot up Route 93 will deliver you to Vermont's **Northeast Kingdom,** New England's unspoiled outback. Alight in **Saint Johnsbury,** a prosperous trade-route holdover where, starting in the 1830s, the Fairbanks family used the proceeds from their scale factory to attempt to build a mini-Boston, complete with its own institutions of higher learning. Presiding over Main Street are the **Fairbanks Museum and Planetarium** (802–748–2372; www.fairbanksmuseum.com), an 1889 Ricardsonian Romanesque temple to natural history, open Monday through Saturday 10:00 A.M. to 4:00 P.M., and Sunday 1:00 to 5:00 P.M., with extended summer hours, and the **St. Johnsbury Athenaeum** (802–748–8291; www.stjathenaeum.org), an 1871 library/gallery that lends itself to leisurely delectation. A new stop on the tourist circuit—a relative term here—is the whimsical yet sincere **Dog Chapel** adjoining the **Stephen Huneck Gallery at Dog Mountain** on Spaulding Road (802–748–2700; www.huneck.com/dog_chapel.htm).

LUNCH: Northern Lights Bookshop Cafe, 378 Railroad Street, St. Johnsbury; (802) 748–4463; www.nlightsvt.com. Enjoy a light, bibliophiliac repast.

Afternoon

After browsing a bit in the **Moose River Lake & Lodge Store** at 370 Railroad Street (802–748–2423)—think L. L. Bean meets *Met Home*—continue northward along I–91, which turns into Route 55 at the Canadian border (you only need a driver's license to cross, but it couldn't hurt to carry a passport). In Drummondville, take 20 east as far as Route 73, which heads north to **Quebec City.** Hang a right after the Pont de Québec and follow Route 175 east, which, under various names, will lead you into the walled city of **Vieux-Québec.**

Cruise around a bit to get your bearings, then park near or in the **Chateau Frontenac** (the massive 1893 castle-hotel that dominates the skyline unmissably), and do some more aimless but serendipitous wandering by foot. Directly downhill from the chateau, below the ramparts, is the charming **Quartier Petit-Champlain** (418–692–2613 or 877–692–2613; www.quartier-petit-champlain.qc.ca), the oldest neighborhood in North America. Its rough-and-tumble former life as a red-light district kept it intact until restorationists took an interest in the mid-seventies. It's now a warren of browse-worthy boutiques and *intime* restaurants. At its center is the **Place-Royale,** a natural nexus that had served as a trading post for at least two millennia before Samuel de Champlain set up residence in 1608. With its Information Centre at 27, rue Notre-Dame and the Maison Chevalier museum at 50, rue du Marche-Champlain (418–643–3167; www.mcq.org), both open Tuesday through Sunday 10:00 A.M. to 5:00 P.M., the square is once again a magnet for commerce—this time, the tourist trade.

While you're poking around the Vieux-Port, keep in mind that, in Algonquin, *Kebec* means "where the river narrows." The crossing takes only ten minutes aboard the **Lévis ferry** (418–644–3704; www/traversoers/gpiv/qc/ca). This low-cost mini-cruise departs from 10, rue des Traversiers every thirty to sixty minutes year-round, from 6:30 A.M. to 1:30 A.M., and affords great views.

DINNER: Le Marie-Clarisse, 12, rue du Petit-Champlain; (418) 692–0857; www.marieclarisse.qc.ca. Tucked into a stone cellar at the base of the Escalier Casse-Cou, or "breakneck stairs," and also easily accessible via the **Funicular** (418–692–1132; www.funiculaire.com), this spot provides the quintessential Vieux-Québec dining experience, with a menu that changes daily but might include briny periwinkles you extract with a pin or a classic pear *financière.*

LODGING: Fairmont Le Chateau Frontenac, 1, rue des Carrières; (418) 692–3861 or (800) 441–1414. You'd better spend at least one night here; otherwise you're bound to feel deprived. Encompassing over 600 rooms, plus restaurants, shops, a spa, and endless hallways to roam, this grand hotel is a world unto itself. With any luck, and perhaps some special pleading, you'll get a gargoyle's views of pitched copper roofs and the river beyond.

DAY 2

Morning

BREAKFAST: Fairmont Le Chateau Frontenac. The **Cafe de la Terrasse** (418–691–3763), perched alongside the Dufferin Terrace boardwalk above the ramparts, serves a fine buffet breakfast. Here, in the winter, from 11:00 A.M. to 11:00 P.M., you'll spot skaters and tobogganers on the open-to-the-public **Patinoire** and **Glissades de la Terrasse** (418–694–9487); you may be tempted to join in.

Soon it's time to tear yourself away from the old town, temporarily. About one mile back east along Route 175, the **Musée du Québec** at the Parc des Champs-de-Bataille (418–643–2150 or 866–220–2150; www.mdq.org), open daily in-season from 11:00 A.M. to 6:00 P.M. (it's closed Mondays in winter), is a must-see art museum that occupies a contemporary aerie linking a neoclassical 1933 gallery to a dour 1860s stone jail. The narrow cells make interesting exhibition spaces, as well as a fun place to faux-imprison friends and family. Be sure to climb all the way up into the jail's turret, for dizzying views of the river and the Plains of Abraham, where the French and British fought one last, decisive tug-of-war in 1759. These 250 acres are now a lovely place to stroll—or bike, rollerblade, skate, sled, or cross-country ski—year-round. Vélo Passe-Sport Plein Air at 22, côte du Palais (418–692–3643) can provide the necessary means.

A ten-minute drive northeast of town, the **Parc de la Chute-Montmorency** at 2490, avenue Royale in Beauport (418–663–3330; www.chutemontmorency.qc.ca) was once the late eighteenth-century estate of the Duke of Kent. Now it's a pleasantly proletarian playground, with an aerial tram and a ledgeside trail that lead to a 273-foot waterfall. In summer the torrent effuses a cooling, indeed often drenching mist; in winter the spray forms a conical sugarloaf long popular for sliding and snowshoeing (rentals are available on-site).

LUNCH: Le Manoir Montmorency, 2490, avenue Royale, Beauport; (418) 663–3330; www.chutemontmorency.qc.ca. Sunday brunch buffets are a popular family pastime at this recreation of the Kent residence after it became a colonnaded hotel: a magician circulates to keep the *enfants* amused. For a real treat enjoy a formal meal in the panoramic dining room overlooking the falls.

Afternoon

The views might entice you further along the Saint-Lawrence: an hour's drive will bring you to the scenic **Charlevoix** region, where the Laurentian mountains tumble toward the river. Upon returning to town, pick a promising neighborhood and stroll some more. **Rue Saint-Jean** is often described as Quebec's SoHo, and it's comparably packed with eateries, shops, and clubs. Those seeking vestiges of Canadian tradition would do well to cruise the antiques shops lining **Rue Saint-Paul,** tucked below the northern ramparts. Primitive furniture—prized for its hard-knocks beauty—has become rare-unto-unfindable in New England, but Canada's back country is still yielding treasures. Also at this end of town is the bustling—from March through November—**Marché du Vieux-Port** at 160, quai Saint-André (418–692–2517), where you can stock up on local delicacies.

Rue Saint-Paul hugs the northern ramparts.

Time permitting, gain a deeper understanding of the country's past and present at the dazzling **Musée de la Civilisation** at 85, rue Dalhousie (418–643–2158; www.mcq.org), open daily in-season from 10:00 A.M. to 7:00 P.M., and Tuesday through Sunday 10:00 A.M. to 5:00 P.M. off-season. This Moshe Safdie gem encapsulates local color in an array of changing but reliably intriguing exhibitions. The museum fronts the **Promenade de la Pointe-à-Carcy,** a riverside boardwalk conducive to sunset strolls.

DINNER: Laurie Raphaël, 117, rue Dalhousie; (418) 692–4555; www.laurie raphael.com. At Daniel Vézina's playfully modernist restaurant every dish is brilliantly conceived and presented. Gourmets owe themselves the pleasure of a seven-course "Tour of Quebec" tasting menu, which changes monthly to make the most of seasonal provender.

LODGING: Hotel Dominion, 126, rue Saint-Pierre; (418) 692–2224 or (888) 833–5253; www.hoteldominion.com. This nineteenth-century warehouse—

just around the corner from the restaurant—has been transformed into a sleek hotel of cutting-edge design and superb creature comforts.

DAY 3

Morning

BREAKFAST: The Hotel Dominion. Enjoy the lovely continental breakfast (espresso, fresh croissants) in the luxurious lobby; you're sure to find yourself in interesting company.

Meander a bit more—whatever you missed. Then, if a nonstop return drive seems inconceivable, consider a half-way overnight at a luxurious auberge in Quebec's Eastern Townships (just north of the Vermont border) or at one of the Northeast Kingdom's exquisite country inns.

THERE'S MORE

Adventures. New World Quebec at 825, chemin du Hibou in Stoneham (418–848–4144 or 800–267–4144; http://futurix.clic.net/com/nworld) organizes rafting trips. Les Excursions & Méchouis Jacques-Cartier at 978, avenue Jacques-Cartier Nord in Tewkesbury (418–848–RAFT; www.excursions jcartier. com) offers the same, plus canoeing, kayaking, and equitation. Le Mythe des Glaces at 737, boulevard Du Lac in Charlesbourg (418–849–6131; http://www.quebecweb.com/mythe), offers the unique experience of ice canoeing. The Ascensation rock-climbing school has indoor facilities at 2350, avenue du Colisée in Québec (418–647–4422 or 800–762–4967) and mounts excursions into the countryside. In the vast Parc de la Jacques-Cartier north of the city, Faune Aventure (418–848–5099) runs wildlife tours featuring nocturnal wolf-calling and moose safaris.

Kid stuff. You can count on one happy, albeit pruny child if you take him or her to the Valcartier Vacation Village at 1860, boulevard Valcartier in Valcartier (418–844–1220; www.valcartier.com), a vast water and amusement park featuring dozens of slides, a wave pool, "adventure river," go-karts, trampolines, and more—and, in winter, their frozen equivalents, including dog-sled and horse-drawn carriage rides.

Nightlife. Cabaret, dance clubs, theater, *grands spectacles*—Quebec has them all. International headliners, from classical to pop, appear at the Grand

Théâtre de Québec, 269, boulevard Réné-Levesque Est (418–643–8131; www.grandtheatre.qc.ca), which also houses the Théâtre du Trident (418–643–5873). Théâtre Périscope at 2, rue Crémazie Est (418–529–2183) hosts a changing roster of French-language acting companies. As for the scores of smaller performance venues in town, you can find current listings in free publications such as *Voir* (www.voir.ca).

Skiing. An ardent downhill skier could follow a zigzagging trail of worth-while mountains, starting in northeastern Vermont. Future Olympians train at Burke in East Burke (802–626–3322 or 800–922–BURK; www.skiburke.com), and Jay Peak in Jay (802–988–2611 or 800–451–4449; www.jaypeakresort.com) is a challenging mega-mountain. Two good-sized areas—Owl's Head (514–292–3342; www.owlshead.com) and Mt. Orford (819–843–6548 or 800–567–2772 or www.mt-orford.com)—flank Lake Memphremagog in the Eastern Townships region. Arced around Quebec City are the easy-to-reach Stoneham (418–848–2411 or 800–463–6888; www.ski-stoneham.com); intensely developed Mont Sainte-Anne (418–827–4281 or 800–463–1568; www. mont-sainte-anne.com); and, over-looking the St. Lawrence an hour northeast in Charlevoix, pristine Le Massif (418–632–5879 or 877–LE-MASSIF; www.lemassif.com). Nordic skiers have their pick of over 2,000 kilometers of groomed trails, with heated shelters, in the Greater Quebec area; for listings, consult the Regroupement des Stations de Ski de Fond (418–653–5875; www.rssfrq.qc.ca).

SPECIAL EVENTS

Early February. Carnaval de Québec; (418) 626–3716; www.carnaval.qc.ca. Feasts, parades, snow sculptures, and a canoe race across the Saint-Lawrence.

Mid-July. Quebec Summer Festival; (418) 692–5200; www.infofestival.com. Over 600 performing artists bring world music to Vieux-Québec.

Early August. Les Fêtes de la Nouvelle-France, Quebec; (418) 694–3311; www.nouvellefrance.qc.ca. Performers render tribute to Quebec's illustri-ous past.

Late August to early September. Quebec International Film Festival; (418) 694–9920. An indie extravaganza.

OTHER RECOMMENDED RESTAURANTS AND LODGINGS

Ayer's Cliff, Eastern Townships

Ripplecove Inn, 700 Ripplecove Road; (819) 838–4296, or (800) 668–4296; www.ripplecove.com. This beautifully decorated inn serving exquisite French cuisine sits on a twelve-acre lakeside peninsula.

Beaupré, Quebec

Auberge La Camarine, 10947, boulevard Sainte-Anne; (418) 827–5703 or (800) 567–3939; www.camarine.com. Pleasant lodgings and phenomenal *cuisine de mère* at the foot of Mont Sainte-Anne.

Coventry, Vermont

Heermansmith Farm Inn, Hermansmith Farm Road (off Route 5); (802) 754–8866; www.scenesofvermont.com/heermansmith. A remote country inn serving elaborate, locally grown cuisine.

Craftsbury, Vermont

Craftsbury Bed & Breakfast on Wylie Hill; (802) 586–2206; www.scenes ofvermont.com/craftsburybb. This quilt-bedecked 1860s farmhouse offers a homey alternative to pricier options in town.

Craftsbury Outdoor Center, Lost National Road; (802) 587–7767 or (800) 729–7751; www.craftsbury.com. Plain, dorm-style accommodations, accompanied by masterful training in various outdoor sports spanning 140 acres.

Craftsbury Common, Vermont

The Inn on the Common, Main Street; (802) 586–9619 or (800) 521–2223; www.innonthecommon.com. A cluster of Federal buildings proffering luxury lodgings and elegant communal power dinners.

East Burke, Vermont

The Inn at Mountain View Creamery, Darling Hill Road; (802) 626–9924 or (800) 572–4509; www.innmtnview.com. A 440-acre country estate with stylish lodgings and a delightful restaurant, Darling's, in an 1890 brick creamery.

Georgeville, Quebec

Auberge Georgeville, 71, Chemin Channel; (819) 843–8683 or (888) 843–8686; www.fortune1000.ca/georgeville. A turreted lakeside painted lady (pink) serving Cordon Bleu/eclectic cuisine.

Greensboro, Vermont

Highland Lodge, Caspian Lake Road; (802) 533–2647; www.thehighlandlodge. com. A small-scale, Victorian-era lakeside resort, as prized for its cross-country network as it is for lazy summering.

Lower Waterford, Vermont

Rabbit Hill Inn, Route 18; (802) 748–5168 or (800) 76BUNNY; www.rabbit hillinn.com. A romantically enhanced Greek Revival inn serving exquisite candlelit dinners.

Lyndonville, Vermont

The Wildflower Inn, Darling Hill Road; (802) 626–8310 or (800) 627–8310; www.wildflowerinn.com. A spacious 1796 farmhouse set amid 500 hilltop acres, with pool, petting zoo, and supervised kids' activities—familial bliss.

La Malbaie, Quebec

Fairmont Le Manoir Richelieu, 181, rue Richelieu; (418) 665–3703; www. fairmont.com. A far-from-rustic resort overlooking the St. Lawrence, since 1899.

North Hatley, Quebec

Auberge Hatley, 325 C.P. 330 chemin Virgin; (819) 842–2451; www.relais chateaux.fr/hatley. A gabled lake-view country house serving exquisite classical French cuisine.

Manoir Hovey, Lake Massawippi (819) 842–2421 or (800) 661–2421; www. manoirhovey.com. A twenty-five-acre Mount Vernon–style lakeside estate, with glorious gardens and killer *cuisine de terroir*.

Quebec City, Quebec

A la Table de Serge Bruyère, 1200, rue Saint-Jean; (418) 694–0618. Since 1980, consistently top-caliber (if pricy) contemporary cuisine.

Auberge du Trésor, 20, rue Sainte-Anne; (418) 694–1876 or (800) 566–1876; www.aubergedutresor.com. A European-style pension, offering classicist dishes plus cabaret.

Auberge Saint-Antoine, 10, rue Saint-Antoine; (418) 692–2211 or 888–692–2211; www.saint-antoine.com. Romantic rooms in the Old Port.

Auberge Saint-Pierre, 79, rue Saint-Pierre; (418) 694–7981 or (888) 268–1017; www.auberge.qc.ca. Stone walls and jacuzzis, fluffy duvets, and gourmet breakfasts—historic lodgings for modern softies.

Café-Restaurant du Musée du Québec, Parc de Champs-de-Bataille; (418) 644–6780. Artful presentations of regional specialties.

Hotel le Priori, 15, rue Sault-au-Matelot; (418) 692–3992 or (800) 351–3992; www.hotellepriori.com. Stylish exposed-brick rooms with splashes of color.

Initiale, 54, rue Saint-Pierre; (418) 694–1818. A bank turned elegant—and accomplished—restaurant.

L'Echaudé, 73, rue du Sault-au-Matelot; (418) 692–1299; www.echaude.com. A blend of traditional/nouvelle cuisine.

Le Café du Clocher Penché, 203, rue Saint-Joseph Est; (418) 640–0597. A lively all-day bistro in the up-and-coming Art Zone.

Le Lapin Sauté, 52, rue Petit-Champlain; (418) 692–5325. Country-style feasting, with an emphasis on game.

Poisson d'Avril, 115, quai Saint-André; (418) 692–1010 or (877) 692–1010; www.poissondavril.net. Proximity to the Vieux-Port market ensures the freshest of seafood—including all-you-can-eat mussels.

Saint-Cathérine, Quebec

Ice Hotel-Quebec; (418) 661–4522; www.icehotel-canada.com. And now for something completely different (and frozen): a hotel made of ice, complete with movie theater and bar.

Saint-Laurent, Quebec

Le Canard Huppé, 2198, chemin Royal; (418) 828–2292. An idyllic country inn-and-restaurant on the nearby Ile d'Orléans.

Moulin de Saint-Laurent, 754, chemin Royal; (418) 829–3888 or (888) 629–3888; www.moulinstlaurent.qc.ca. Traditional French and Canadian cuisine in a converted 1720 watermill, plus riverside cottages.

Stoneham, Quebec

Domaine la Truite du Parc, 7600 Boulevard Talbot (Route 175); (418) 848–3732; www.traineauxchiens.qc.ca. A sporting camp—where you can cleep in a teepee or igloo.

Westmore, Vermont

Willough Vale Inn, Route 5A; (802) 525–4123 or (800) 594–9102; www.willoughvale.com. A handsome neo-traditional inn with lakeview dining.

Woodbury, Vermont

Kahagon, Nichols Pond Road; (802) 472–6446. A former Procter (of Procter & Gamble) estate, this 460-acre hideaway combines rustic charm and *Gourmet*-worthy cuisine.

FOR MORE INFORMATION

Greater Quebec Area Tourism & Convention Bureau, 835, avenue Wilfrid-Laurier, Quebec, Canada G1R 2L3; (418) 522–3511; www.quebec region.com.

Northeast Kingdom Chamber of Commerce, 357 Western Avenue, St. Johnsbury, VT 05819; (802) 748–3678 or (800) 639–6379; www.nek chamber.org.

Vermont Department of Tourism and Marketing, 6 Baldwin St., Montpelier, VT 05602; (802) 828–3236 or (800) VERMONT; www.1-800-VERMONT.com.

VERMONT
ESCAPES

ᴇꜱᴄᴀᴘᴇ ᴏɴᴇ

VERMONT

The "West Coast"

SLOPES TO SHORE

2 NIGHTS

The highest Green Mountains • New England's inland sea
Ice cream heaven • A pack rat's paradise

Northwestern Vermont has everything one could possibly require of a great
escape: dramatic scenery, quaint towns, luxurious inns, and phenomenal food.
The back-to-the-landers who fled to these hills in the sixties and seventies
brought with them city-honed tastes for all the finer things. Hence the ascen-
dance of Burlington as mecca for the hipoisie. From Church Street, a Euro-
style pedestrian mall lined with convivial cafes, to its invitingly renewed
waterfront, this once drab port seems to get livelier by the year.

  Of course, you didn't come all this way—it's about a three-hour drive—
merely to recapture Boston-in-the-boonies. This itinerary focuses primarily
on what you won't find in the metropolis: peace, quiet, and the promise of
renewal rooted in a bounteous land.

DAY 1

Morning

Head up I–93 past Manchester, New Hampshire, and take I–89 northwest
into Vermont, exiting at **Montpelier**, the nation's smallest state capital. You
could tour the gold-domed 1859 State House (802–828–2228; www.leg.state.
vt.us./sthouse), open 9:00 A.M. to 4:00 P.M. weekdays year-round, as well as
the nearby **Vermont Historical Society Museum** at 109 State Street (802–
828–2291; www.state.vt.us/vhs/museum), which conveys a historic overview

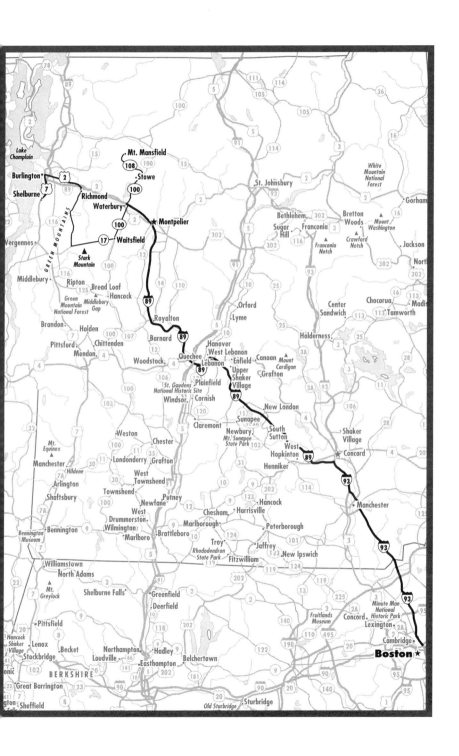

through regional particularities; it's open Tuesday through Friday 9:00 A.M. to 4:30 P.M., Saturday 9:00 A.M. to 4:00 P.M., and Sunday noon to 4:00 P.M. A few blocks east, on College Street, is the **T. W. Wood Art Gallery** (802–828–8743), which showcases Vermont art work past and present; the WPA-era holdings are particularly strong. Part of the Norwich University campus, the gallery is open Tuesday through Sunday from noon to 4:00 P.M.

LUNCH: Main Street Grill & Bar, 188 Main Street, Montpelier; (802) 223–3188; www.neculinary.com. Montpelier is home to the nationally renowned New England Culinary Institute, and you can nab a fantastic lunch at its learning-lab restaurants. The Grill offers exciting New American bistro fare at a fairly brisk pace and affordable prices; upstairs is the more formal Chef's Table (802–229–9202). For a light bite, check out **La Brioche Bakery,** NECI's cafe at 89 Main Street (802–229–0443).

Afternoon

Continue northwest on I–89 as far as **Waterbury,** and pull into **Ben & Jerry's Ice Cream Factory** about a mile north on Route 100 (802–244–TOUR; www. benjerry.com) for a fun tour culminating in free samples. Continue along Route 100, making optional stops for further tastings at the **Cold Hollow Cider Mill** (802–244–8771 or 800–3–APPLES; www.coldhollow.com), where—depending on the season—you can watch apples being pressed or try a cider donut; and at the **Green Mountain Chocolate Company** (802–244–8356 or 800–686–8783; www.greenmountainchocolate.com), where a complimentary nibble is sure to lead into temptation.

You can work it all off in **Stowe,** about 10 miles north via Route 100. Renowned for its snow sports, Stowe actually makes a great summer playground as well. A recreational path squiggles from the lively, shop-riddled center of town some 5½ miles along the West Branch River toward the **Stowe Mountain Resort** (802–253–3000 or 800–253–4754; www.stowe.com)—itself a smorgasbord of recreational options. The most challenging of these is the in-line skate park at Spruce Peak, complete with half-pipes and its own little rope tow: yes, you can slalom down. A slightly tamer charge can be had in Spruce Peak's alpine slide: you take the chairlift up and careen down concrete chutes on a heavy plastic sled, controlling the speed. Both Spruce Peak and neighboring Mount Mansfield offer lift-assisted mountain biking. Armchair view-lovers may drive the winding toll road that climbs the ridge of Mount Mansfield, or hop a gondola to its craggy peak—at 4,393 feet, Vermont's highest point.

DINNER: Blue Moon Cafe, 35 School Street, Stowe; (802) 253–7006. Relaxed-chic dining.

LODGING: Inn at the Round Barn Farm, 1661 East Warren Road, Waitsfield; (802) 496–2276; www.innatroundbarn.com. Retrace route 100 past I–89 to **Waitsfield;** cross the covered bridge in the center of the village to reach this ideal country retreat. Rooms range from relatively simple to country-luxe, complete with skylit whirlpools, and everyone enjoys the same pretty hilltop setting.

DAY 2

Morning

BREAKFAST: Inn at Round Barn Farm.

After strolling (or skiing) the grounds and checking out the rare 1910 round barn, now home to the **Green Mountain Cultural Center** (802–496–7722), head back into the village, perhaps pausing at the **Bridge Street Bakery** (802–496–0077 or 877–767–4752; www.vtcakes.com) to indulge in the commendable Tyrolean tradition of *zweites frühstück* ("second breakfast") or to cadge a few treats for later. Assorted studios occupy the Bridge Street Marketplace at the corner of Route 100, including that of **Elisabeth von Trapp** (802–496–3171), a third-generation singer-songwriter. And around the corner, east on Route 100, is **The Store** (802–496–4465; www.vermontstore.com), an 1834 meetinghouse that's now an upscale emporium whose wares span beautifully distressed antiques and esoteric comestibles. A bit farther east, on summer Saturdays, you'll come upon the **Mad River Green Farmers' Market,** a delightful mix of prize produce, baked goods, local crafts, and music.

Take Route 17 west out of town for a dazzling view of lush Addison County from the height of the Appalachian Gap. In fact, get out and do some crest-walking if you're in the mood: a 2½-mile hike along the **Long Trail,** south of the road, will bring you to the peak of 3,662-foot **Stark Mountain.** If you're not ready to allot four to five hours, just gawk and drive on. On the far side of the gap, follow country roads north through Huntington, with an optional detour to the **Green Mountain Audubon Nature Center** on Sherman Hollow Road (802–434–3068; www.thecompass.org/audubon) to stretch your legs while exploring 255 acres of varied habitats, including beaver ponds and maple groves (you can help with the sugaring in-season—i.e., spring). A few miles farther north is the town of **Richmond,** noted for its

1813 **Round Church,** past the center of town on Bridge Street; this sixteen-sided architectural marvel was the first ecumenical chapel in the country. To the west, Route 2 traverses the Historic District town of **Williston Village** and ultimately leads to **Burlington,** past the **University of Vermont** on the heights and down toward the waterfront. Pull over near the **Church Street Marketplace** (802–863–1648; www.churchstmarketplace.com), a pedestrian mall thronged with over a hundred inviting shops and restaurants.

LUNCH: NECI Commons, 25 Church Street, Burlington; (802) 862–NECI; www.neculinary.com. Enjoy observing—and scarfing up—further genius-in-training within the open kitchens of the New England Culinary Institute.

Afternoon

Stroll downhill to the shore of **Lake Champlain,** aka "the Sixth Great Lake." The **Burlington Community Boathouse** at the foot of College Street (802–865–3377), a charming neo-Victorian folly, offers the opportunity to catch a cruise, rent a craft, or just toast the sun as it descends behind the dramatic scrim of the Adirondacks. Eight miles of recreational paths flank the lake here, leading to swimmable beaches. Bikes, skates, and kayaks can be rented from **Skirack,** nearby at 85 Main Street (802–658–3313 or 800–882–4530; www.skirack.com), which also offers free parking.

Cultural mavens will soon want to hightail it south to Shelburne on commercialized Route 7 to catch the vast and varied holdings of the **Shelburne Museum** (802–985–3346; www.shelburnemuseum.org), open 10:00 A.M. to 5:00 P.M. daily from mid-May to late October and 1:00 to 4:00 P.M. in the shoulder seasons. New York socialite Electra Havemeyer Webb, who in the early nineteenth century summered where you'll be sleeping tonight, was proven prescient rather than eccentric once the scope of her collectomania could be appreciated. The cache currently stands at some eighty thousand *objets*—from folk art to French Impressionism—housed in three dozen historic buildings on forty-five acres. In some instances the structures themselves—including a stone lighthouse, a country store, a vintage train, and an entire sidewheel steamboat—constitute collectors' items.

DINNER AND LODGING: The Inn at Shelburne Farms, 1611 Harbor Road, Shelburne; (802) 985–8498; www.shelburnefarms.org. The sixty-room Queen Anne-style Shelburne House, built by Seward and Lila Vanderbilt Webb in 1899, sits on 1,000 acres landscaped by Frederick Law Olmsted. Rather than see this extraordinary property carved up for condos, the Webb heirs

The Burlington Community Boathouse on Lake Champlain

transformed it into a model ecology-oriented farm, whose educational out-reach efforts the inn helps fund. Whereas ordinary visitors are limited to a tour, guests are able to roam the grounds freely, play tennis, swim, and partake of elegant meals—in other words, live much as the Webbs might have, if only temporarily.

DAY 3

Morning

BREAKFAST: Inn at Shelburne Farms. Continue to savor the good life as you gaze across Lake Champlain.

Just take it easy today before heading home. At most retrace your steps to enjoy further the panoply of pleasures already sampled. You can always come back.

THERE'S MORE

Adventures. Umiak Outfitters on Mountain Road in Stowe (802–253–2317; www.umiak.com) can set you up for everything from mountaineering and snowshoeing to canoeing or kayaking, by moonlight if you wish; Clearwater Sports on Route 100 in Waitsfield (802–496–2708; www.clearwatersports.com) rents out mountain bikes, canoes, kayak, and sailboards. The Sugarbush Polo Club (802–496–8938) not only mounts matches in the Mad River Valley but arranges lessons for the curious. The Vermont Icelandic Horse Farm in Waitsfield (802–496–7141) harbors a stableful of small, gentle-gaited mounts ideal for jaunts of a half-day or more, regardless of the season; in winter, you might try "ski-joring"—cross-country with an equine assist. To get a glider's-eye view of the dramatic countryside, look to Sugarbush Soaring at Warren Airport (802– 496–2290; www.sugarbush.org). Would-be paragliders can find tutelage through Parafly Paragliding at 98 Severance Road in Colchester (802– 879–3507 or 800–PARAFLY; www.paraflypg.com). The maritime equivalent of a super-highway, Lake Champlain is littered with nineteenth-century wrecks; to get a peek, join a snorkeling or SCUBA expedition mounted by Waterfront Diving at 214 Battery Street in Burlington (802– 865–2771).

Bargain shopping. Burlington offers prime second-hand pickings. Check out Battery Street Jeans at 182 Battery Street (802–865–6223) for all sorts of vintage clothing; the Architectural Salvage Warehouse at 212 Battery Street (802–658–5011; www.architecturalsalvagevt.com) for decorative elements; and the Outdoor Gear Exchange at 131 Main Street (802–860–0190) for used and/or marked-down equipment. Also, don't overlook the perfectly tasty seconds at the Lake Champlain Chocolates factory store at 750 Pine Street (802–864–1807; www.lakechamplainchocolate.com).

Cultural events. The 1899 Barre Opera House (802–476–8188; www.barreoperahouse.org) hosts a broad range of performing arts. Montpelier's Lost Nation Theater, based at City Hall Arts Center at 39 Main Street (802–229–0492), mounts provocative plays and musicals. Occupying the bulk of tiny Johnson, the Vermont Studio Center (802–635–2727; www.vermontstudiocenter.com) hosts extraordinary guest artists and authors. Saint Michael's Playhouse at 56 College Parkway in Colchester (802–654–2281; www.saintmichaelsplayhouse.com) has operated as an Equity summer stock company since 1947. The art deco Flynn Theatre for the Performing Arts at 153 Main Street in Burlington (802–86–FLYNN; www.flynntheatre.org) hosts concerts, films, and plays, including acclaimed performances by the Vermont Stage Company (802–862–1497; www.vtstage.org). For news of the latest doings, check *Seven Days,* Burlington's free alternative weekly (802–864– 5684; www.sevendaysvt.com).

Curiosities. At the still-active Rock of Ages Quarry on Route 14 in Barre (802–476–3119; www.rockofages.com), you can view the source of the granite that helped build New England, and the country. First tapped in 1812, this cache continues to supply a third of the national gravestone market. Also in Barre, Hope Cemetery on Merchant Street shelters life-size sculptures created by stonecutters over the past century. The Robert Hull Fleming Museum at the University of Vermont in Burlington (802–656–0750; www.uvm.edu/~fleming) is a gallimaufry spanning sciences as well as arts, and primitive artifacts in addition to American art past and present. The interactive Lake Champlain Basin Science Center at 1 College Street (802–864–1848; www.lakechamplaincenter.org) harbors scores of local species, including the prehistoric longnose gar. The Vermont Wildflower Farm on Route 7 in Charlotte (802–985–9455; www.american meadows.com) offers six acres of colorful plantings to explore and emulate. Occupying a nineteenth-century stone schoolhouse in Basin Harbor, the Lake Champlain Maritime Museum (802–475–2022; www.lcmm.org) illuminates the lake's historical role through the centuries; the hands-on exhibits will appeal to children.

Excursions. Lake Champlain Shoreline Cruises at the Burlington Community Boathouse offers various scenic tours aboard the replica paddle-wheeler *Spirit of Ethan Allen II* (802–862–8300; www.soea.com), some with food and entertainment. For a budget alternative, catch the Lake Champlain Ferries' *Champlain* (802–864–9804; www.ferries.com) over to Port Kent, New York—about an hour each way.

Historic houses. A few minutes north of Burlington on Route 127, the Ethan Allen Homestead (802–865–4556; www.ethanallen.together.com) is where the homebred firebrand spent his final years. In Ferrisburgh, south of Shelburne on Route 7, the Rokeby Museum (802–877–3406; www. rokeby.org) is a farmstead owned by a single Quaker family from the 1790s to 1961; it served as a stop on the Underground Railroad.

Snow sports. The craggy peaks of northern Vermont offer New England's steepest slopes. Each area has its own special character and forte. Spanning two sizable peaks, Sugarbush in Warren (802–583–SNOW or 800–53–SUGAR; www.sugarbush.com) covers the most extensive and most varied terrain. Mad River Glen in Waitsfield (802–496–3551; www.madriverglen.com) will delight ski-Luddites up to the challenge of telemarking frozen chutes; there's also plenty of beginner/intermediate terrain. Bolton Valley (802–434–3444; www.boltonvalley.com) is a 6,000-acre Alpine village setup catering mainly to families, plus a smattering of extreme skiers. Stowe (802–253–3000 or 800–253–4754; www.stowe.com) still boasts a commendable classicism: cut by Civilian Conservation Corps crews in the thirties, its precipitous, sinuous "Front Four" trails need no improvement. Stowe actually hooks up with Smugglers' Notch in Jefferson (802–644–8851 or 800–451–8752; www.smuggs.com). The strong of leg can ski over, while others will need to drive by way of Morrisville (the narrow notch road is closed in winter). All these areas maintain extensive cross-country networks as well, and some—notably, Smugglers'—turn into family playgrounds come summer.

SPECIAL EVENTS

Early June. Burlington Discover Jazz Festival, (802) 86–FLYNN; www.discoverjazz.com. More than 150 class acts, many of them playing for free.

Late June. One World One Heart Festival, Warren; (800) BJFESTS. Ice cream moguls Ben & Jerry host nationally known performers, social-action exhibits, and, of course, ample tastings, all for free.

Late June. Vermont Quilt Festival, Northfield; (802) 485–7092; www.vqf.org. Norwich University hosts one of the premier quilting shows in the country.

Late October. Vermont International Film Festival, Burlington; (802) 660–2600; www.vtiff.org. A multinational invitational.

December 31. First Night, Burlington; (802) 863–6005 or (800) 639–9252; www.firstnightburlington.com. The city goes all out in a communal celebration.

OTHER RECOMMENDED RESTAURANTS AND LODGINGS

Barre

A Single Pebble, 135 Barre-Montpelier Road; (802) 476–9700; www.central-vt. com/web/pebble. Boutique-style Chinese food, by a California-trained aficionado.

Bristol

Mary's at Baldwin Creek, Route 116; (802) 453–2432; www.marysatbc.com. An utterly charming farmhouse restaurant/inn dedicated to the art of regional cuisine.

Burlington

The Daily Planet, 15 Center Street; (802) 862–9647. This playful, post-hippie solarium synthesizes Burlington chic with a wide-ranging, well-priced menu.

Fresh Market, 400 Pine Street; (802) 863–3968 or (800) 447–1205. A perfect place to put together a picnic or catch a light bite.

Isabel's on the Waterfront, 112 Lake Street; (802) 865–2522. A popular spot for lakeside feasting.

Leunig's Bistro, Church Street; (802) 863–3759. Old-fashioned Euro-atmosphere in spades, accompanied by forward-thinking cuisine.

Mirabelles, 198 Main Street; (802) 658–3074. A charming cafe/patisserie.

Smokejacks, 156 Church Street; (802) 658–1119; www.smokejacks, 156 Church Street; (802) 658–1119; www.smokejacks.com. It really is a smokehouse (try the salmon or duck), despite the art deco decor.

Trattoria Delia, 152 St. Paul Street; (802) 864–5253; www.trattoriadelia.com. Artfully rustic Italian dishes, with a side of romance.

Willard Street Inn, 349 South Willard Street; (802) 651–8710 or (800) 577–8712; www.willardstreetinn.com. A grand 1882 Victorian mansion overlooking the lake.

Colchester

Libby's Blue Line Diner, Route 7: (802) 655–0343. A classic Worcester lunch car, circa 1953, serving three meals, including a knockout breakfast.

Essex

Inn at Essex, 70 Essex Way; (802) 878–1100 or (800) 727–4295; www.innatessex. com. A large, luxurious hotel with outstanding cuisine provided by the staff and fledgling chefs of the New England Culinary Institute, who sometimes host hands-on learning weekends.

Jeffersonville

Three Mountain Lodge, Route 108; (802) 644–5736; www.threemountain lodge.com. Generous regional fare in a Civilian Conservation Corps–era ski dorm turned inn.

Marshfield

Rainbow Sweets Bakery & Cafe, Route 2; (802) 426–3531. A quirky but worthwhile out-of-the-way cafe.

Montpelier

Inn at Montpelier, 147 Main Street; (802) 223–2727; www.innatmontpelier. com. A pair of Federal houses provides elegant lodging and dining to match.

Shelburne

Café Shelburne, 5573 Shelburne Road; (802) 985–3939; www.cafeshelburne. com. Chef-owner Patrick Grangien trained at three-star establishments in France.

South Burlington

Pauline's, 1834 Shelburne Road; (802) 862–1081 or (800) 491–1281. A superb New American restaurant improbably plunked down amid a strip mall.

Stowe

Chelsea Grill, Route 108; (802) 253–3075. Pretty citified for these parts, with California flair.

Fiddler's Green Inn, 4859 Mountain Road; (802) 253–8124 or (800) 882–5346; www.fiddlersgreeninn.com. An atmospheric 1820 lodge offering good home-cooked meals.

Green Mountain Inn, Main Street; (802) 253–7301 or (800) 253–7302; www. greenmountaininn.com. An 1833 inn at the center of town, with all modern amenities and an ambitious restaurant, the Whip.

Restaurant Swisspot, 128 Main Street; (802) 253–4622. Specializing in fondues conducive to tête-à-têtes.

Ski Inn, 5037 Mountain Road (Route 108); (802) 253–4050; www.ski-inn.com. One of Stowe's oldest ski inns, colorful and comfy as ever.

Stowehof Inn, Edson Hill Road; (802) 253–9722 or (800) 932–136; www. stowehofinn.com. This fanciful hilltop hotel looks vaguely Austrian-Balinese and boasts glorious views.

Ten Acres Lodge, 14 Barrows Road; (802) 253–7638 or (800) 327–7537. A terrific regional restaurant distinguishes this 1826 farmhouse; rooms range from rustic to luxury.

Topnotch, 4000 Mountain Road; (802) 253–8585 or (800) 451–8686; www. topnotch-resort.com. The name suits this world-class resort encompassing spa, stables, tennis, and two outstanding restaurants.

La Toscana Country Inn, 4080 Mountain Road; (802) 253–9776 or (800) 245–5118. The 1859 farmhouse is also home to Trattoria La Festa (802–253–8480; www.trattorialafesta.com), run by the Rome-born and trained De Vito brothers.

Trapp Family Lodge, 700 Trapp Hill Road; (802) 253–8511 or (800) 826–7000; www.trappfamily.com. The lodge has long since lost any sense of intimacy, but *Sound of Music* fanatics probably won't mind.

Vergennes

Basin Harbor Club, Basin Harbor Road; (802) 475–2311 or (800) 622–4000; www.basinharbor.com. A 700-acre lakeside resort in operation since 1886—traditionalist in spirit, fresh and pampering in execution.

Christophe's On the Green, 5 North Green Street; (802) 877–3413. Innovative chef Christophe Lissarrague hails from the Pays Basque.

The Strong House Inn, 94 West Main Street (Route 22A); (802) 877–3337; www.stronghouseinn.com. An 1830s Federal honey with distinctive, sumptuous rooms.

Waitsfield

The Inn at Mad River Barn, Route 17; (802) 496–3310 or 800–631–0466; www.madriverbarn.com. A classic 1948 ski lodge with period pub and game room.

John Egan's Big World Lodge, Pub & Grill, Route 100; (802) 496–3033; www. bigworldvermont.com. Basic rooms and well-priced international fare— named for the famed extreme skier, a local.

Lareau Farm Country Inn, Route 100; (802) 496–4949 or (800) 833–0766; www.madriver.com/lodging/lareau. A friendly 1852 farmhouse; the adjoining barn houses American Flatbread (802–496–8856; www.americanflat bread.com), source of crunchy wood-fired pizzas.

The Spotted Cow, Bridge Street Marketplace; (802) 496–5151. Elegant dinners in a hand-crafted space.

Warren

Chez Henri, Sugarbush Village; (802) 583–2600. An atmospheric and authentic French bistro at the base of Sugarbush.

The Common Man, German Flats Road; (802) 583–2800; www.common manrestaurant.com. Country-sophisticate fare in a rustic barn lavished with crystal chandeliers.

The Pitcher Inn, 275 Main Street; (802) 496–6350 or (888) TO–PITCH; www. pitcherinn.com. A well-camouflaged 1998 inn—a Relais & Chateaux gem— hides extraordinary themed rooms and a stellar restaurant.

West Hill House, West Hill Road; (802) 496–7162 or (800) 898–1427; www.westhillhouse.com. A gabled 1862 farmhouse, nicely opened up.

Waterbury

The Inn at Blush Hill, Blush Hill Road; (802) 244–7529 or (800) 736–7522; www.blushhill.com. An ideal B&B, offering charming rooms and gourmet breakfasts in a 1790 keeping room.

Mist Grill, 92 Stowe Street; (802) 244–CAFÉ. An 1807 gristmill, turned foodie find.

Villa Tragara, Route 100; (802) 244–5288; www.stoweinfo.com. Superb "Vermont Italian" fare.

Winooski

Waterworks, Champlain Mill Shopping Center, 1 Main Street; (802) 655–2044. A former woolen mill houses a handsome contemporary restaurant.

FOR MORE INFORMATION

Lake Champlain Regional Chamber of Commerce, 60 Main Street, Burlington, VT 05401; (802) 863–3489; www.vermont.org.

Stowe Area Association, Main Street, Stowe, VT 05672; (802) 253–7321 or (800) 24–STOWE; www.gostowe.com.

Sugarbush Chamber of Commerce, Route 100, Waitsfield, VT 05673; (802) 496–3409 or (800) 82–VISIT; www.madrivervalley. com.

Vermont Department of Tourism and Marketing, 6 Baldwin Street, Montpelier, VT 05602; (802) 828–3683 or (800) VERMONT; www.1-800-VERMONT.com.

Midstate

THE GOOD LIFE

---

2 NIGHTS

Revivified mills • Nineteenth-century luxury
Tidy farms and wild things
Hanging with the horsy set • Where writers roam

There's nothing middling about Vermont's midstate. While the southern seg-
ment may vaunt its picturesque villages and the northern part its dramatic
mountainscapes, the midsection can boast a bit of both. So zealously did summering Rockefellers guard the beauty of Woodstock, for instance, that utility
lines were placed underground—the better to preserve the town's nineteenth-
century mien. With six connected peaks, Killington is by far the largest ski area
in Vermont. Though its access road is rather appallingly built up, it's the one
area in New England that approaches the scope of western resorts, offering
the energetic a good week's worth of varied terrain to explore.

While the more commercial towns—such as Rutland—tend toward char-
acterless sprawl, the region abounds in charming villages. Sloping from a spine
of Green Mountains toward the headwaters of Lake Champlain on one side
and the historic water route of the Connecticut River on the other, this land
has remained prosperous and remarkably unspoiled over the centuries. Its
keenest pleasures are of a quiet variety.

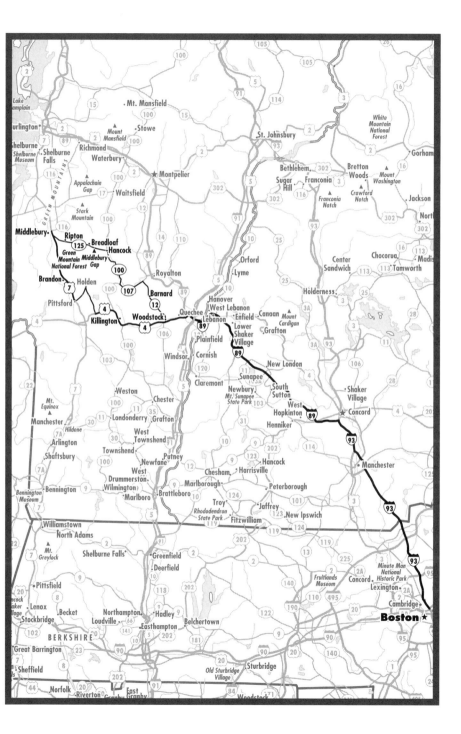

DAY 1

Morning

Take I–93 north past Manchester, New Hampshire (under an hour), and pick up I–89 into Vermont (the same). A few miles past the border (i.e., the river), turn off on Route 4 and head west toward **Quechee.** Souvenir shops will alert you to the presence of **Quechee Gorge,** a mile-long, 162-foot ravine flanking the Ottauquechee River. Stop long enough to gawk, as generations have before you. If you're up for a dip, you can clamber down to a swimming hole from the southwest end of the bridge.

Accessed by a replica covered bridge, Quechee's tidy little Main Street is dominated by an old brick mill building renovated to accommodate the **Simon Pearce Glass Factory** (802–295–2711 or 800–774–5277; www. simonpearce.com). You can watch, up close and toasty, as glassblowers produce the designs of this Irish-born artist, or stock up on seconds—firsts, if you can afford them—in the factory's handsome showrooms.

LUNCH: Simon Pearce Restaurant, Quechee; (802) 295–1470. You can road test the glassware—thumbprint celadon pottery, too—while enjoying a river view. The menu is New American, with a few Irish flourishes, such as the must-try apple cake.

Afternoon

A few miles west along Route 4 is **Woodstock,** a trove of Federal architecture and a fashionable summer spot for well over a century. You have to troll the trendy shops and galleries, if only as a survey course in the good life, country-contemporary style. Antiques tend to be choice, if pricy, in this neck of the woods, so they're always worth a look. The 1807 **Dana House** (802–457–1822; www.vmga.org/windsor/woodhs), the Woodstock Historical Society's showhouse at 26 Elm Street, gives a good idea of the relative sumptuousness of postrevolutionary life in this rural shire town; the museum is open Monday through Saturday from 10:00 A.M. to 5:00 P.M. and Sundays 2:00 to 5:00 P.M., mid-May through late October. The local lifestyle only got grander with the advent of the summer crowd in the post–Civil War years. The 1890s **Billings Farm & Museum** on River Road north of Route 12 (802–457–2355; www.billingsfarm.org) embodies the rational approach to farming that captured the imagination of the era's gentry. From breeding and sheepshearing to woodlot management, no agrarian activity was left to chance or habit.

Woodstock's model Billings Farm is set in the heart of horse country

In some ways this scientific approach laid the groundwork for the ecology movement, and it's interesting to observe the farm's ongoing operation—on view daily from 10:00 A.M. to 5:00 P.M., May through October and occasional winter weekends.

For a walk on the wild side, also visit the **Vermont Institute of Natural Science** on Church Hill Road south of town (802–457–2779; www.vinsweb. org), of special interest for its Raptor Center, which houses several dozen wild birds—from owls to eagles—too injured to release into the wild. You may spot their cousins in the course of a guided bird walk. The institute is open from 10:00 A.M. to 4:00 P.M. Monday through Saturday

DINNER AND LODGING: The Kedron Valley Inn, Route 106, South Woodstock; (802) 457–1473 or (800) 836–1193; www.innformation.com/vt/kedron. The rooms are truly romantic, the regional cuisine brilliant.

DAY 2

Morning

BREAKFAST: Kedron Valley Inn. Enjoy a splendid breakfast, and take some time to study the innkeepers' museum-quality collection of antique quilts.

Regaining Route 4 by way of Woodstock, continue west, stopping to ascend **Killington**'s colorful gondola (802–422–6200 or 800–621–MTNS; www.killington.com) for a staggering view from the 4,241-foot summit. It's atop this peak, in 1763, that Reverend Samuel Peters alit upon the name "*verd mont*" ("green mountain" in French). Adventurous sorts might want to do some lift-assisted mountain biking; rentals are available on-site.

In Mendon take a detour north through Chittenden and Holden, to skirt the **Green Mountain National Forest** rather than slog through Rutland's urban sprawl. In Pittsford you can pick up Route 7 north, which in about 26 miles will deliver you to **Middlebury,** where you can explore such stores as **Greenfields Mercantile** at 46 Main (802–388–2150), purveyors of tasteful "hemptations," from stationery to linenlike clothing, and the **Frog Hollow Vermont State Craft Center,** 1 Mill Street (802–388–3177; www.frog hollow.org), featuring the *crème de la* crafts.

During your explorations, stop in at the **Sheldon Museum** at 1 Park Street (802–388–2117; www.middlebury.edu/~shel-mus), a quarry mogul's 1829 manse that now serves as a repository for regional folk art and historical arti-facts; it's open Monday through Friday 10:00 A.M. to 5:00 P.M., Saturday till 4:00 P.M., in season. **Middlebury College,** just down the road, also has an art museum too interesting to miss (plus it's free): the permanent collection spans Moses Soyer and Fernando Botero. The museum, open Tuesday through Fri-day 10:00 A.M. to 4:00 P.M. and Saturday and Sunday noon to 5:00 P.M., is housed in the dazzling **Middlebury College Center for the Arts** (802–443–3168; www. middlebury.edu/~cfa).

LUNCH: The Storm Café, 3 Mill Street; (802) 388–1063. Stylish eats in an 1840 stone mill.

Afternoon

Circle back westward, by way of the scenic **Middlebury Gap.** Along steeply winding Route 125 you'll pass the tiny town of **Ripton,** with its ca. 1890 country store and the **Homer Noble Farm,** where Robert Frost lived and wrote from 1939 to 1963; a National Recreational Trail, posted with six poems, commemorates his sojourn there. Just up the road is Middlebury College's **Bread Loaf** campus, a former summer hotel where writers—from accomplished to would-be—have convened annually since 1926. The very meadows seem to exude inspiration.

Once you emerge from the national forest in Hancock, continue your country drive along Routes 100 south, 107 east, and 12 south, to Barnard.

DINNER AND LODGING: Twin Farms, Barnard; (802) 234–9999 or (800) 894–6327; www.twinfarms.com. Sinclair Lewis's 235-acre country retreat has been transformed into a ultra-luxurious compound of lavishly decorated cottages. Included in the admittedly exorbitant per diem is exquisite food and wine, equipment and instruction for sports ranging from croquet to skiing onsite, and visiting privileges with an extraordinary art collection.

DAY 3

Morning

BREAKFAST: To be taken in your private Shangri-La or the grand dining room. Linger on, making the utmost of this once-in-a-lifetime experience.

THERE'S MORE

Antiques and collectibles. The Vermont Salvage Exchange on 2 Gates Street in White River Junction (802–295–7616; www.vermontsalvage. com) is a font of intriguing architectural elements. Jigsaw puzzle fans will want to view and perhaps purchase some of the most artful examples being made today, at Stave Puzzles on Main Street in Norwich (802–295–5200; www.stave.com). The Antiques Collaborative at Waterman Place on Route 4 in Quechee (802–296–5858) presents the finds of sixty dealers.

Bargain shopping. The headquarters for Pompanoosuc Mills on Route 5 in East Thetford (802–785–4851 or 800–841–6671; www.pompanoosuc.com), a handcrafted furniture chain, offers some seconds. Quechee's Fat Hat Factory on Route 4 (802–296–6646; www.fathat.com) whips up all sorts of garments in cuddly Polarfleece. The Claire Murray Showroom on Route 5 in Ascutney (802–674–9280 or 800–252–4733; www.clairemurray.com) doubles as a factory outlet, showcasing Murray's colonially inspired textiles, from rugs to quilts.

Family pastimes. The changing hands-on exhibits at the Montshire Museum of Science on Montshire Road in Norwich (802–649–2200; www. montshire.net) will engage all ages, and there are one hundred riverside acres—plus a tree house—to explore. It's also fun to tour the University of Vermont Morgan Horse Farm at 74 Battell Drive in Weybridge (802–338–2011; www.uvm.edu/cals/farms/mhfarm).

Performing arts. Northern Stage offers professional theater at the Briggs Opera House in White River Junction (802–291–9009; www.northern stage.org). The Pentangle Council on the Arts (802–457–3981; www.pen tanglearts.org) mounts a varied program—music, theater, dance—in Woodstock's Town Hall Theater. Randolph's 1907 Chandler Music Hall (802–728–6464; www.randolphvt.com/chandler) hosts musical and theatrical performances year-round.

Sporting sites. Terrainwise, Killington (802–422–3333 or 800–621–MTNS; www.killington.com) is the best and biggest ski area in the East; in summer, it converts into a fun park, with water and alpine slides, and a skate park. Ascutney in Brownsville (802–484–7711 or 800–243–0011; www. ascutney.com) and Okemo in Ludlow (802–228–5571 or 800–78–OKEMO; www.okemo.com) are both good family-scale mountains. Kedron Valley Stables on Route 106 in South Woodstock (802–457–1480 or 800–225–6301; www.kedron.com) arranges horseback tours, some inn to inn.

SPECIAL EVENTS

Mid-June. Quechee Hot Air Balloon Festival and Crafts Fair; (802) 295–7900 or (800) 295–5451; www.quechee.com. A fleet of colorful balloons, a phalanx of artisans, and free music (including a fiddler's contest).

Mid-September. World's Fair, Tunbridge; (802) 889–5555; www.tunbridge fair.com. This classic agricultural fair has gone by this rather sweeping name since 1867.

Late November. Bradford United Church of Christ Wild Game Supper; (802) 222–5913. A massive feast featuring foods fresh from the woods.

Early December. Wassail Celebration, Woodstock; (802) 457–3555 or (888) 496–6378; www.woodstockvt.com. A carriage parade, plus dances, dinners—and caroling, of course.

OTHER RECOMMENDED RESTAURANTS AND LODGINGS

Brandon

Brandon Inn, 20 Park Street; (802) 247–5766 or (800) 639–8685; www. brandoninn.com. This tastefully restored brick inn, built in 1892, boasts a winning restaurant, five acres of peaceful grounds, and a pool.

Brownsville

The Pond House, Shattuck Hill Farm; (802) 484–0011; www.pondhouse inn.com. An 1830s Cape on ten rolling acres; skiers and horses are welcome, and savory meals are offered.

Chittenden

Mountain Top Inn, Mountain Top Road; (802) 483–2311 or (800) 445–2100; www.mountaintopinn.com. A family-scale resort on 500 acres, ideal for horseback riding and cross-country skiing.

East Middlebury

Waybury Inn, Route 125; (802) 388–4015 or (800) 348–1810; www. wayburyinn.com. An 1810 inn still succoring wayfarers with superior room and board.

Goshen

Blueberry Hill Inn, off Route 125; (802) 247–6735 or (800) 448–0707; www. blueberryhillinn.com. This cross-country mecca amid Green Mountain National Forest serves gourmet communal meals.

Killington

Cortina Inn, 103 US Route 4; (802) 773–3331 or (800) 451–6108; www. cortinainn.com. A luxurious modern hotel with pretty country-motif rooms, a health club and indoor pool, eight tennis courts, and two excellent restaurants.

Hemingway's Restaurant, Route 4; (802) 422–3886; www.hemingways restaurant.com. Some of the finest cuisine in the region is elegantly presented within this unprepossessing 1860 farmhouse.

The Inn at Long Trail, Route 4; (802) 775–7181 or (800) 325–2540; www. innatlongtrail.com. New England's first ski lodge is the pine-paneled core of this complex, encompassing a range of rooms (basic to luxury) and a congenial Irish pub.

Mendon

Red Clover Inn, 7 Woodward Road; (802) 775–2290 or (800) 752–0571; www.redcloverinn.com. An 1840 inn on thirteen peaceful acres, with a pool and acclaimed restaurant.

Middlebury

The Swift House Inn, 25 Stewart Lane, Middlebury; (802) 388–9925; www. swifthouseinn.com. Built for a governor in 1895, with some luxurous updates.

Norwich

Norwich Inn, 225 Main Street; (802) 649–1143; www.norwichinn.com. A 1797 stage stop sheltering a brew pub and fine restaurant.

La Poule à Dents, Main Street; (802) 649–2922; www.lapoule.com. French Mediterranean fare in a charming 1820s house.

Quechee

The Quechee Inn at Marshland Farm, Quechee Main Street; (802) 295–3135 or (800) 235–3133; www.pinnacle-inns.com. This 1793 farmstead has everything: handsome neo-Colonial rooms, a tavern restaurant with a progressive culinary bent, and an on-site outdoor sports center.

Randolph

Three Stallion Inn, Lower Stock Farm Road; (802) 728–5575 or (800) 424–5575; www.3stallioninn.com. An 1840s farmhouse, with a New American restaurant, centers a sports-oriented resort on 1,300 acres.

Woodstock

Jackson House Inn, 1143 Senior Lane; (802) 457–2065 or (800) 448–1890; www. jacksonhouse.com. Dining has become a very serious—and delightful—

business at this 1890 farmhouse, and the rooms (some with whirlpool baths) are Euro-luxurious.

The Prince & the Pauper, 24 Elm Street; (802) 457–1818; www.princeand pauper.com. The "creative continental" menu changes daily but always dazzles.

Woodstock Inn & Resort, 14 The Green; (802) 457–1100 or (800) 448–7900; www.woodstockinn.com. Laurence Rockefeller built this luxury resort, adorned with Americana and featuring an eighteen-hole Robert Trent Jones golf course, a swimming pool, fitness center, and even its own ski area, Suicide Six.

FOR MORE INFORMATION

Vermont Department of Tourism and Marketing, 6 Baldwin Street, Montpelier, VT 05602; (802) 828–3683 or (800) VERMONT; www.1-800VER MONT.com.

Woodstock Area Chamber of Commerce, 18 Central Street, Woodstock, VT 05091; (802) 457–3555 or (888) 496–6378; www.woodstockvt.com.

Southern Vermont

A PATCHWORK OF PLEASURES

2 NIGHTS

*Post-hippie havens • Art repositories • World-class fishing holes
Mountaintop monasteries • Catchall country stores*

Southern Vermont was welcoming summer visitors in style long before the
fad for "rustication" arose. Although the area was never to enjoy—or perhaps
suffer—the social cachet of a Newport or Lenox, this neck of the New England woods attracted moneyed visitors starting in the 1840s, when wealthy
hypochondriacs began flocking to Brattleboro to take the mineral-rich
waters. Manchester Village, with its elegant marble sidewalks, was likewise a
spa town; it was even set to serve as a summer White House in 1865, but the
president was unavoidably detained.

Because a combination of Yankee thrift and recurrent depressions kept the
area's historic strata—from Colonial to Gilded Age and beyond—intact, it's
possible today to enjoy a panoply of picture-perfect villages. Prime time, of
course, is during foliage (mid-October), but that's also when all the inns are
apt to be booked solid. Virtually any time—save perhaps amid the dreariness
of mud season early in the spring—is a good time to visit.

DAY 1

Morning

Take Route 2 west to Greenfield, and I–91 into Vermont. At the first exit (it's
about a two-hour trip), follow Route 5 into the heart of **Brattleboro,** a rather
unlovely town rendered lively and colorful by several decades' worth of post-

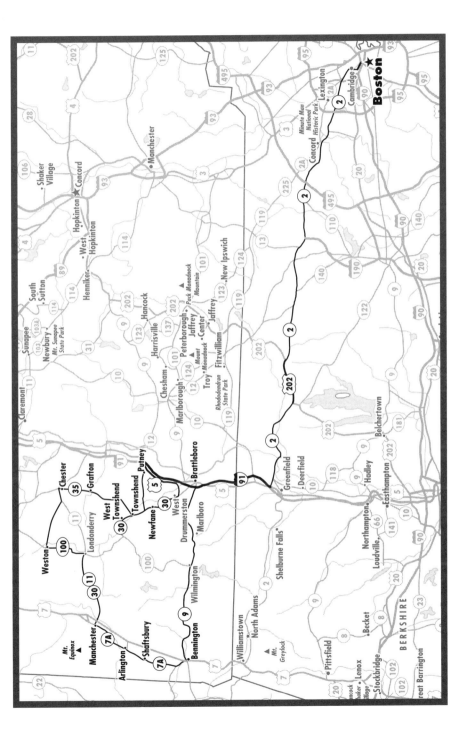

hippie occupation. At the **Brattleboro Museum & Art Center**, housed in a 1915 railroad station at the foot of Main Street (802–257–0124; www. brattleboromuseum.org), you're likely to find exhibits illuminating the town's illustrious past, as well as shows attesting to a thriving current art scene; it's open Tuesday through Sunday noon to 6:00 P.M. mid-May through October. Ascending Main Street, you'll encounter the **Windham Art Gallery** at number 69 (802–257–1881), a co-op occasionally featuring local luminaries such as Wolf Kahn. You might want to shop for sundry essentials at **Sam's Army & Navy** (802–254–2933), at 74 Main Street since the thirties, pause for a latte at **Mocha Joe's** at number 82 (802–257–7794; www.mochajoes.com), or check out **Vermont Artisan Designs**, which has taken over an old department store at 106 Main Street (802– 257–7044) with an array of art-level crafts. Continue to wander around the smallish downtown, a canyon of brick buildings dating to the late nineteenth century, when Brattleboro ruled—as it does once again—as a regional center of commerce.

LUNCH: The Common Ground, 25 Elliot Street, Brattleboro; (802) 257–0855. The best way to catch the pulse of town is to break multigrain bread at this communal natural-foods restaurant founded in 1971. If you'd rather picnic as you wander, stop by the **Brattleboro Food Co-op** back at the foot of Main Street (802–257–0236; www.brattleborofoodcoop.com)—a far cry from its brown-rice-by-the-pound origins, and in fact downright decadent.

Afternoon

Take Route 9 west of town, past the hamlet of **Marlboro** (famed for its music festival), through touristy **Wilmington,** and on to **Bennington**—about 40 up-and-down miles all told. Get your bearings atop the 306-foot **Bennington Battle Monument** at 15 Monument Circle (802–447–0550), a 306-foot granite monolith erected in 1891 to commemorate a pivotal Revolutionary War battle; it's open daily 9:00 A.M. to 5:00 P.M. mid-April through October. You can see actual vestiges of the era, including the oldest known Revolutionary flag, at the **Bennington Museum** on West Main Street (802–447–1571; www.benningtonmuseum.com), open daily 9:00 A.M. to 5:00 P.M. This in-triguing hodgepodge of state memorabilia includes an old schoolhouse containing a sizable showing of the works of native naif artist Grandma Moses.

Returning to the center of town, poke around **Bennington Potters** at 324 County Street (802–447–7531 or 800–205–8033; www.manchester vermont.net/bennpots), which for decades has presented a vision of uncluttered modern design fully compatible with traditional settings.

Follow Route 7A north about 20 miles, pausing as necessary for promising antiques shops, including the **Chocolate Barn** in Shaftsbury (802–375–6928). A few miles past Arlington, turn left onto the **Mount Equinox Skyline Drive** (802–362–1114; www.equinoxmountain.com), a 5-mile toll road that will take you up a 3,848-foot peak owned and occupied by Carthusian monks. The mountain actually belongs to the Taconic range but affords sweeping views of Vermont's namesake Green Mountains.

DINNER AND LODGING: The Equinox, Route 7A, Manchester Village; (802) 362–4700 or (800) 362–4747; www.equinoxresort.com. This grand hotel had its origins in a Revolutionary tavern. The toffs are on top again: enjoy the elegant common spaces, the full facilities (including a spa, tennis, and a restored 1927 golf course), and especially the spectacular regional cuisine in the elegant Colonnade dining room.

DAY 2

Morning

BREAKFAST: The Equinox. Try the hearth-lit Marsh Tavern, within the inn, for a cozy, substantial breakfast.

Start your day by exploring the **Equinox Shops** opposite the hotel, including the **Frog Hollow Vermont State Craft Center** (802–362–3321; www.froghollow.org) and **Walters & Wray Antiques** (802–362–4944). Manchester is noted for its scads of factory outlet stores (800–955–SHOP; www.manchestervermont.com), mostly upmarket. Field-and-stream fanatics will want to make a special pilgrimage to **Orvis,** up Route 7A (802–362–3750; www.orvis.com), to be outfitted in style, and perhaps instructed, for encounters of the piscine kind. Two doors up from the Equinox is the **American Museum of Fly Fishing** (802–362–3300; www.amff.com), where intricate hand-tied flies and celebrity rods—including Eisenhower's and Hemingway's—are on display daily from 10:00 A.M. to 4:00 P.M. May through October.

Historic-house fans will want to visit **Hildene,** south on Route 7A (802–362–1788; www.hildene.org), a Georgian Revival mansion built by Robert Todd Lincoln, the president's eldest son. Even if you forgo the tour, offered daily from 9:30 A.M. to 4:00 P.M. mid-May through October, you'll want to explore the grounds—400-plus acres with lush formal gardens and, in winter, extensive cross-country trails.

Robert Todd Lincoln's Hildene estate recalls Manchester's glory days.

This sylvan area has long attracted artists, and the cream of regional art is on view at the **Southern Vermont Art Center** on West Road (802–362–1405; www.svac.org), a Georgian Revival mansion set amid another 400-odd wooded acres, with a sculpture garden and botany trail. The center is open Tuesday through Saturday 10:00 A.M. to 5:00 P.M. and, in summer, Sunday noon to 5:00 P.M.; it often hosts performing artists as well.

Post-Manchester, follow Route 11 west to Londonderry, where you can pick up Route 100 north to **Weston.** On the right as you enter town is the **Vermont Country Store** (802–824–3184; www.vermontcountrystore.com), representing the first wave of restoration fever to sweep Vermont in the mid-1940s, and still going strong as a source of handy gadgets and retro essentials. The **Weston Fudge House** (802–824–3014; www.westonfudge.com) also dates from that era and is enduringly enticing. Perched beside the oval village green is the **Farrar-Mansur House** (802–824–6624). Open daily July–August and weekends in the shoulder seasons, this 1797 tavern is worth viewing not only for its period details, but for murals installed by Work Projects Administration artists in the 1930s, depicting the town in its 1840s heyday. North of town, off Route 155, is the **Weston Priory** (802–824–5409; www.weston priory.org), a Benedictine retreat where visitors are welcome to attend services in a stone chapel—Mass is usually accompanied by Gregorian chants—and to visit a gift store featuring recordings and crafts.

About 10 miles east of Weston is the pretty town of **Chester,** distinguished by its many stone houses, a relative rarity in Vermont. These were built pre–Civil War and are thought to have played a role in the Underground Railroad. There's an especially striking concentration north of the Victorian railroad station on Depot Street.

LUNCH: Raspberries and Tyme, 90 The Common, Chester; (802) 875–4486. Tucked into a Victorian manse flanking the narrow green, this old-fashioned tea room features a newfangled menu.

Afternoon

Some 7 miles south of Chester via Route 35, **Grafton** is Vermont's most painstakingly preserved nineteenth-century village. Decimated by the Civil War and an 1869 flood, the town lay dormant like Sleeping Beauty's castle for close to a century. In the mid-sixties a legacy from a wealthy summerer gave rise to the Windham Foundation, which has gradually set the town to rights, highlighting the **Old Tavern at Grafton** (802–843–2231 or 800–843–1801; www.old-tavern.com), an 1801 stage inn which still serves weary wayfarers in rather more exalted style. The rockers lining the porch can be claimed by all comers, and a stroll through town might include the tiny, curiosity-packed **Grafton Nature Museum** (802–843–2111; www.nature-museum.org) and the **Grafton Historical Society Museum** (802–843–2489), both open weekends 1:00 to 4:00 P.M. late May to mid-October. South on Route 35, the **Grafton Ponds Nordic Ski & Mountain Bike Center** (802–843–2400; www.old-tavern.com/recreation) offers access to a 40-kilometer network of trails. Also in this direction is **Gallery North Star** (802–843–2465), featuring interesting work by area artists.

Continue another 7 miles to reach old-fashioned **Townshend** with its spacious green. A few miles west on Route 30, drive across the Townshend Lake Dam to do some sunning, swimming, or exploring amid the 856-acre **Townshend State Park** (802–365–7500 or 800–299–3071; www.state.vt.us/ anr/fpr/parks/htm/townsend).

DINNER AND LODGING: The **Windham Hill Inn,** 311 Lawrence Drive, West Townshend; (802) 874–4080. The embodiment of a perfect country inn, set on a 160-acre hilltop, with luxurious quarters, astounding dining, and plenty of room for roaming.

DAY 3

Morning

BREAKFAST: Windham Hill Inn. Breakfast in the mullion-windowed dining room is every bit as fabulous as dinner.

It's time to head homeward, with a few fun stops en route. In good weather, make a beeline for the **Newfane Flea Market,** about 10 miles south on Route 30 (802–365–7771); it's among the longest-lasting of its ilk and still a good bet for unusual finds. Continue a mile south on Route 30 to view **Newfane** itself—Vermont's veritable poster town, with its glorious green ringed by Greek Revival edifices. Here you'll find some serious acquirables, at **Schommer Antiques** (802–365–7777), as well as ephemera, musty books, and more at the **Nu-Tique Shop** (802–365–7677), both on Main Street.

You could then continue south on Route 30, cross the covered bridge in West Dummerston, and wend through apple orchards to meet up with Route 5 heading north to **Putney.** Alternately, for a bit more adventure, go back to the flea market, take the turnoff, turn right past Grassy Brook, and take the unmarked road up and over **Putney Mountain.** The road soon turns to dirt, makes some scary switchbacks, and eventually reaches the top, where there's room to pull over and follow a footpath about a half-mile to the scoured-granite summit. The descent down the other side is a little less precipitous, but still nothing you'd want to attempt in anything but good weather. A left at the base will take you past the **Putney School,** a pioneering progressive board-ing school, into its namesake town—in the early nineteenth century the site of the free-love-embracing, silver-smithing Oneida Community. Though these early communards were pretty much drummed out of town in 1847, more recent endeavors took firmer root, and Putney is once again a hotbed of crafts. Pull into any studios that look promising, including the **Green Moun-tain Spinnery** at 7 Brickyard Lane (802–387–4528 or 800–321–WOOL; www.spinnery.com), where locally grown wools are naturally processed and dyed, much as they might have been a century ago.

LUNCH: Curtis' Barbecue, Route 5, Putney; (802) 387–5474. This bright-blue schoolbus parked beside a gas station is *the* place to eat, late spring through foliage season. It's the real thing, slow-cooked in wood-fired pits to succulent perfection. Should Curtis be closed, consider a healthy-gourmet picnic-to-go from the **Putney Food Co-op** (802–387–5866; www.putney.net/coop). Be open to serendipity: there's a palpable magic to this place.

THERE'S MORE

Adventures. Connecticut River Safari off Route 5 north of Brattleboro (802–257–5008) rents out canoes for exploring the placid "Meadows" where the West River approaches the Connecticut beside the Brattleboro Retreat, a sanatorium founded in 1834. Kimberly Farms in Shaftsbury (802–442–4354; www.netcolony.com/members/kimberlyfarm/rides) offers customized horseback outings. BattenKill Canoe Ltd. on River Road off Route 7A in Arlington (802–362–2800 or 800–421–5268; www.battenkill.com) outfits expeditions on that particularly pic-turesque—and trout-rich—river.

Curiosities. The Southern Vermont Natural History Museum on Route 9 between in Marlboro (802–464–0048) incorporates the Luman Nelson Wildlife Collection, an extensive—if creepy—taxidermy display; a few live raptors are in residence as well. Occupying a turreted Victorian at 75 School Stree in Chester, the National Survey Charthouse (802–875–2121; www.vermontel.net/~nat/surv) has been making maps since 1912; they're still among the best.

Excursions. The *Belle of Brattleboro* (802–254–1263), a mahogany-trimmed riverboat moored by the West River Bridge north of Brattleboro, cruises the backwaters beside the Brattleboro Retreat. The Green Mountain Rail-road (802–463–3069 or 800–707–3530; www.rails-vt.com) offers two scenic vintage train rides linking Bellows Falls with Chester Depot, and Man-chester with Arlington or North Bennington.

For families. Brattleboro's Farmers' Market (802–257–1272)—held summer Saturdays from 9:00 A.M. to 2:00 P.M. in a dell off Route 9 just west of I–91—is not to be missed, for the prize produce, ethnic foods, and general good vibes. The Adams Farm at 15 Higley Hill Road in Wilmington (802–

464–3762; www.adamsfamilyfarm.com), founded in 1865, offers fun farm activities including pony rides and hay mazes. Dwight Miller & Son in Dummerston (802–254–9158) is a seventh-generation farmstead where you can pick strawberries, peaches, and apples in season.

Performing arts. The Vermont Jazz Center (802–254–9088; www.vtjazz. org) occupies a former shoe factory at 72 Cotton Mill Hill in Brattleboro. Wilmington's Memorial Hall Center for the Arts (802–464–8411; www. visitvermont.com/memorialhall), a compact McKim, Meade, and White Dutch Colonial theater built in 1903, hosts local and touring performers. The Vermont Theatre Company (802–258–1344; www.geocities.com/ broadway/booth/1360) mounts plays year-round; venues include the Hooker Dunham Theatre at 139 Main Street in Brattleboro (802–254– 9276; www.wildrootarts.org). The Oldcastle Theatre Company (802–447– 0564; www.oldcastle.org) puts on a varied summer and fall season at the Bennington Center for the Arts on Route 9 (802-442-7158; www.vermont artscenter.org). Founded in 1927, the Dorset Theatre Festival on Cheney Road (802–867–5777; www.theatredirectories.com/fest) is an Equity straw-hat theatre. The Weston Playhouse (802–824–5288; www.westplay. com), dating back to 1937, presents a summer lineup of Broadway shows and concerts. In July faculty and students at the well-regarded Kinhaven Music School in Weston (802–824–4332; www.kinhaven.org) put on free concerts.

Potables. Brattleboro boasts two breweries: the Windham Brewery within the Latchis Hotel (see below) and McNeill's Brewery in a retrofitted fire-house at 90 Elliot Street (802–254–2553). Maple Leaf Malt & Brewing, in a former general store at 3 North Main Street in Wilmington (802–464–9900), produces boutique beers. Occupying an 1850s farmhouse on Route 112 in Jacksonville, the North River Winery (802– 368–7557; www.vtnatural.com) specializes in fruit wines, including "Vermont Harvest" apple with a lick of maple syrup. The specialty at the Putney Mountain Winery on Holland Hill Road in Putney (802–376–4610) is apple cider "champagne."

Sporting sites. Brattleboro's Living Memorial Park (802–257–2311) encompasses a skating rink, a 6-mile cross-country trail lit for night skiing, and even a small downhill slope served by a T-bar. Big downhill resorts include the venerable Bromley in Peru (802–824–5522; www.bromley.com); sprawling Stratton in Bondville (802–297–2200 or 800–STRATTON; www.

stratton.com); roughhewn Magic Mountain in Londonderry (802–824–5645; www.magicmtn.com); and massive Mount Snow in Dover (802–464–3333 or 800–245–SNOW; www.mountsnow.com). The latter offers summertime activities, including mountain biking and in-line skating.

SPECIAL EVENTS

Mid-July to mid-August. Marlboro Music Festival; (802) 254–2394; www.marlboromusic.org. Performers of international renown flock to tiny, rural Marlboro College to make beautiful music together.

Early August. Grace Cottage Hospital Fair Day, Townshend; (802) 365–7357; www.gracecottage.org. A unique country fair, featuring an auction, free pony rides, and a birthday parade (local deliveries of all ages).

Vermont Wine & Food Festival, Stratton Mountain; (800) STRATTON; www.vermontwineandfood.com. New England's hot chefs convene to show and share their stuff.

Late August. Bondville Fair; (802) 297–1882. An agrarian classic, with livestock contests, antique tractor pulls, and more.

Early September. Music Festival, Guilford; (802) 257–1969. The Friends of Music at Guilford put on free and often stellar barn concerts.

Mid-October. Apple Pie Festival, Dummerston Center; (802) 254–9158. The good ladies (and gentlemen) of the Congregational Church crank out some 1,500 mouthwatering pies.

Late November. Putney Craft Tour and Sale; (802) 387–4032; www.putney crafts.com. A score of studios open their doors.

December 31. Last Night, Brattleboro; (802) 254–5808. Music, fireworks, and snow sports ring in the new year.

OTHER RECOMMENDED RESTAURANTS AND LODGINGS

Arlington

The Arlington Inn, Route 7A; (802) 375–6532 or (800) 443–9442; www.arlingtoninn.com. A gracious 1848 Greek Revival mansion, with nicely appointed rooms and romantic fireside dining.

West Mountain Inn, Route 313; (802) 375–6516; www.westmountaininn. com. A country home on 150 hilltop acres with good country cuisine.

Bennington

Allday & Onions, 519 Main Street; (802) 447–00443; www.thisisvermont. com/pages/alldays. A comfy cafe featuring rich food and modest prices.

Blue Benn Diner, Route 7; (802) 442–5140. This 1940s chrome-and-neon diner serves contemporary as well as time-honored fare.

Brattleboro

Latchis Hotel, 50 Main Street; (802) 254–6300; www.brattleboro.com/latchis. A 1938 art deco complex with reasonable rooms, bistro, and movie palace.

The Marina, 28 Springtree Road (off Route 5); (802) 257–7563; www. vermontmarina.com. A fun spot offering casual food on a waterside dock.

Peter Havens, 32 Elliot Street; (802) 257–3333. A New American bistro beloved of locals.

Riverview Café, 3 Bridge Street; (802) 254–9841; www.riverviewcafe.com. New American fare—including vegetarian options—made from scratch.

T. J. Buckley's, 132 Elliot Street; (802) 257–4922. An elegant diner serving fancy prix fixe dinners.

Dorset

Barrows House, Route 30; (802) 867–4455 or (800) 639–1620; www.barrows house.com. A rambling country inn with a swimming pool, two tennis courts, and an esteemed New American restaurant.

Inn at West View Farm, 2928 Route 30; (802) 867–5715 or (800) 769–4903; www.innatwestviewfarm.com. Four-poster beds and further culinary competition.

Dummerston

Naulahka, 19 Terrace Street; (802) 257–7783 or (800) 848–3747. Rudyard Kipling's ark-like 1893 estate, much as he left it in 1896, fleeing a legal dispute with his brother-in-law. The Landmark Trusts rents it out by the week.

Jamaica

Three Mountain Inn, 180 Main Street; (802) 874–4140 or (800) 532–9399; www.threemountain.com. A 1790s inn with updated bedrooms, an atmospheric keeping room/bar, and a restaurant offering polished regional fare.

Landgrove

Meadowbrook Inn, 24 Route 11; (802) 824–6444 or (800) 498–6445; www.meadowbinn.com. Romantic rooms and pampering breakfasts.

Londonderry

Frog's Leap Inn, Route 100; (802) 824–3019 or 877–FROGSLEAP; www.frogsleapinn.com. A pretty rural estate with swimming pool, tennis court, and appealing dinners.

Manchester Center

Bistro Henry, Routes 11/30; (802) 362–4982; www.bistrohenry.net. The atmosphere is casual and cheery; the Mediterranean cuisine most appetizing.

Chantecleer, Route 7A; (802) 362–1616. Acclaimed Continental cuisine in a transformed nineteenth-century dairy barn.

The Perfect Wife, 2594 Depot Street; (802) 362–2817; www.perfectwife.com. A fun place boasting "free-style cuisine."

Up for Breakfast, 4935 Main Street; (802) 362–4204; www.upforbreakfast.com. *Gourmet*-worthy day-starters.

Manchester Village

1811 House, Route 7A; (802) 362–1811 or (800) 432–1811; www.1811house.com. A Federal-era inn, decorated for the period.

Inn at Ormsby Hill, 1842 Main Street; (802) 362–1163 or (800) 670–2841; www.ormsbyhill.com. A spiffily decorated 1764 Colonial; breakfasts are superb.

The Reluctant Panther, 17–39 West Road; (802) 362–2568; www.reluctantpanther.com. The unmissable lavender facade heralds the fancy rooms and evolved Continental cuisine within.

Skylight Lodge, 52 Routes 11/30; (802) 362–2566. A classic fifties ski dorm with a sense of fun.

Village Country Inn, Route 7A; (802) 362–1792 or (800) 370–0300; www. villagecountryinn.com. A porch-encircled inn offering frilly rooms and a pleasing restaurant.

Wilburton Inn, River Road; (802) 362–2500 or (800) 648–4944; www. wilburton.com. Recreate the robber-baron lifestyle, including lavish dinners, at this turn-of-the-century brick mansion.

Marlboro

Skyline Restaurant, Route 9; (802) 464–5535. All-you-can-eat pancake and waffle breakfasts, with plenty of pure maple syrup and a 100-mile view.

Newfane

The Four Columns Inn, 21 West Street; (802) 365–7713 or (800) 787–6633; www.fourcolumnsinn.com. Set beside one of Vermont's most picturesque town greens, this 1830 Greek Revival mansion is famed for luxury lodgings, as well as exquisite creative cuisine.

Peru

Johnny Seesaw's, Route 11; (802) 824–5533 or (800) 424–CSAW; www. jseesaw. com. A 1926 dancehall turned atmospheric ski lodge; dinners are substantial and well priced.

Putney

The Putney Inn, off I–91; (802) 387–5517 or (800) 653–5517; www. putneyinn.com. Motelish rooms camouflaged by traditional furnishings and a superior restaurant housed in an old farmhouse.

South Londonderry

Londonderry Inn; (802) 824–5226; www.londonderryinn.com. This 1826 homestead has been a big old country inn since the forties, as pleasant for summer sightseers as it is for skiers.

Three Clock Inn, 95 Middletown Road; (802) 824–6327; www.threeclock inn.com. Robust classic French cuisine.

West Brattleboro

Chelsea Royal Diner, 487 Marlboro Road; (802) 254–8399. Affordable home cooking in a restored 1938 lunchcar.

Max's, 1052 Western Avenue (Route 9); (802) 254–7747; www.maxs restaurant.com. Italian "fusion"—at once casual and complex.

West Dover

Deerhill Inn, Valley View Road; (802) 464–3100 or (800) 99DEER9; www. deerhill.com. Exuberant country decor and generous portions of home-cooked contemporary Continental cuisine.

Doveberry Inn, Route 100; (802) 464–5652; www.doveberryinn.com. An intimate inn serving Northern Italian-influenced innovations.

The Inn at Sawmill Farm, Cross Town Ridge and Route 100; (802) 464–8131 or (800) 493–1133; www.vermontdirect.com/sawmill. This Relais & Chateaux property practically invented country elegance, and the dining room yields superb regional cuisine.

Snow Goose Inn, Route 100; (802) 464–3984 or (888) 604–7964; www. snowgooseinn.com. The luxury quarters feature Jacuzzi tubs and wood-burning fireplaces.

Weston

The Inn at Weston, Route 100; (802) 824–6789; www.innweston.com. Tasteful lodging and excellent dining.

Wilmington

The Hermitage, Coldbrook Road; (802) 464–3759; www.hermitageinn.com. An inn and cross-country/hunting preserve, with a restaurant known for its game birds and stellar cellar.

Le Petit Chef, Route 100; (802) 464–8437. Luscious French cuisine in an 1850 farmhouse.

Trail's End, 5 Trail's End Lane; (802) 464–2727 or (800) 859–2585; www.trails endvt.com. A nicely updated fifties ski lodge with a massive fieldstone hearth, clay tennis court, and swimming pool.

FOR MORE INFORMATION

Brattleboro Area Chamber of Commerce, 180 Main Street, Brattleboro, VT 05301; (802) 254–4565; www.brattleboro.com.

Manchester & the Mountains Chamber of Commerce, 2 Main Street, Manchester Center, VT 05255; (802) 362–2100, www.manchesterandmtns.com.

Vermont Department of Tourism and Marketing, 6 Baldwin Street, Montpelier, VT 05602; (802) 828–3683 or (800) VERMONT; www.1-800-VERMONT.com.

RHODE ISLAND
ESCAPE

RHODE ISLAND

Coast to Coast

LEARNING AND LUXURY

2 NIGHTS

*Bohemia by the bay • Foodie meccas • A temple to tennis
The yachting life • Gilded Age mansions and Colonial gems*

With its 400 miles of coastline, New England's smallest state is perfectly suited to weekend getaways. This is, after all, where restless Puritans like Roger Williams and Anne Hutchinson fled the strictures of Bay Colony conformity—inspiring the epithet "Rogues' Island." Until fairly recently, the gritty, graft-ridden city of Providence seemed determined to live up to Cotton Mather's assessment of it as "the sewer of New England." With a recent influx of civic pride, artistic endeavor, and all-around hipness, however, Providence seems to have set its sights on becoming New England's Venice.

Newport, a natural harbor on the large island that the Wampanoags dubbed Aquidneck, or "Isle of Peace," has never lacked for prosperity. In the early eighteenth century, as a key point in the infamous Triangle Trade, Newport ranked as the fifth largest city in the Colonies. Independent to the core, Rhode Islanders were the first to cast off royal rule—though later the last to accept the U.S. Constitution. All the more ironic, then, that Newport should become, in the late nineteenth century, a nexus for obscenely rich summerers seemingly intent on recreating a royalty all their own. Their excesses are everywhere evident: the Europeanate mansions along Bellevue Drive are object lessons in overweening ostentation.

All this show tends to overshadow a more modest and appealing Newport, where traces of Colonial life persist and nature's majesty still prevails.

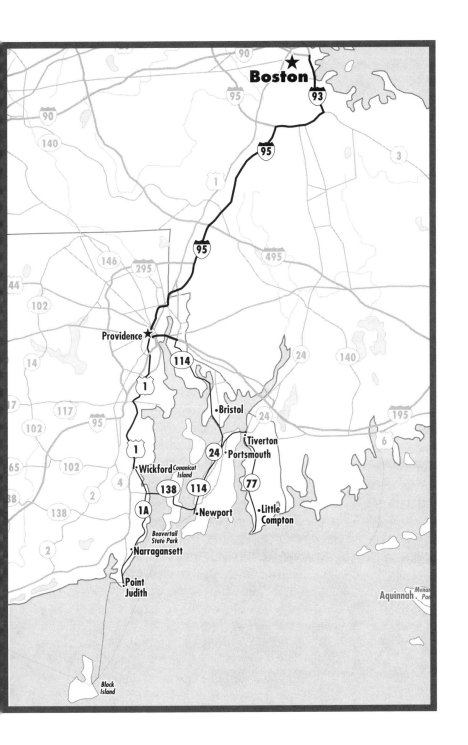

DAY 1

Morning

Providence is only about an hour's drive from Boston, via I–95. Southeast of the tourable gold-domed **State Capitol** at 82 Smith Street (401–222–2357; www.state.ri.us/tours) is the hill occupied by **Brown University** and, at its foot, the "Mile of History" known as **Benefit Street,** packed with Colonial and Federal houses. In addition to maintaining the 1786 **John Brown House** at 52 Power Street, notable for its fine Rhode Island furniture and China trade treasures, the Providence Preservation Society (401–831–7440; www. providencepreservation.org) also offers guided walking tours. There's plenty to see if you just roam on your own. Definitely stop in at the **Rhode Island School of Design Museum** at 224 Benefit Street (401–454–6100; www. risd.edu), not only for worthwhile contemporary shows but for its small and outstanding permanent collection; hours vary seasonally, so call ahead. Just up the street, at number 251, is the charming 1836 Greek Revival **Providence Athenaeum** (401–421–6970; www.providenceathenaeum.org), in whose stacks Edgar Allan Poe courted Sarah Whitman—his "Annabel Lee."

LUNCH: Raphael Bar-Risto, 1 Cookson Place, Providence; (401) 421–4646. This Italo-chic bistro, housed in a transformed train station, perfectly embodies the new Providence, with retro modern decor in marble and maple, Bellini martinis, and truly inspired progressive cuisine.

Afternoon

You could spend the remainder of the day here "downcity," perhaps visiting **RISD/Works** at 10 Westminster Street (401–277–4949; www.risdworks.com), which showcases the output of famous alums like fashion designer Nicole Miller and New Yorker cartoonist Roz Chast; profits go toward scholarships. Also check out **The Arcade** at 65 Weybosset Street (401–598–1199), the country's oldest mall housed in a Greek Revival structure built in 1828. It's now owned by **Johnson & Wales University,** whose students run **Johansson's Bakery** there. The college also maintains an interesting repository, the **Culinary Archives and Museum,** on its campus at 315 Harborside Boulevard (401–598–2805; www.culinary.org), which is open for one-hour guided tours Tuesday through Saturday 9:00 A.M. to 4:00 P.M. Foodies will also want to tour Atwells Avenue on **Federal Hill,** Providence's Little Italy.

Having tasted your way through town, you might want to while away an hour or two on the city's canals—especially if it's a **WaterFire** night (401–272–3111; www.waterfire.org), a unique experience involving bonfires and eerie music. With or without the special effects, stroll the four-acre **Waterplace Park** (401–785–9450); rent a canoe or kayak on-site, or leave the rowing to a gondolier (401–421–8877; www.gondolari.com).

DINNER: Empire, 123 Empire Street; (401) 621–7911; www.empireprovidence. com. The Italianate inventions within this former Packard showroom across from Trinity Rep are as lush as the setting is minimalist-cool.

LODGING: What Cheer! Bed and Breakfast, 73 Holden Street; (401) 351–6111; www.providence-suites.com. Cheerful indeed, with every comfort attended to. This updated 1890 house is centrally located, too.

Evening

The main reason to spend the night in Providence is to enjoy its unique nightlife. If tickets are available, you owe yourself a performance at the **Trinity Square Repertory Theatre**, one of the most exciting regional companies in the country, housed in talkies-era movie house at 201 Washington Street (401–351–4242; www.trinityrep.com). Afterwards, sample the musical offerings at the legendary **Lupo's Heartbreak Hotel** at 239 Westminster Street (401–272–LUPO). Consult the *Providence Phoenix*—cousin to Boston's— for other club-scene leads.

DAY 2

Morning

BREAKFAST: What Cheer!

This morning you have a choice of garden spots to explore; true mavens might want to squeeze in all three. In Bristol, about 15 miles southeast along Route 114, **Blithewold** at 101 Ferry Road (401–253–2707; www.blithewold. org) is a 1908 summer cottage modeled on a seventeenth-century English manor house. The forty-five-room mansion—palpably cozier than its Newport counterparts—is open for self-guided tours Tuesday through Saturday 10:00 A.M. to 4:00 P.M. April to mid-October, as is its extraordinary 33-acre bayside arboretum. After crossing onto Aquidneck Island in another few miles, you could take a detour through **Tiverton Four Corners** (www.tiverton. org)—stop to pick up gourmet nibbles at **Provender** (401–624–8084) and check the **Virginia Lynch Gallery** upstairs (401–624–3392; www.vlynch gallery.com)—and south along Route 77 to visit **Sakonnet Vineyards** at 162 West Main Street in **Little Compton** (401–635–8486; www.sakonnetwine. com). Alternatively, continue south along Route 114, pausing in **Portsmouth** to visit the **Green Animals Topiary Gardens** on Cory's Lane (401–683–1267; www.newportmansions.org), where for close to a century scores of yew and privet hedges have been trimmed into fantastical creatures. The complex, which also includes a small museum of Victorian toys, is open daily in-season from 10:00 A.M. to 5:00 P.M. Detour onto Route 138 for refreshments at **Greenvale Vineyards,** headquartered in a glorious Victorian barn at 582 Wapping Road (401–847–3777; www.greenvale.com).

Another 10 miles or so brings you into **Newport,** where the best place to get oriented is the compact **Museum of Newport History**, housed within the neoclassical 1772 Brick Market at 82 Touro Street (401–846–0813; www.newporthistorical.com), open Tuesday through Friday from 9:30 A.M. to 4:30 P.M. and Saturday 9:30 to noon. Here, interactive exhibits span the community's 350-year history, from Colonial port to international watering place. A short walk northwest of the museum is the 1748 **Hunter House** at 54 Washington Street (401–847–1000; www.newportmansions.org), an architectural treasure in its own right and also a repository for some of Newport's renowned—and now invaluable—Townsend-Goddard furniture. It's open daily 10:00 A.M. to 5:00 P.M. May through September, and weekends April and October. The entire Point area is beautiful, a remarkable concentration of homespun houses dating back centuries.

Heading back past the Brick Market, hang a left to view the **Old Colony House** on Washington Square, the country's second-oldest capitol building, built in 1729. Continuing down Thames Street, you'll probably want to poke around **Bowen's Wharf** and **Bannister's Wharf;** if you can overlook all the T-shirt shops, there are some pretty appealing emporia here.

LUNCH: The Mooring, Sayer's Wharf, Newport; (401) 846–2260; www. mooringrestaurant.com. Right in the neighborhood and right on the waterfront (opt for a dockside table), this restaurant occupies the former headquarters of the New York Yacht Club. Seafood staples rule.

Afternoon

Newport is best seen from the water: the 72-foot replica schooner *Madeleine* (401–847–0299 or 800–395–1343; www.cruisenewport.com), berthed at

Bannister's Wharf, is one of many boats offering brief "sight sailing" tours of the bay. Or continue exploring Thames Street, perhaps checking the collectibles inventory at **Armory Antiques** at number 365 (401–848–2398) or the eccentric architectural salvage and replicas at **Aardvark Antiques** at number 475 (401–849–7233; www.aardvarkantiques.com). Definitely stop by the **International Yacht Restoration School** at number 449 (401–848–5777; www.iyrs.org) to observe old wooden beauties getting a new lease on life.

If you wander up Mill Street, past the **Old Stone Mill**—a Colonial structure, not Viking, longstanding legend notwithstanding—you'll happen upon the **Redwood Library & Athenaeum** at 50 Bellevue Avenue (401–847–0292; www.redwood1747.org). Modeled on a Roman temple in 1749–50 by native architect Peter Harrison, who would later go on to design Touro Synagogue and the Brick Market, it survives as the oldest continuously used library in the country; its art holdings also warrant a visit. Down the street, at 76 Bellevue Avenue, is the **Newport Art Museum** (401–848–8200; www. newportartmuseum.com), housed in an 1862 Richard Morris Hunt stick-style mansion. Showing contemporary work as well as a standing collection, it's open Monday through Saturday 10:00 A.M. to 5:00 P.M. and Sunday noon to 5:00 P.M.

Further along Bellevue, at number 194, is yet another relic of Newport's Golden Age, the **International Tennis Hall of Fame** (401–849–3990; www.tennisfame.org), within the grand 1880 shingle-style Newport Casino, designed by Stanford White. The exhibits, on view daily from 9:30 A.M. to 5:00 P.M., are fascinating, and amazingly, the thirteen grass courts are open to hoi polloi by reservation. From here on down Bellevue, it's mostly mansions: one, **Vernon Court** (number 492), houses the fledgling **National Museum of American Illustration** (401–851–8949; www.american-illustration.org), viewable by reservation.

The Preservation Society of Newport County (401–847–1000; www.new portmansions.org) maintains nearly a dozen of these sacred monsters, the showiest of which, **The Breakers,** runs to seventy rooms. Most are open daily 9:00 A.M. to 5:00 P.M. in season; call ahead for details. The **Astors' Beechwood Mansion** at 580 Bellevue Avenue (401–846–3774; www.astors-beechwood. com) is the only cottage to attempt living history. In this comparatively modest 1852 manse, it is perpetually 1891, and Mrs. Astor—self-proclaimed arbiter of who was who—is always entertaining. For a "backdoor" glimpse of the mansions, and a scenic, invigorating hike along the rocky coast, follow the 3½-mile **Cliff Walk** from Easton Beach, off Memorial Boulevard, to Bailey's

Beach, long the preserve of local gentry. The billionaires' views along the way are yours for free.

DINNER AND LODGING: Vanderbilt Hall, 41 Mary Street, Newport; (401) 846–6200 or (888) VAN–HALL; www.vanderbilthall.com. Cornelius Vanderbilt built a fancy Colonial Revival YMCA for the town of Newport in 1909. The old Y makes a dazzling new hotel. The cramped quarters of old have been transformed into fifty luxurious rooms, and the dining rooms—ultraformal **Alva** and the more casual **Orangery**—are by far the best in town. Even the pool is put to good use.

DAY 3

Morning

BREAKFAST: Vanderbilt Hall. Enjoy a lush breakfast in the conservatory.

The day is yours to squander. Fit in a few more Newport sights, such as an **Ocean Drive** drive, or better yet, bike trek (rentals are available at Ten Speed Spokes, 18 Elm Street, 401–847–5609; www.tenspeedspokes.com). At some point you'll want to head west on Route 138, across the Newport Bridge, and onto **Conanicut Island.** For a pleasant hiking jaunt, drive through **Jamestown Harbor** and south on Beavertail Road to **Beavertail State Park** (401–423–9941; www.riparks.com/beaverta) on the southern end, where a rocky 3-mile trail crosses the coast below an 1856 granite lighthouse. Continuing across the West Bay on Route 138, take Route 1A south to **Narragansett,** perhaps pausing at 174-acre **Conanchet Farm** on Boston Neck Road to visit **South County Museum,** (401–783–5400; www.southcountymuseum.org), which commemorates nineteenth-century rural Rhode Island life; it's open Wednesday through Saturday 10:00 A.M. to 4:00 P.M. and Sunday noon to 4:00 P.M. May through October. As you pass through Naragansett, note **The Towers** at 3606 Ocean Road (401–782–2597)—all that's left of a once-grand McKim, Mead, and White-designed Narragansett Casino, and now the site of occasional evening dances.

Narragansett Pier is a classic seaside town—Newport's populist mirror image, minus the Colonial underpinnings and Gilded Age excess, but with a boardwalk thrown in for picturesqueness. The town beach right beside the pier is one of the premier surfing spots on the East Coast, even off-season. If a taste of the sea has only made you hunger for more, you could continue south to **Point Judith** and take an hour-long ferry over to **Block Island**

(401–783–4613; www.blockislandferry.com). Or save that for another trip, and instead head Boston-ward on Route 1A, making one last stop about 6 miles north to admire the Colonial and Federal houses in the pretty coveside village of **Wickford.**

LUNCH: Wickford Gourmet, 21 West Main Street, Wickford; (401) 295–8190. Tarry over exquisite cafe fare or pick up *délices*-to-go.

THERE'S MORE

Antiques and collectibles. In Tiverton check out the Cottage at Four Corners at 384 Main Road (401–625–5814) and Peter's Attic at 8 Neck Road (401–625–5912). Newport is riddled with antiques shops; Franklin and Spring Streets present especially rich veins. The Newport Bookstore at 116 Bellevue Avenue (401–847–3400; www.nptbooks.com) has a wonderful selection of vintage tomes. In Wickford peruse the Wickford Antique Centre at 16 Main Street (401–295–2966).

Crafts. Collage, a crafts gallery at 25 Bowen's Wharf in Newport (401–849–4949), attracts RISD grads. Another Newport must-visit is J.H. Breakell & Co. silversmiths at 132 Spring Street (401–849–3522 or 800–767–6411; www.breakell.com).

Family fun. The Providence Children's Museum at 100 South Street (401–273–KIDS; www.childrenmuseum.org) is full of hands-on and clamber-on opportunities. Covering 430 acres, the Roger Williams Park, Museum, and Zoo at 950 Elmwood Avenue in Providence (401–785–3510; www.rwp zoo.org) is a Victorian legacy nicely updated with relatively "natural" environments, including a rain forest. Coggeshall Farm, an eighteenth-century farmstead within the 460-acre Colt State Park in Bristol (401–253–7482; www.riparks.com/colt), features period crafts and activities. Also check out the Audubon's Society's Environmental Education Center at 1401 Hope Street in Bristol (401–245–7500; www.asri.org), which features a walk-in whale. Newport's Easton Beach has not only a ¾-mile stretch of surfable beach, but a carousel and miniature golf; it's also home to the New England Aquarium Exploration Center, operated under the aegis of Boston's New England Aquarium (401–940–8430; www.neaq.org/visit/newport). The Flying Horse Carousel on Bay Street in Watch Hill (401–596–7761) has delighted little ones since the 1860s.

Historic buildings. Portsmouth's Old School House on East Main Road (401–683–9178) is the country's oldest, dating to 1716. Newport's oldest surviving dwelling, built circa 1675, is the Wanton-Lyman-Hazard House at 17 Broadway (401–846–0813). The Samuel Whitehorne House at 416 Thames Street (401–847–2448), the 1811 Federal mansion of a leading slave trader, is packed with Townsend-Goddard furniture and chinoiseries. Newport also boasts venerable, first-of-their-kind places of worship such as the circa 1729 Seventh Day Baptist Meeting House at 82 Touro Street (401–846–0813; www.newporthistorical.com/the) and the 1763 Touro Synagogue at 85 Touro Street (401–847–4794; tourosynagogue.org). Wickford harbors two historic houses: the Gilbert Stuart Birthplace on Gilbert Stuart Road (401–294–3001; www.gilbertstuartmuseum.com) and Smith's Castle (401–294–3521; www.smithcastle.org), a 1678 farmstead begun as a trading post by Roger Williams.

Horseback riding. Stables providing lessons and wooded trail rides include Roseland Acres Equestrian Center at 594 East Road in Tiverton (401– 624– 8866; www.horserentals.com/roselandacres) and Glen Farm at 163 Glen Farm Road in Portsmouth (401–847–7090; www.glenfarmequestrian.com). The Newport Equestrian Academy at 287 Third Beach Road in Middletown (401–847–7022) and Rustic Rides on West Side Road on Block Island (401–466–5060) also offer trail rides on the beach.

Performing arts. The Providence Performing Arts Center, a 1928 Loew's movie palace at 220 Weybosset Street (401–421–ARTS; www.ppacri.org), hosts shows and concerts year-round. The Perishable Theatre at 95 Empire Street in Providence (401–331–2695; www.perishable.org) puts on fresh new work; Brown University's Leeds Theatre at 77 Waterman Street (401– 863–2838) mounts interesting productions throughout the year. Newport has the Newport Repertory Theater (401–847–8412; www.newport rep.org) and a resident dance troupe, the Island Moving Company (401–847–4470). The Granite Theatre occupies a grandly columned 1839 Greek Revival church at 1 Granite Street in Westerly (401–596–2341; www.granitetheatre.com). The Greenwich Odeum Theater, a 1926 vaudeville house at 59 Main Streat in East Greenwich (401–885–9119; www.greenwichodeum.org), hosts theater, dance, and music of all genres.

Water sports. The Sakonnet Boathouse at 169 Riverside Drive in Tiverton (401–624–1440; www.sakonnetboathouse.com) rents various craft for exploring both branches of the Westport River. The Saltwater Edge at 559

Thames Street in Newport (401–842–0062; www.saltwateredge.com)
offers saltwater fly-fishing expeditions on the bay and beyond. The nonprofit Sail Newport (401–846–8385; www.sailnewport.com) rents out
sailboats and kayaks at Fort Adams State Park. Northeast Kitesurfing is
based at 74 Narragansett Avenue in Narragansett (401–474–3880; www.
northeastkitesurfing.com). The Kayak Centre at 9 Phillips Street in Wickford (401–295–4400 or 888–SEA KAYAK; www.kayakcentre.com) can set
you up to paddle about Wickford Cove and the West Bay; among the many
guided tours available are some by full moon.

SPECIAL EVENTS

Late January to early February. Newport Winter Festival; (401) 847–7666;
www.newportevents.com. Ten days of doldrums antidotes, including a
citywide scavenger hunt and polar bear plunge.

April. Easter Egg Hunt and Brunch, Newport; (401) 847–1000; www.
newportmansions.org. Rosecliff, a 1902 Stanford White mansion, welcomes children and their parents.

Early May. Garden Favorites Plant Sale, Bristol; (401) 253–2707; www.
blithewold.org. The gardeners at Blithewold Mansion divide their prize
perennials while dispensing advice.

Mid–May. Debutante Ball, Block Island; (401) 466–5200, or (800) 383–BIRI;
www.blockislandinfo.com. To celebrate spring the islanders "come out" in
costume—whether white, creative, or drag—for a wild night of dancing.

Early June. Federal Hill Stroll, Providence; (401) 274–1636; www.providence
cvb.com. A chance to sample the fare of area restaurants.

Newport International Film Festival; (401) 619–0112; www.newportfilm
festival.com. The cream of the indies.

Early July. Newport Music Festival; (401) 849–0700; www.newportmusic.
org. Two weeks, three concerts a day, of classical music played in mansions.

Early August. Providence/Rhode Island International Film Festival; (401)
847–7590; www.film-festival.org. To celebrate—and enhance—Rhody's
growing popularity as a backdrop.

Newport Folk Festival, Newport; (401) 847–3700; www.newportfolk.
com. The top acts in the country, acoustic or not.

Mid-August. JVC Jazz Festival, Newport; (401) 847–3700; www.festival productions.net. The cream of contemporary jazz.

Mid-September. Convergence (401) 724–2200; www.caparts.org. A statewide contemporary arts festival.

December 31. First Night, Providence; (401) 521–1166; www.firstnight providence.org. A family-values shindig all over town, with fireworks and multiple performances.

OTHER RECOMMENDED RESTAURANTS AND LODGINGS

Block Island

Atlantic Inn, High Street; (401) 466–5883 or (800) 224–7422; www.atlanticinn. com. A grand old 1879 hotel, nicely updated, with a sophisticated New American restaurant.

The Oar, 221 Jobs Hill Road; (401) 466–8820; www.blockisland.com/biresorts. This popular eatery overlooking New Harbor is hung with oars painted by victorious sailors.

The 1661 Inn and Hotel Manisses, 1 Spring Street; (401) 466–2421 or (800) MANISSE; www.blockisland.com-biresorts. A luxuriously restored clapboard house cozies up to a quintessential-Victorian 1872 grand hotel featuring notable cuisine and a dazzling ocean view.

Little Compton

The Commons Lunch, The Commons; (401) 635–4388. A down-home diner specializing in local dishes such as jonnycakes and quahog pie.

Narragansett

Crazy Burger Café, 144 Boon Street; (401) 783–1810. All sorts of smart combos, including vegetarian.

Newport

Asterix and Obelix, 599 Thames Street; (401) 841–8833. Mediterranean-Asian fusion in a charming sidewalk cafe.

The Black Pearl, Bannister's Wharf; (401) 846–5264. This onetime boathouse makes a classic harborside tavern serving continental fare.

Boulangerie Obelix, 382 Spring Street; (401) 846–3377. A charming French bakery/cafe.

Castle Hill Inn, 590 Ocean Drive; (401) 849–3800; www.castlehill.com. An 1874 bayside manse on a forty-acre peninsula boasting fabulous views and an accomplished New American restaurant.

Clarke Cooke House, Bannister's Wharf; (401) 849–2900. Smack in the middle of the tourist track, this 1790 Colonial offers superior creative American cuisine, in a formal or bistro setting.

The Francis Malbone House, 392 Thames Street; (401) 846–0392 or (800) 846–0392; www.malbone.com. A 1760 Georgian brick mansion with period furnishings.

George Champlin Mason House, 31 Old Beach Road; (401) 877–7081 or (888) 834–7081; www.georgemasonhouse. A favored local architect, Mason built this gingerbready 1873 confection for himself; the three guest rooms are beauties.

Hotel Viking, 1 Bellevue Avenue; (401) 847–3300 or (800) 678–8946; www.hotelviking.com. Built in 1926 to house surplus guests for the "Newport 100" (the gentry whose mansions would seem capable of housing whole battalions), the Viking again holds its own.

Ivy Lodge, 12 Clay Street; (401) 849–6865; www.ivylodge.com. This 1886 shinglestyle cottage, designed by Stanford White, gives a glimpse of Gilded Age living.

Le Bistro, Bannister's Wharf; (401) 849–7778; www.lebistronewport.com. A charming French cafe in a loft above the bustling harbor.

The Melville House, 39 Clarke Street; (401) 847–0640; www.melvillehouse.com. A tasteful 1750 Colonial serving gourmet breakfasts.

Rose Island Lighthouse; (401) 847–4242; www.roseislandlighthouse.org. A chance to rough it on a tiny island in the middle of Narragansett Bay.

Scales & Shells, 527 Thames Street; (401) 846–FISH; www.scalesandshells.com. Seafood prepared and presented with panache.

Steaming Bean Express Cafe, 515 Thames Street; (401) 849–5255. A congenial spot in the quiet end of town.

22 Bowen's, 22 Bowen's Wharf; (401) 841–8884, www.22bowens.com. A big, bold, steak-and-seafood house with modernist leanings.

White Horse Tavern, 26 Marlborough Street; (401) 849–3600. A prime contender for the title of oldest U.S. tavern, this 1673 institution has a distinctly modern dedication to fine cuisine.

Providence

AcquaViva EuroBistro, 286 Atwells Avenue; (401) 273–8664. An exuberant Italian restaurant with courtyard; upstairs is La Locanda del Coccio (401–273–2652; www.chefwalter.com), Walter Potenza's hommage to his Jewish-Italian roots.

Adesso, 161 Cushing Street; (401) 521–0770. A stylish "Cal/Ital" cafe just off Thayer Street, Brown University's Harvard Square.

Agora, 1 West Exchange Street; (401) 598–8011; www.westinhotels.com. An Escoffier-influenced hit.

Al Forno, 577 South Main Street; (401) 273–9767. This ristorante virtually kickstarted the craze for rustic Italian.

CAV, 14 Imperial Place; (401) 751–9164. Creative fare in a loft decked out with antiques (some for sale).

Gatehouse, 4 Richmond Square; (401) 521–9229 or (888) 333–4283. A romantic river-view Mediterranean bistro.

Hemenway's Seafood Grille, 1 Washington Providence Plaza; (401) 351–8570. A bright airy space serving fresh slabs of fish.

L'Epicureo, 238 Atwells Avenue; (401) 454–8430. A former butcher shop turned modernist Italian eatery.

Meeting Street Cafe, 220 Meeting Street; (401) 273–1066. A bright and friendly noshing spot, with great portions and prices.

Montego Bay on the Hill, 422 Atwells Avenue; (401) 751–3040. Low-priced, authentic Caribbean fare.

Naissance, 242 Atwells Avenue; (401) 272–9610. International tapas and creative fondues.

Neath's, 262 South Water Street; (401) 751–3700; www.neaths.com. Cambodian delicacies with French polish in a restored riverside warehouse.

New Rivers, 7 Steeple Street; (401) 751–0350. Outstanding New American fare, a stone's throw from RISD.

Olga's Cup and Saucer, 103 Point Street; (401) 831–6666. Casual, creative, and tasty.

Pot au Feu, 44 Custom House Street; (401) 273–8953. Neoclassical French fare upstairs, homey bistro below.

Rue De L'Espoir, 99 Hope Street; (401) 751–8890. Exuberant French/Californian finesse.

State House Inn, 43 Jewett Street; (401) 361–6111; www.providence-inn.com. A B&B with Shaker-style furnishings.

XO Café, 125 North Main Street; (401) 273–9090; www.xocafe.com. An artsy, fusiony international bistro.

Watch Hill

Olympia Tea Room Cafe, 74 Bay Street; (401) 348–8211. A prized institution since 1916.

Westerly

Three Fish, 37 Main Street; (401) 348–9700. An ambitious neobistro.

The Villa, 190 Shore Road; (401) 596–1054 or (800) 722–9240; www.thevillaat westerly.com. Plush Mediterranean-motif digs, with pool.

FOR MORE INFORMATION

Newport County Convention & Visitors Bureau, 23 America's Cup Avenue, Newport, RI 02840; (401) 849–8048 or (800) 976–5122; www. go newport.com.

Providence Tourism Council, 55 Dorrance Street, Providence RI 02903, (401) 861–0100 or (800) 562–9895; www.tourprovidence.com.

Rhode Island Tourism Division, 1 West Exchange Street, Providence, RI 02903; (401) 222–2601 or (800) 556–2484 or 888–U–UNWIND; www.visitrhodeisland.com.

CONNECTICUT
ESCAPES

ESCAPE ONE
CONNECTICUT

The Maritime Coast
LIVING OFF THE SEA

2 NIGHTS

Preserved ports • Theatrical shrines • Impressionist graffiti
Riverine adventures • Odd vessels • Colonial feasting

Two mighty rivers debouch in the southeastern corner of Connecticut. Over the centuries, the broad Thames, with its deep harbor at New London, was able to keep pace with international commerce and—unfortunately for respite-minded tourists—the Industrial Revolution and its gritty aftermath. The state's namesake river, on the other hand, was too shallow to permit anything but local traffic. Although the waterway developed into a 400-mile trade route through the whole of New England, the coastal region managed to stay out of the mainstream.

It is here, in a cluster of charming villages, that the paths of pioneers, seafarers, artists, and summerers intersected. Much loveliness is left.

DAY 1

Morning

I–95 south through Providence will lead you, in about 1½ hours, to **Stonington Borough,** a nineteenth-century seafaring town preserved in all its Federal and Greek Revival glory along a mile-long peninsula. Stroll down Water Street, browsing the shops and stopping to take in a bit of local lore at the **Old Lighthouse Museum** at number 7 (860–535–1440; www.stoningtonhistory.org). The striking 1823 stone structure is open daily in July and August from 10:00 A.M. to 5:00 P.M., with reduced hours in the shoulder seasons.

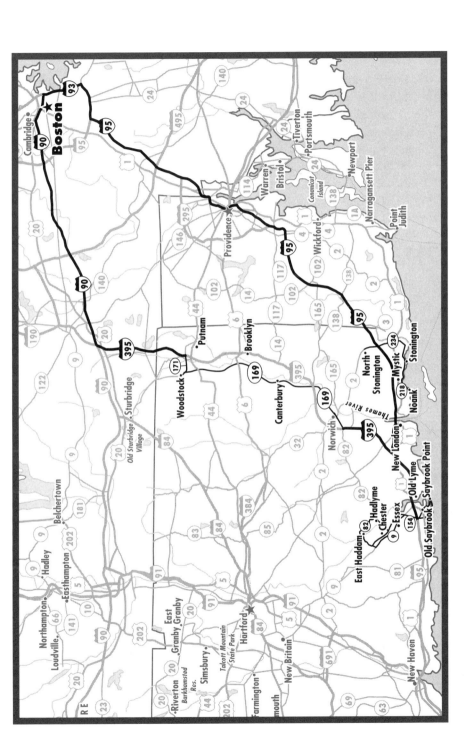

A few more miles along coastal Route 1 will bring you to **Mystic,** home to **Mystic Seaport** at 50 Greenmanville Avenue (806–572–5315 or 888–9–SEAPORT; www.mysticseaport.org). Something of a Sturbridge-by-the-sea, this seventeen-acre maritime museum enfolds a reassembled nineteenth-century seafaring village encompassing twenty-two buildings serving various functions and hundreds of vintage vessels. Pride of place goes to the 1841 *Charles W. Morgan,* America's last surviving wooden whale ship, which you can clamber aboard; explore the cramped quarters and imagine what it might be like to set out for years at a stretch, in search of "greasy luck." We like to wander about and see what's up: a raucous dance in the tavern, perhaps, or a cradle under construction at the shipcarver's shop. Several galleries complement the living-history complex. The one not to miss is the Wendell Building, with its folk-sculpture figureheads. To complete the experience, you might also want to tour the harbor. Options include a gaff-rigged schooner, a coal-fired wooden vessel (the last of its kind), and an antique motor launch. Mystic Seaport is open daily year-round from 9:00 to 5:00 P.M.

LUNCH: Abbott's Lobster in the Rough, 117 Pearl Street, Noank; (860) 536–7719; www.abbotts-lobster.com. A classic shack on the waterfront, a little more than a mile southwest via Route 215. No summer is complete without a pilgrimage.

Afternoon

Return to the town of Mystic, worth perusing for its shops and a 1922 drawbridge which rises dramatically to make way for passing boats; while you're waiting, consider a homemade cone at **Drawbridge Ice Cream,** 2 West Main Street (860–527–9798). Back past the Seaport, near I–95, the **Mystic Aquarium/Institute for Exploration** at 55 Coogan Boulevard (860–572–5955; www.mysticaquarium.org) beckons with some 4,000 specimens of undersea life. Variegated species swirl within a 30,000-gallon coral reef tank; African black-footed penguins command their own pavilion; Atlantic bottle-nosed dolphins and beluga whales are put through their paces in the marine theater; and outdoors, harbor seals swoop around Seal Island. For an added ripple visitors can simulate a 3,000-foot underwater descent aboard *Titanic* discoverer Robert Ballard's *Explorer.* The aquarium is open 9:00 A.M. to 6:00 P.M daily in summer, with reduced hours the rest of the year.

DINNER AND LODGING: Stonecroft Country Inn, 515 Pumpkin Hill Road, Ledyard; (800) 772–0774; www.stonecroft.com. Gorgeous lodgings in an 1807

Georgian Colonial and renovated grange keep pace with Drew Egy's dazzling international cuisine.

DAY 2

Morning

BREAKFAST: Stonecroft Country Inn.

Regaining I–95 south, head westward into **New London,** where exit 83 will lead you to **Monte Cristo Cottage** at 325 Pequot Avenue along the Thames River shoreline (860–443–0051). Named for his actor father's bread-and-butter role, Eugene O'Neill's childhood home inspired such plays as the faux-nostalgiac *Ah! Wilderness* and later the harrowing *Long Day's Journey into Night.* Call for hours, which vary. Also in the vicinity is the **Lyman Allyn Museum** at 625 Williams Street (860–443–2545; www.lymanallyn.conncoll.edu), a small but stirring cache of international antiquities, Old Master drawings, and American Impressionist paintings open Tuesday through Saturday 10:00 A.M. to 5:00 P.M. and Sunday 1:00 to 5:00 P.M.

Consider it a preview—a teaser—for the **Florence Griswold Museum** at 96 Lyme Street in **Old Lyme** (860–434–5542; www.flogris.org), about 10 miles southwest along I–95. A sea captain's daughter reduced in circumstances, Miss Griswold opened her grand 1817 mansion—a colonnaded Late Georgian—to guests at the turn of the century. It proved especially popular with a circle of painters including Childe Hassam; their legacy can be found painted directly on the panels of the dining room, and in an impressive collection that keeps their impoverished patron's memory alive. The museum—open Tuesday to Saturday 10:00 A.M. to 5:00 P.M. and Sunday 1:00 to 5:00 P.M., with reduced hours off-season—is but one vestige of the artistic endeavor that still prevails here. Walking about the pretty town, you'll also come upon the **Lyme Art Association** at 90 Lyme Street (860–434–7802) and the **Lyme Academy of Fine Arts** at number 84 (860–434–5232; www.lymeacademy.edu).

LUNCH: Bee & Thistle Inn, 100 Lyme Street, Old Lyme; (860) 434–1667 or (800) 622–4946; www.beeandthistleinn.com. This exceptionally elegant and cozy 1756 Colonial, next door to the museum, serves contemporary American cuisine. After a memorable meal, wander through five acres of English gardens down to the peaceful riverside, and you'll have some notion of what drew the Impressionists.

New London's Lyman Allyn Museum of Art

Afternoon

A few miles west of Old Lyme is **Old Saybrook.** Take a scenic drive south on Route 154 and around **Saybrook Point,** perhaps pausing for a refreshment at the **James Pharmacy** at 2 Pennywise Lane (860–388–2566), a 1896 soda fountain. Then follow Route 154 as it loops back north through **Essex** (on tomorrow's agenda) and **Chester,** which boasts some home-decor and antiques shops worth browsing. East of Chester, Route 148 leads to a narrows along the Connecticut, where some sort of ferry has been in service continuously since 1769. These days it's a tiny, nine-car boat (860–526–2743; www.chesterct. com/ferry), which makes the crossing in five minutes, pulling up beneath the fantastical **Gillette Castle** at 67 River Road in Hadlyme (860–526–2336). Actor William Gillette, renowned for playing Sherlock Holmes, built this fieldstone folly—it resembles a giant's sandcastle—in 1919, and it remains the centerpiece of a 184-acre state park. The terraced gardens, with their sweeping river valley views, are open from 8:00 A.M. until sundown.

Routes 146 north and 82 west will take you into **East Haddam.**

DINNER: Gelston House, 8 Main Street, East Haddam; (860) 873–1411. With its view of the Goodspeed Opera House (tonight's ultimate destination) and under the same management, this contemporary-grill restaurant within an 1853 hostelry is *the* place for dinner. In fact you'll probably want to return for dessert, often accompanied by an après-show cabaret.

LODGING: Bishopsgate Inn, 7 Norwich Road, East Haddam; (860) 873–1677; www.bishopsgate.com. This quiet and tasteful 1818 shipwright's home has plentiful fireplaces; one suite even has its own sauna.

Evening

Though you'd better reserve tickets way in advance, you'd no more want to miss the **Goodspeed Opera House** at Goodspeed Landing (860–873–8664; www.goodspeed.org) than go to New York and bypass Broadway. That's where a goodly number of the Goodspeed's fledgling musicals tend to end up, in fact, as did a cute little show called *Annie.* A banking tycoon plunked a theater atop his showy Second Empire warehouse, built in 1876, and imported actors from New York by riverboat. Some patrons still arrive by boat—private yacht—and the little theater has been an SRO hit since it was rescued from the wrecker's ball in the early 1960s. If tonight's tryout pans out, you can say you saw it first.

DAY 3

Morning

BREAKFAST: The Bishopsgate Inn. The generous breakfast will get you off to a good start, but pace yourself; brunch looms.

Essex, about 8 miles south on Route 154, is a town entirely dedicated to "messing about in boats"—and, on the side, catering to the boating class with shops and attractions. Local maritime and natural history is showcased in the **Connecticut River Museum** (860–767–8269; www.ctrivermuseum.org), housed in an 1878 dockhouse at the foot of Main Street and open Tuesday to Sunday 10:00 A.M. to 5:00 P.M. Highlights include a full-scale replica of the *American Turtle,* a wooden submarine that was a world first in 1775.

BRUNCH: Griswold Inn, 36 Main Street, Essex; (860) 767–1776; www. griswoldinn.com. The inn was built a year later—a banner year, as it happened. "The Gris" upholds the British tradition of a Sunday Hunt Breakfast—a killer buffet that has its own loyalists; reservations are highly recommended.

Afternoon

Head back to Boston by way of Connecticut's "quiet corner. "A quick highway zip along Routes 9 south, I–95 north, and 395 north will let you skip the cities and escape to Route 169 off exit 83A northeast of Norwich, a centuries-old turnpike now protected as a National Scenic Byway. About 7 miles north, on **Canterbury**'s green, the **Prudence Crandall Museum** (860–546–9916), a handsome beige 1805 Federal house, stands as a memorial to a brave headmistress who admitted a black student in 1832. Undaunted when her white patrons withdrew their daughters in protest, she established New England's first academy for African-American girls, which lasted only a year; lawsuits and a mob attack shut it down. The house is open February to mid-December, Wednesday to Sunday 10:00 A.M. to 4:30 P.M.; the memories are palpable.

Six miles north in **Brooklyn,** look for the 1770 **Congregational Meeting House,** a glorious example of Connecticut's civic architecture, and, farther along, the **New England Center for Contemporary Art** (860–774– 8899), housed in a massive Colonial barn; it's open, free, Wednesday through Friday 10:00 A.M. to 4:00 P.M., weekends 1:00 to 5:00 P.M.

Fifteen more miles brings you to **Woodstock,** home to the shocking-pink **Bowen House** (860–928–4074; www.spnea/org). This 1846 gingerbread Gothic Revival confection, also known as **Roseland Cottage,** was quite the party house in its day: the barn boasts a vintage bowling alley. Four presidents attended various celebrations during the early years, and the Society for the Preservation of New England Antiquities continues to host occasional revelries. The house (hourly tours) and grounds are open from 11:00 A.M. to 5:00 P.M. Wednesday to Sunday June through mid-October.

Southeast about a mile off Route 171, the once derelict mill town of **Putnam** deserves the comeback-of-the-decade award. The boarded-up buildings along Route 44 are now filled to bursting with antiques and collectibles. For a guide to the score of shops, harboring hundreds of vendors, contact the Putnam Antique Association (800–514–3448). Among the must-visits are the **Putnam Antiques Exchange** at 75–83 Main Street (860–928–1905), where you'll find whole rooms ready to appropriate, and the **Antiques Marketplace** at 109 Main Street (860–928–0442), where the revival originated.

DINNER: Vine Bistro, 85 Main Street, Putnam; (860) 928–1660. Stop in for stylish refreshment—including flavor-intensive Italian sorbets—before picking up Route 395 north and heading back to Boston via the Mass Turnpike.

THERE'S MORE

Airborne Adventures. Eagle Aviation at the Goodspeed Airport in East Haddam (860–873–8568 or 800–564–2FLY) offers airplane and seaplane rides. Brighter Skies Balloon Co. (860–963–0600 or 800–677–5114) operates out of Woodstock.

Bargain shopping. It's worth heading farther west along the coast to plunder the Clinton Crossing Premium Outlets on Route 81 in Clinton (860–664–0700; www.chelseagca.com), where tenants range from Barneys to BCBG.

Excursions. Voyager Cruises at Mallory Wharf in Mystic (860–536–0416) sends *The Argia,* a replica gaff-rigged schooner, into Fisher's Island Sound. Captain John's at 15 First Street in Waterford (860–443–7259; www. sunbeamfleet.com) sends out various craft in search of whales, seals, and eagles, depending on the season. The Essex Steam Train & Riverboat, based at Railroad Avenue on Route 154 (860–767–0103; www.essexsteamtrain. com), offers a relaxed way to tour upriver. Hook up with Down River Sports & Canoes at 1697 Old Saybrook Road in Haddam (860–345–8355) to canoe the Connecticut.

Kid stuff. Maple Breeze Park on Route 2 in Pawcatuck (860–599–1232) will fulfill every last kidly craving, from miniature golf to go-karts, bumper boats, and water slides. In New London, families will enjoy the beach, boardwalk, and waterslide at Ocean Beach Park (860–447–3031 or 800–510–7263), as well as the Lyman Allyn Dolls & Toys annex downtown at 165 State Street (860–437–1947; www.lymanallyn.conncoll.edu). For rainy days and restless tots (eight and under), there's also the Children's Museum of Southeastern Connecticut at 409 Main Street in Niantic (860–691–1111, www.childrensmuseumsect.org). With its touch tanks and walking trail, the Meigs Point Nature Center at Hammonasset Beach State Park in Madison (860–245–8743) is both educational and fun.

Museums. Funded by the casino-enriched tribe whose history it traces, the $193 million Mashantucket Pequot Museum & Research Center off Route 214 (860–396–6800 or 800–411–9671; www.mashantucket.com) is a staggering experience, rich in sensory impressions and straightforwardly factual enough to offset lifelong exposure to standard American history. The Denison Homestead Museum on Pequotsepos Road in Mystic (860–536–9248; www.visitmystic.com/denisonhomestead) is a sampler of decorative styles, ranging from a Colonial kitchen to an early twentieth-century living room. The Mystic Art Association enjoys a lovely setting at 9 Water Street (860–536–7601; www.mystic-art.org). Allegra Farm on Route 82 in East Haddam (860–873–9658; www.allegrafarm.com) is a living history museum devoted to horse-drawn travel—which you can experience on-site. The Slater Memorial Museum at the Norwich Free Academy, 108 Crescent Street (806–887–2505), contains antiquities from various cultures, including Native American, and American art and furniture from Colonial to contemporary.

Naval perks. The free Nautilus Memorial and Submarine Force Museum at the U.S. Naval Submarine Base on Route 12 in Groton (860–694–3174 or 800–343–0079; www.ussnautilus.org) includes a tour of the world's first nuclear-powered sub, built in 1954.

Performing arts. The Pequot-owned Foxwoods Resort Casino off Route 214 in Mashantucket (800–200–2882; www.foxwoods.com) books Las Vegas–level headliners. The Wolf Den within the Mohegan Sun Casino in Uncasville (888–226–7711; www.mohegansun.com) presents as stellar a lineup. The Garde Arts Center at 325 State Street in New London (860–444–7373; www.gardearts.org), a vaudeville holdover, presents theater, dance, music, and independent films. The Eugene O'Neill Theatre Center at 305 Great Neck Road in Waterford (860–443–5378; www.eugeneoneill.org) hosts summer readings and workshop productions of new plays. The National Theatre of the Deaf, 5 West Main Street, Chester (860–724–5179 or 800–300–5179; www.ntd.org), draws enthusiastic audiences as they tour all over the country; every June, they offer free performances in their hometown. The Ivoryton Playhouse at 103 Main Street in the Ivoryton section of Essex (860–767–7318; www.essexct.com/playhouse) mounts summer stock and hosts concerts.

Potables. Stonington Vineyards at 523 Taugwonk Road in Stonington (860–535–1222 or 800–421–WINE; www.stoningtonvineyards.com) has been a standard setter for New England's burgeoning wine industry; it offers tours and tastings daily, as does Chamard Vineyards at 115 Cow Hill Road in Clinton (860–664–0299; www.ctwine.com/chamard). Open during the fall harvest, Clyde's Cider Mill at 129 North Stonington Road in Old Mystic (860–536–3354) is the only surviving steam-powered press in New England. The Sharpe Hill Vineyard off Route 97 in Pomfret (860–794–3549; www.sharpehill.com) spans seventy-two acres and boasts a restaurant.

SPECIAL EVENTS

Mid-February. Connecticut River Eagle Festival, Essex; (860) 767–2848; www.ctaudubon.org. The Connecticut River Museum hosts activities including viewing tours.

Mid-July to late August. Summer Music at Harkness Memorial State Park, Waterford; (860) 443–7373; www.gardearts.org. The beachside gardens of the forty-two-room Eolia Mansion are given over to renowned performers.

Mid-October. Arts & Crafts Festival, Woodstock; (860) 928–4074; www.spnea. org. Roseland Cottage hosts a convocation of artisans and entertainers.

December. Mystic Seaport Lantern Light Tours; (860) 572–5315 or (888) 9–SEAPORT; www.mysticseaport.org. Carriage tours of the candlelit town, complete with stories.

OTHER RECOMMENDED RESTAURANTS AND LODGINGS

Centerbrook

Steve's Centerbrook Cafe, 78 Main Street; (860) 767–1277. Chef Steve Wilkinson spans classical French and up-to-date global cuisine.

Chester

Restaurant du Village, 59 Main Street; (860) 526–5301. Transporting French legerdemain in an auberge-style setting.

Deep River

Riverwind Inn, 209 Main Street; (860) 526–2014; www.riverwindinn.com. A 1760 home-plus-annex packed with antiques and charm.

East Lyme

Flanders Fish Market, 22 Chesterfield Road (Route 161); (860) 739–8866 or (800) 638–8189; www.flandersfish.com. A no-frills roadhouse serving super-fresh fish.

Essex

Black Seal, 29 Main Street; (860) 767–0233. A contemporary bistro with a nautical bent.

Ivoryton

Copper Beech Inn, 46 Main Street; (860) 767–0330 or (888) 809–2056; www. copperbeechinn.com. A superb French restaurant within a luxurious 1890 home; some rooms come with a private garden-view deck.

Mystic

House of 1833, 72 North Stonington Road; (203) 536–6325 or (800) FOR–1833; www.houseof1833.com. A truly grand, pillared house, plus pool and tennis court.

The Inn at Mystic, Routes 1 and 27; (860) 536–9604 or (800) 237–2415; www.innatmystic.com. This curious but inviting complex comprises a pillared 1904 Colonial Revival mansion, where Bogie and Bacall spent their honeymoon; a modern motel with waterview tennis court; and the Flood Tide, a contemporary Continental restaurant.

Mystic Pizza, 56 West Main Street; (860) 536–3700; www.mysticpizza.com. The piled-high pies here inspired the 1988 film starring Julia Roberts.

Steamboat Inn, 73 Steamboat Wharf; (860) 536–8300; www.visitmystic.com/ steamboat. Perched right over the harbor, the handsome, cathedral-ceilinged quarters feel like a private schooner, only roomier.

Whaler's Inn, 20 East Main Street; (860) 536–1506; www.whalersinnmystic. com. A cluster of nicely rehabbed eighteenth-century inns near the docks, with a New Italian restaurant, Bravo Bravo (860–536–3228).

New London

Lighthouse Inn, 6 Guthrie Place; (860) 443–8411 or (888) 600–5681; www. lighthouseinnct.com. A steel magnate's semicircular 1902 Mediterranean manse makes the most of its Long Island Sound views; grounds by Frederick Law Olmsted.

North Stonington

Randall's Ordinary, Route 2; (860) 599–4540 or (877) 599–4540; www. randallsordinary.com. This 1685 "ordinary," or tavern, still practices the all-but-lost art of hearth cookery. The rooms, with period furnishings, include a silo suite with fireplace and Jacuzzi in an 1819 barn.

Norwich

The Spa at Norwich Inn, 607 West Thames Street; (860) 886–2401 or (800) ASK–4–SPA; www.thespaatnorwichinn.com. A stylishly updated turn-of-the-century inn with a world-class modern spa.

Old Lyme

Old Lyme Inn, 85 Lyme Street; (860) 434–2600 or (800) 434–5352; www. oldlymeinn.com. An 1850s Victorian mansion rivaling the Bee & Thistle with dazzling seasonal dishes.

Old Saybrook

Cafe Routier, 1080 Boston Post Road (Route 1); (860) 388–6270. An unprepossessing setting conceals some fairly fancy French cuisine.

Saybrook Point Inn & Spa, 2 Bridge Street; (860) 395–2000 or (800) 243– 0212; www.saybrook.com. A spiffy neotraditional hotel with its own marina, smashing water views, a spa with indoor and outdoor pools, and an elegant contemporary-Mediterranean restaurant, Terra Mar.

Pomfret

Celebrations Inn, 330 Pomfret Street; (860) 928–5492 or (877) 928–5492; www.celebrationsinn.com. An 1885 Queen Anne Victorian offering themed rooms and afternoon tea (or herb cordial).

Fireside Tavern, 108 Wade Road; (860) 794–3549; www.sharpehill.com. An antique-filled loft restaurant, part of the fledgling Sharpe Hill Vineyard.

The Harvest, 37 Putnam Road; (860) 928–0008; www.harvestrestaurant.com. A fancy, forward-looking restaurant in a 1765 house.

The Inn at Gwyn Careg, 68 Wolf Den Road; (860) 928–7758. An expanded 1760 Colonial inn and restaurant, luxuriously updated, on thirty acres with spectacular gardens.

Stonington

The Inn at Stonington, 60 Water Street; (860) 535–2000; www.innatstonington.com. Twelve spiffy rooms, all with fireplace, most with Jacuzzi; out back is the 1929 restaurant Skipper's Dock (860–535–0111), which specializes in fish, naturally, often Frenchified.

Noah's, 113 Water Street; (860) 535–3925; www.noahsrestaurant.com. Breakfast through dinner, on the rarefied side, in a casual cafe setting.

Water Street Cafe, 142 Water Street; (860) 535–2122. A stylish New American eatery fit for a picturebook town.

Thompson

Lord Thompson Manor, Route 200; (860) 923–3886; www.lordthompsonmanor.com. This 1917 English-style manor house has handsome rooms and forty-two Olmsted-designed acres.

Westbrook

Water's Edge Resort, 1525 Boston Post Road (Route 1); (860) 399–5901 or (800) 222–5901; www.watersedge-resort.com. A shoreline inn-and-condo complex with its own sliver of beach and fine New American cuisine.

Woodstock

Inn at Woodstock Hill, 94 Plaine Hill Road; (806) 928–0528; www.wood stockhill.com. An 1816 Christopher Wren–style country manor with a worthwhile Continental restaurant.

FOR MORE INFORMATION

Connecticut Office of Tourism, 505 Hudson Street, Hartford, CT 06106; (860) 270–8080 or (800) CT–BOUND; www.ctbound.org.

Connecticut River Valley & Shoreline Visitors Council, 393 Main Street, Middletown, CT 06457; (860) 347–0028 or (800) 486–3346; www.visit-ct-river-shore.org.

Connecticut's Mystic & More, 470 Bank Street, New London, CT 06320; (860) 444–2206 or (800) TO ENJOY; www.mysticmore.com.

Northeast Connecticut Visitors District, 13 Canterbury Road, Brooklyn, CT 06234; (860) 779–6383 or (888) 628–1228; www. ctquietcorner.org

Litchfield County

FARMLAND

FOR THE RICH AND FAMOUS

2 NIGHTS

Exquisite inns • Killer antiques • Showy gardens
Esoteric teas • Underground explorations

Northwestern Connecticut is where Manhattan muckamucks, from William Buckley to Meryl Streep, like to play country squire. Thanks to a depression that descended on the region after a Colonial mining boom, the countryside remains remarkably unspoiled and incredibly beautiful—like a flashback to the early nineteenth century. Winding roads through rolling meadows will suddenly reveal a pristine Federal farmhouse, setting off acquisitive urges of the severest sort. Most properties, of course, are already spoken for, and at a considerable price. However, it doesn't hurt to dream.

Like similar New England enclaves of quiet good taste, the region abounds in fine restaurants and inns, notable antique troves, and truly exceptional gardens—all the accouterments of the good life, neo-bucolic-style. En route or in returning, you can enjoy the cultural riches of Hartford.

DAY 1

Morning

Take the Mass Pike west to where it meets I-84, and follow that to exit 54 in downtown **Hartford.** Keep an eye out for the "boat building"—the world's first two-sided building, built for the Phoenix Mutual Life Insurance Company

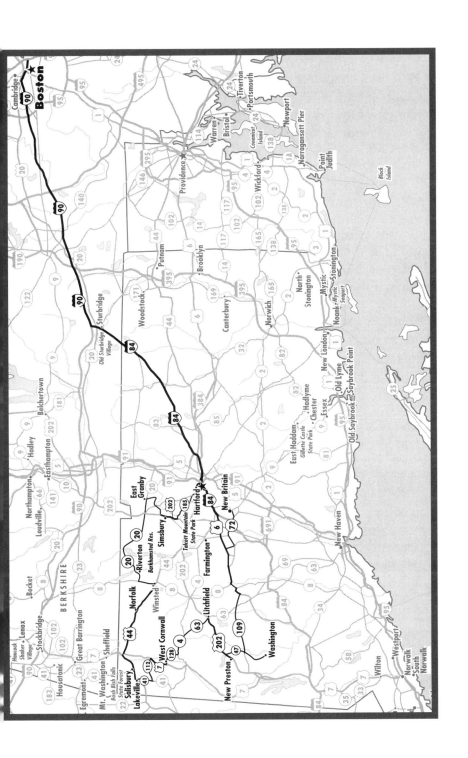

in 1963. To the west, at 800 Main Street, is the **Old State House** (860–522–6766; www.cga.state.et.us), the oldest such structure in the country, designed by Charles Bulfinch in 1796. The Amistad trial, among other notable historic events, took place here; today the plaza hosts concerts and farmers' markets in season.

A few blocks south, the **Wadsworth Atheneum** at 600 Main Street (860–278–2670; www.wadsworthatheneum.org) is not only the nation's oldest public art museum—founded in 1842—but also one of the most intriguing. Though relatively small, it packs in some 45,000 works of art covering 5,000 years, from mummies to Warhol and beyond. Antiques aficionados will swoon over the decorative arts collection, highlighting fine Connecticut Valley furniture. The museum is open Tuesday through Friday 11:00 A.M. to 5:00 P.M. and weekends 10:00 A.M. to 5:00 P.M. On the plaza outside, look for Alexander Calder's hulking *Stegosaurus*, always a hit with the childlike at heart, who will also warm to the **Bushnell Park Carousel** (860–585–5411; www.the carouselmuseum.com/bushnell park) on Jewell Street several blocks west of the museum. This 1914 treasure, open seasonally, is set amid the nation's first municipal park, a thirty-seven-acre beauty designed by Frederick Law Olmsted.

About a mile west of the downtown area, the Nook Farm neighborhood was once home to two famous, dissimilar writers. The **Harriet Beecher Stowe House,** an 1871 Gothic villa at 77 Forest Street at Farmington Avenue (860–525–9317; www.harrietbeecherstowecenter.org), housed the author of *Uncle Tom's Cabin*. While writing thirty-two books and raising seven children, Stowe somehow also found time to pioneer the practice of "domestic science." Her house's plain, sensible kitchen is modeled on the precepts set forth in *The American Woman's Home,* a book she coauthored with her sister. Around the corner is the **Mark Twain House** at 351 Farmington Avenue (860–247–0998; www.marktwainhouse.org), a gaudy 1881 Gothic Revival mansion structured like a steamboat, where Twain wrote several novels, including *Adventures of Huckleberry Finn*. Showy as it is, with fancy brickwork and Tiffany windows and interiors, this house reads more playful than impressive. The children's school room is a charming creative hodgepodge, and the billiards room doubled as Twain's study. He is said to have played—while cogitating, no doubt—up to twelve hours a day. Both houses offer hour-long tours Monday through Saturday 9:30 A.M. to 5:00 P.M. and Saturday noon to 5:00 P.M. May through October; call for off-season hours.

Follow Farmington Avenue to its namesake town, about 3½ miles southwest, to visit the **Hill-Stead Museum** at 35 Mountain Road (860–677–4787;

www.hillstead.org). Theodate Pope, an alumna of Farmington's prestigious Miss Porter's School, so loved the town that she insisted her parents move east, then helped architect-du-jour Stanford White design them a 1901 neo-Colonial house; she went on to become the country's first female licensed architect. Though the interior's a bit oppressive, it's worth taking the hour-long tour to view the Popes' prescient French Impressionist purchases. Pope also designed the 152-acre grounds, which are glorious. Hill-Stead is open Tuesday through Sunday 10:00 A.M. to 5:00 P.M. in-season, and closes one hour earlier off-season.

LUNCH: Ann Howard's Apricots, 1593 Farmington Avenue, Farmington; (860) 673–5405. The Hartford area's favorite New American restaurant.

Afternoon

As an alternative (or, better yet, supplement) to the Wadsworth Atheneum, also consider a stop in **New Britain,** off I-84 a few miles south of Farmington. Open Tuesday through Sunday from noon to 5:00 P.M., and a bit more (Wednesday till 7:00 P.M., Saturday from 10:00 A.M. on), the **New Britain Museum of American Art** at 56 Lexington Street (860–229–0257; www.nbmaa.org) houses 5,000 American works from 1740 to the present, spanning Sargent and Cassatt, Hassam and Homer. The primitive portraits are riveting, and there's also an unusual collection of illustration art (the field in which Homer started out). Take a moment after touring to stroll through the Olmsted-designed **Walnut Hill Park.** Tonight's lodging lies about 20 miles west, via Routes 72, 6, and 109.

DINNER AND LODGING: Mayflower Inn, 118 Woodbury Road (Route 47), Washington; (860) 868–9466; www.relaischateaux.fr/mayflower. What started life as an 1894 boarding school has evolved into the grandest hotel in the region, with exquisite classicist decor and cuisine to match. Twenty-five sui generis rooms are surrounded by twenty-eight acres of English gardens.

DAY 2

Morning

BREAKFAST: Mayflower Inn. Enjoy a dazzler at the inn.

Circle **Washington's** pretty hilltop town green, ringed with venerable houses. To picture the 10,000-year-old history that preceded them, head a half-mile south on Route 199 to visit the **Institute for American Indian Studies** at 38 Curtis Road (860–868–0518). Considerably less flashy than the Mashantucket Pequot Museum flanking the Foxwoods Casino, this research facility—open Monday through Saturday 10:00 A.M. to 5:00 P.M. and Sunday noon to 5:00 P.M. year-round—does an excellent job of conveying the spirit of a tight-knit, indigenous community.

Two miles northwest of Washington, **New Preston** is a tiny village positively riddled with antique shops and other chichi decor emporia; it's a browser's paradise. Among the many venues worth investigating are **J. Seitz & Co.** (860–868–0119; www.jseitz.com) for Santa Fe–style chic, and the **Garden House** (860–868–6790) for dazzling rustic remnants suitable for indoor/outdoor use. From here it's about a 7-mile journey northeast along Route 202 to the county seat of **Litchfield.** Make a brief detour along the way to stretch your legs at the **White Memorial Foundation and Conservation Center Museum,** 80 Whitehall Road (860–567–0857; www.whitememorialcc.org), the state's largest wildlife sanctuary, with 35 miles of trails spanning 4,000 acres and five distinct ecosystems.

An important Colonial crossroads, Litchfield was a proud town long before the New York glitterati started showing up. A good place to begin your explorations is at the **Litchfield History Museum** at 7 South Street (860–567–4501). Open Tuesday through Saturday from 11:00 A.M. to 5:00 P.M. and Sunday 1:00 to 5:00 P.M. in season, this well-presented collection gives a good overview of town history. The Litchfield Historical Society also maintains the **Tapping Reeve House** at 63 South Street, where America's first law school was founded in 1773. Wander down West Street to survey an appealing array of shops, including the museum-quality **Jeffrey Tillou Antiques** at number 33 (860–567–9693) and **Les Plaisirs de la Maison,** a French country cache at West and Main Streets (860–567–2555).

LUNCH: **West Street Grill,** 43 West Street, Litchfield; (860) 567–3885. Trendily black and white, with big-city panache and exciting regional fare.

Afternoon

On your way out of town, dip south a little on Route 63 to take in **White Flower Farm** (860–496–9624; www.whiteflowerfarm.com), where the premier gardening catalog maintains 10 acres of showy plantings. A few miles east of town, on Buell Road off East Litchfield Road, the Cotswold-style estate

Litchfield's White Flower Farm

Topsmead (860–567–5694), now part of **Topsmead State Forest** (http://dep.state.ct.us/rec/parks/ctforests), boasts magnificent gardens.

It's a scenic country drive, northwesterly along Routes 63, 4, and 128 to the charming town of **West Cornwall,** custom-made for strolling. The **West Cornwall Covered Bridge,** Connecticut's largest, was built of native oak in the mid–nineteenth century and has been in service ever since; there's a swimming hole just downriver, below the rapids. Bibliophiles won't want to miss **Barbara Farnsworth, Bookseller,** a collection of 40,000 or so vintage books at 407 Route 128 (860–672–6571).

Routes 7, 112, and 41 will lead you to **Lakeville,** where you can enjoy an educational as well as refreshing tea tasting at **Harney & Sons,** an importer of national renown located at 23 Brook Street (860–435–5050 or 800–TEA–TIME; www.harney.com). You might peruse the holdings of **Burton Brook Farm Antiquarians** at 299 Main Street (860–435–9421). Further finds await a mile up Route 44 in **Salisbury,** where **Buckley & Buckley** at 84 Main Street (860–435–9919) specializes in American "high country" furniture dating from 1680 to 1860.

DINNER AND LODGING: White Hart Inn, Village Green, Salisbury; (860) 435–0030; www.whitehartinn.com. Three in-house restaurants of varying formality serve vibrant New American cuisine at this early nineteenth-century hostelry smartly spiffed up with scads of chintz.

DAY 3

Morning

BREAKFAST: White Hart Inn. Fresh pastries will perk your appetite.

The day is geared to relaxation. About 10 miles east of Salisbury on Route 44, **Norfolk** is a pleasant, pretty town that serves as summer headquarters for the Yale music department; it's Connecticut's Lenox. If there happens to be a concert scheduled for the afternoon within the 1906 redwood-and-cedar music shed at the **Ellen Battell Stoeckel Estate** (860–542–3000), definitely stick around. In any case you're welcome to wander the forested 70-acre grounds and perhaps catch snatches of a rehearsal.

Horticultural cognoscenti will want to make a pilgrimage to Frederick McGourty's **Hillside Gardens** at 515 Litchfield Road, Norfolk (860–542–5345), to admire thousands of unusual perennials, imaginatively landscaped. Stop by, and your garden will be grateful.

Route 44 will also lead further east to Winsted, where you can pick up Route 20 for a meandering drive through the state forests that surround Barkhamsted Reservoir. For an unusual frisson, alight to explore the **Old New-Gate Prison Museum** at 115 Newgate Road in East Granby (860–653–3563). The name is not quite so complicated—and oxymoronic—as it sounds. Here America's first copper mine (chartered in 1707) became the colony's primary prison—named for the notorious London gaol—in 1773; in an ironic reversal, British prisoners of war were sent to Newgate during the revolution. The subterranean passages, some 50 feet underground, proved a secure if punitively dank stronghold until 1827, when prisoners were finally transferred to slightly more humane quarters. The tunnels—open Wednesday through Sunday 10:00 A.M. to 4:30 P.M. in-season—are fun to visit, though you wouldn't want to stay there.

BRUNCH: Simsbury Inn, 397 Hopmeadow Street, Simsbury; (860) 651–5700 or (800) 634–2719; www.simsburyinn.com. Head a couple of miles southwest along Routes 187, 189, 315, and 10 toward Simsbury, having booked ahead for the award-winning spread at **Evergreens** within this luxurious neo-country hotel.

Afternoon

Heading eastward (i.e., homeward) on Route 185, take a short southerly detour to climb **Talcott Mountain**—by car, then foot (about 1½ more miles). At the very top is the 165-foot **Heublein Tower** (860–242–1158), built in 1914 as a private summer house. Open Thursday to Sunday 10:00 A.M. to 4:30 P.M. Memorial Day through Labor Day and daily during foliage season, it offers a heady view of four states, and some intimation of what personal power felt like early in the twentieth century.

THERE'S MORE

Aerial adventures. Get a crow's-eye view of the countryside via hot-air balloon with Airvertising & Airventures in West Simsbury (860–651–4441 or 800–535–2473).

Antiques. Route 6 in Woodbury is flanked by dozens of superb if high-end antique shops, including Grass Roots at 12 Main Street North (203–263–3983), and Country Loft Antiques at 557 Main Street South (203–266–4500). Running Saturdays mid-March to mid-December, the Woodbury Antiques & Flea Market at 787 Main Street South (203–263–2841; www.woodburyfleamarket.com) might yield a diamond in the rough.

Arts and crafts. The Farmington Valley Arts Center at 25 Arts Center Lane off Route 44 in Avon (860–678–1867) is an old explosives plant turned gallery and studio complex. The Brookfield Craft Center, housed in a 1780 gristmill at 286 Whisconier Road (Route 25) in bucolic Brookfield (203–775–4526; www.brookfieldcraftcenter.org), is not only a source of interesting work, but a great place to study. The little town of Kent, near the New York border, has become an improbable arts center, spearheaded by the international-caliber Paris–New York–Kent Art Gallery on Route 7 (860–927–4152), housed in a creatively recycled nineteenth-century caboose.

Carriage Rides. Loon Meadow Farm at 41 Loon Meadow Drive off Route

44 in Norfolk (860–542–6085; www.loonmeadowfarm.com) offers carriage rides—the elegant way to get about town—as well as hayrides and sleigh rides accompanied by mulled cider. Flamig Farm (860–658–5070; www. flamigfarm.com) can introduce you to Simsbury in a similar fashion.

Family fun. At Dinosaur State Park on West Street in Rocky Hill (860–529–8423), a giant geodesic dome shelters hundreds of 200-million-year-old Jurassic dinosaur tracks amid a forty-acre nature preserve. Open since 1846, Lake Compounce at 822 Lake Avenue in Bristol (860–583–3300, www.lakecompounce.com) is the oldest continuously operating amusement park in the country. Quassy Amusement Park on Route 64 in Middlebury (203–758–2913 or 800–FOR–PARK; www. quassy.com), built in 1909, is on the small side but holds plenty of thrills for little kids, including a multispecies turn-of-the-century carousel.

Garden spots. At the Elizabeth Park Rose Gardens at 915 Prospect Avenue in Hartford (860–722–6514; www.elizabethpark.org), some 800 varieties bloom. Offering heirloom seeds, Comstock, Ferre & Co. at 263 Main Street in Wethersfield (860–571–6590; www.comstockferre.com), has been in business since 1820.

Historic houses. About 2 miles south of Hartford, Wethersfield—the state's first permanent settlement—is a surprise preserve of seventeenth- and eighteenth-century houses, including the three that constitute the Webb-Deane-Stevens Museum at 211 Main Street (860–529–0612). The Glebe House on Hollow Road off Route 6 in Woodbury (203–263–2855; www. woodburyct.org/woodburyglebehouse) is a circa 1750 minister's farmhouse with simple Colonial furnishings and the only garden in the United States designed by legendary British horticulturalist Gertrude Jekyll. The Holley House Museum at 15 Millerton Road in Lakeville (860–435–2878) focuses on women's roles during the nineteenth century.

Performing arts. For out-of-the-ordinary performance and fine arts, check out Real Art Ways at 56 Arbor Street in Hartford (860–232–1006; www. realartways.org). Hartford Stage at 50 Church Street (860–527–5151; www.hartfordstage.org) is highly acclaimed for its imaginative classic-to-contemporary productions.

Potables. The rocky hillsides have proved well suited to viniculture. Oenophiles will want to visit the Hopkins Vineyard at 25 Hopkins Road in New Preston (860–868–7954; www.hopkinsvineyard.com) and the Haight Vineyard at 29 Chestnut Hill Road off Route 118 in Litchfield (860–567–4045).

Racing and riding. Lime Rock Park in Lakeville (860–435–5000, or 800–RACE–LRP) is where race car amateurs like Paul Newman like to test their mettle. Lee's Riding Stable at 57 East Litchfield Road in Litchfield (860–567–0785) guides trail rides through an adjoining state forest.

Water sports. North American Canoe Tours (860–693–6465) has a tubing concession on the Farmington River at Satan's Kingdom State Recreation Area in New Hartford (the region's name derives from the bandits who used to bedevil stagecoaches taking the Albany Turnpike). By far the eeriest excursion is offered by Underground Canoe Trips of Collinsville (860–693–0385), along the Park River as it tunnels under Hartford.

SPECIAL EVENTS

Late June. Taste of Litchfield Hills; (860) 567–4045. Twenty top local restaurants are represented at this two-day feast, held at the Haight Vineyard.

Early August. Litchfield Jazz Festival, Goshen; (860) 567–4162; www.litchfieldjazzfest.com. Performers, food, and microbrews at the Fairgrounds.

Early October. Washington Antiques Show; (860) 868–7586; www.biblio.org/gunn. Litchfield County's elusive celebrities emerge to splurge.

December 31. First Night, Hartford; (860) 728–3089. A ten-hour arts extravaganza.

OTHER RECOMMENDED RESTAURANTS AND LODGINGS

Avon

Avon Old Farms Hotel, Routes 44 and 10; (860) 677–1651 or (800) 836–4000; www.avonoldfarmshotel.com. This stagecoach inn, considerably expanded, has been welcoming hungry, weary travelers since 1757.

Canaan

The Cannery, 85 Main Street; (860) 824–7333. American bistro innovations, hearty yet imaginative.

Farmington

The Grist Mill Cafe, 44 Mill Lane; (860) 676–8855. The old mill, with its views of the river, lends itself well to romantic French/Italian dinners.

Piccolo Arancio, 819 Farmington Avenue; (860) 674–1224; www.piccolo arancio.com. Northern Italian delicacies, including ravishing ravioli all'arancia.

Hartford

The Goodwin Hotel, 1 Haynes Street; (860) 246–7500 or (800) 922–5006; www.goodwinhotel.com. A luxury hotel in the heart of town.

Mark Twain Hostel, 131 Tremont Street; (860) 523–7255; www.hiayh.org. For travelers on the cheap.

Max Downtown, 185 Asylum Street; (860) 522–2530; www.maxdowntown. com. Hartford's hippest boite.

Museum Cafe, 600 Main Street; (860) 728–5989. The Wadsworth Atheneum's daring New American menu is a match for its progressive art collection.

Lakeville

Charlotte, 223 Main Street; (860) 435–3551. The antique furnishings are for sale; the contempory cuisine, for delectating.

Wake Robin Inn, 104–106 Sharon Road (Route 41); (860) 435–2515; www. wakerobininn.com. A grand 1896 Georgian Colonial on fifteen acres.

New Milford

Adrienne, 218 Kent Road (Route 7): (860) 354–6001; www.adrienne restaurant.com. Chef Adrienne Sussman, formerly of the Waldorf Astoria's Peacock Alley, brings to bear her experience with international cuisines.

Fabled Foods, 59 Bank Street; (860) 354–1144. A delightful New American/ Mediterranean cafe camouflaged by a bakery/deli.

New Preston

The Birches Inn, 233 West Shore Road; (860) 868–1735 or (888) 590–7945; www.thebirchesinn.com. A small, luxuriously updated 1940s inn over-looking Lake Waramaug, with an acclaimed fusion restaurant.

Boulders Inn, East Shore Road (Route 45); (860) 868–0541 or (800) 55–BOULDERS; www.bouldersinn.com. A comfy 1895 lakeview stone mansion serving imaginative cuisine.

The Hopkins Inn, 22 Hopkins Road; (860) 868–7295 or (800) 868–7295; www.thehopkinsinn.com. An 1847 Federal house with plainish rooms but lovely lake views and an Alpine-inclined restaurant.

The Lakeview Inn, 107 North Shore Road; (860) 868–1000. This 1795 Colonial inn offers inspired New American dining and some plush quarters.

Norfolk

Blackberry River Inn, 538 Greenwoods Road, Route 44; (860) 542–5100 or (800) 414–3636; www.blackberryriver.com. Among the charms of this 1763 inn on twenty-seven acres is a cherry-paneled library, a pool, tennis court, and on-site trout fishing.

Manor House, 69 Maple Avenue; (860) 542–5690; www.manorhouse-norfolk. com. An 1898 Tudor mansion lavished with Tiffany stained glass.

Riverton

The Yellow Victorian Restaurant, 6 Riverton Road; (860) 379–7020; www. thevalleybook/dining/yellowvictoriann. Featuring chef-owner Dreama Erisoty's deft New Americana.

Salisbury

The Chaiwalla Tea Room, 1 Main Street; (860) 435–9758. Exotic brews, home-baked goodies, and local color.

Harvest Bakery, 10 Academy Street; (860) 435–1302. An exotic noshery spanning breakfast goodies, soups, salads, and pizzas.

Under Mountain Inn, 482 Undermountain Road; (860) 435–0242. A 1730s farmhouse turned Anglophile haven; decor and dinner alike are unabashedly British.

Simsbury

Simsbury 1820 House, 731 Hopmeadow Street; (860) 658–7658 or (800) TRY–
1820; www.simsbury1820house.com. A Colonial Revival mansion smartly
appointed to suit the period.

Washington Depot

The Pantry, 5 Titus Road; (860) 868–0258. Gourmet paraphernalia, plus a
cafe.

Woodbury

Good News Cafe, 694 Main Street South; (203) 266–GOOD. Carole Peck's
marvelous regional cuisine.

John's Cafe, 693 Main Street South; (203) 263–0188. A modest eatery offering good New American fare.

Longwood Country Inn, 1204 Main Street South; (203) 266–0800; www.
longwoodcountryinn.com. This newly expanded 1789 inn does justice to
Connecticut's "antiques capital"; the restaurant, though, proffers progressive regional fare.

FOR MORE INFORMATION

Connecticut Office of Tourism, 505 Hudson Street, Hartford, CT 06106;
(860) 270–8080 or (800) CT–BOUND; www. ctbound.org.

Greater Hartford Tourism District, 234 Murphy Road, Hartford, CT 06114;
(860) 244–8181 or (800) 793–4480; www.enjoyhartford.com.

Litchfield Hills Visitors Bureau, PO Box 968, Litchfield, CT 06759; (860)
567–4506; www.litchfieldhills.com.

The Gold Coast
WHERE OLD MONEY TALKS

2 NIGHTS

New Haven's cultural cache • The glories of "SoNo"
Colonial taverns • Impressionist hangouts
High-stakes shopping • World-class dining

You don't have to have deep pockets—though it certainly helps—to mine Connecticut's "Gold Coast," a roughly 15-mile appendage of the state which reaches toward New York as if yearning to merge. Despite its Colonial origins as a thriving commercial center (protected harbors ensured its success in the maritime trade), this southernmost corner of New England has for some time harbored more cosmopolitan aspirations. Gilded suburbs nestle alongside gritty industrial towns, and the public benefactors of an age even more ostentatious than ours have left behind an impressive legacy for hoi polloi to plunder.

Don your sensible shoes and prepare for a campaign of museum-hopping and antiquity-shopping up and down the coast. The following, in toto, is probably too full a schedule for all but the fleetest of browsers, but you can pick and choose, and always resume the chase another day.

DAY 1

Morning
Though not strictly Gold Coast, **New Haven**—about 2½ hours southwest of Boston via the Mass Pike and Routes 84 and 91 (get off at exit 3)—is a must stopover for **Yale**'s superb museums. Generally open Tuesday through Saturday from 10:00 A.M. to 5:00 P.M. and Sundays noon to 5:00 P.M., they're free

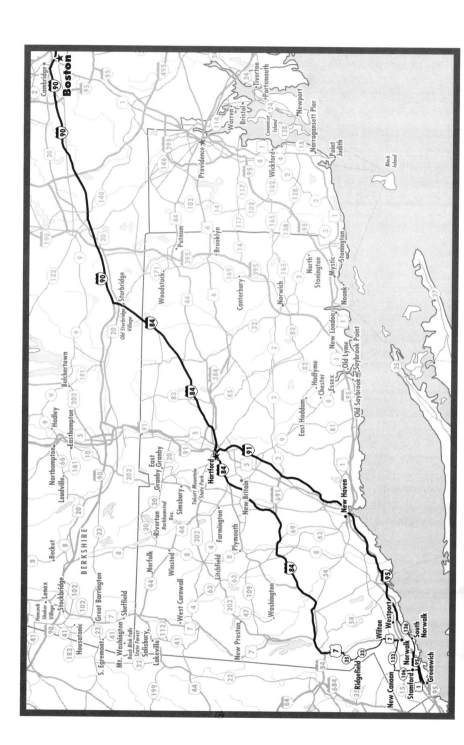

and fun to sample in transit. First-time visitors might want to get their bearings at the university's **Visitor Information Center** at 149 Elm Street (203–432–2300; www.yale.edu/visitor); here, in New Haven's oldest surviving house, a white Colonial facing the town green, you can check current listings and pick up a map for a self-guided tour. Make sure it includes the **Beinecke Rare Book and Manuscript Library** a few zigzag blocks north at 121 Wall Street (203–432–2977), where printed treasures—including a Gutenberg Bible—and manuscripts are safeguarded in an unusual vault with translucent marble windows. Meander south through the late nineteenth-century Gothic "old campus" to reach the **Yale University Art Gallery** at 1111 Chapel Street (203–432–0600; www.yale.edu/artgallery), an 1832 institution now replete with some 100,000 objects, ranging from ancient to contemporary. Americans, from nineteenth-century realists like Eakins to the big names of abstract expressionism, are especially strong. Across the way at 1080 Chapel Street is the equally dazzling **Yale Center for British Art** (203–432–2800), whose holdings date from the reign of Elizabeth I to the present day, with a fine showing of Gainsborough, Reynolds, and Turner.

LUNCH: Union League Cafe, 1032 Chapel Street, New Haven; (203) 562–4299. Savoyard fare within the proletarianized 1854 headquarters of the exclusive Union League Club.

Afternoon

On your way back to the highway, check out the **Audubon Arts District,** centered on the **Creative Arts Workshop** studio/gallery complex at 80 Audubon Street (203–562–4927). You'll find a great many more shops and galleries, considerably more upscale, about an hour further southwest off I–95, in the ultra–Gold Coast town of **Westport.** You could pleasantly spend the rest of the day ogling recherché goods in the village's haute home decor shops.

DINNER AND LODGING: Inn at National Hall, 2 Post Road West, Westport; (203) 221–1351 or (800) NAT–HALL; www.innatnationalhall.com. Tour czar Arthur Tauck, a local, bought a crumbling Italianate 1873 bank at auction in the mid-eighties and transformed it, with the infusion of upwards of $18 million, into a showcase for fanciful decor in the English manor house mode; no luxury has been overlooked. Boston superstar chef Todd English now masterminds the in-house restaurant, **Miramar** (203–222–2267).

DAY 2

Morning

BREAKFAST: Inn at National Hall. Have it delivered to your room before relinquishing the fantasy.

Follow Routes 33 and 136 about 5 miles southwest to **South Norwalk,** a.k.a. "SoNo," a once-derelict neighborhood of century-old storefronts turned trendy shopping/shmoozing destination. The anchor, in mall-speak, is the **Maritime Aquarium at Norwalk,** 10 North Water Street (203–852–0700; www.maritimeaquarium.org), smaller than Boston's but easily as intriguing. Open daily from 10:00 A.M. to 5:00 P.M. (6:00 P.M. July and August), this aquarium/museum/IMAX theater complex, housed in a rehabbed waterside factory, is full of fascinating stuff, ranging from vintage diving suits to treasures recovered from the deep. Amid the changing special exhibits, you can always count on river otters cavorting, harbor seals swooping, sharks cruising, and flounders faking invisibility. Other highlights include a small-scale boat works and a couldn't-be-fresher oyster bar, presided over by Alexander Rummler's semi-naif 1937 mural depicting hard-working shuckers.

LUNCH: Ocean Drive, 128 Washington Street, Norwalk; (203) 855–1665. This stylish pretend beach club has winning ways with seafood.

Afternoon

Follow up with a forage at **United House Wrecking,** at 535 Hope Street in eastern **Stamford** (203–348–5371; www.unitedhousewrecking.com)—about 6 miles southwest off I–95's exit 6. Here you can browse five acres' worth of primo architectural salvage, with plenty of antiques and collectibles—from clawfoot bathtubs to seventeenth-century thrones—thrown in for good measure.

Stamford itself is a real city, kind of a mini-New York North. It even has its own **Whitney Museum of American Art at Champion,** at 1 Champion Plaza (203–358–7630). This small satellite features contemporary art and gallery talks Tuesday through Saturday from 11:00 A.M. to 5:00 P.M. and admission is free. North of town, via Route 137, is the refreshingly rural **Stamford Museum & Nature Center** at 39 Scofieldtown Road (203–322–1646; www.stamfordmuseum.org). Open Monday through Saturday 9:00 A.M. to 5:00 P.M. and Sunday 1:00 to 5:00 P.M., the complex encompasses 3 miles of nature trails covering 118 acres, a nineteenth-century working farm, and a cluster of art and natural history galleries.

A few miles southwest in **Greenwich,** the small but intriguing **Bruce Museum** at 1 Museum Drive (203–869–0376; www.brucemuseum.org) is similarly split: changing art and science exhibits command equal space. Its hours are Tuesday to Saturday 10:00 A.M. to 5:00 P.M. and Sunday 1:00 to 5:00 P.M.

DINNER AND LODGING: Homestead Inn, 420 Field Point Road, Greenwich; (203) 869–7500; www.homesteadinn.com. This 1799 farmhouse turned Carpenter Gothic Victorian confection has long been a favored getaway for jaded New Yorkers, and superb French cuisine at Thomas Henkelmann's namesake restaurant (www.thomashenkelmann.com) only adds to the allure.

DAY 3

Morning

BREAKFAST: Homestead Inn.

Superaffluent Greenwich, oddly, isn't the best of shopping towns, but the same can't be said of **New Canaan,** another high-bracket enclave about 10 miles northeast via Routes 1 and 106. Browse away while the stores are safely locked (usually till noon on Sunday). The antique stores are exemplary if pricy, and the **Whitney Shop** at 100 Elm Street (203–966–4566) offers a veritable crash course in low-profile preppienalia.

BRUNCH: Silvermine Tavern, 194 Perry Avenue, Norwalk; (203) 847–4558; www.silverminetavern.com. The twenty-entree spread at this 1785 tavern is tough to resist, as are the justly legendary sticky buns.

Afternoon

Recover with a constitutional around the surrounding country lanes, dotted with handsome Colonial holdovers. There might be something interesting showing at the **Silvermine Guild Arts Center** at 1037 Silvermine Road (203–966–6668; www.silvermineart.org). A few miles northeast in **Wilton,** a self-guided walking tour of the fifty-seven-acre **Weir Farm National Historic Site** at 735 Nod Hill Road (203–834–1896; www.nps.gov/wefa), open daily in-season from 8:30 A.M. to 5:00 P.M., affords glimpses of the landscape that inspired resident artist J. Alden Weir and such colleagues as Childe Hassam and Albert Pinkham Ryder. Another 7 miles north, in Ridgefield, the **Aldrich Museum of Contemporary Art** at 258 Main Street (203–438–4519; www. aldrichart. org) offers an ever-changing, up-to-the-minute array within a dramatically gutted 1783 clapboard house. The galleries, as well as a two-acre sculpture garden, are open Tuesday through Sunday noon to 5:00 P.M.

DINNER: Elms Inn, 500 Main Street, Ridgefield; (203) 438–2541; www.elms inn.com. It's worth postponing your homeward journey—figure on about three hours along I–84 and the Mass Pike—to partake of chef Brendan Walsh's New American artistry. And consider staying over: the 1799 inn has been refurbished to keep pace with the stellar talent in the kitchen.

THERE'S MORE

Adventures. You could explore the Norwalk Islands with Small Boat Shop Kayak Tours at 144 Water Street (203–854–5223). Also in Norwalk, at thirty-three-acre Calf Pasture Beach (203–854–7806), you can rent a kayak, sailboard, or sailboat.

Excursions. Schooner, Inc. at 60 South Water Street in New Haven (203–865–1737; http://schoonersoundlearning.org) arranges charter cruises aboard the 91-foot gaff-rigged *Quinnipiack*. The Norwalk Seaport Association's *Island Girl* (203–838–9444; www.seaport.org) heads from South Norwalk's Maritime Aquarium out to the Norwalk Islands, with a stopover at the Sheffield Island Lighthouse. The Aquarium's R/V *Oceanic* (203–852–0700; www.maritimeaquarium.org) offers Marine Life Study Cruises on Long Island Sound. *SoundWaters*, a replica schooner berthed at the Brewers Yacht Haven Marine Center in Stamford (203–323–1978), also sets out on hands-on eco-cruises.

Historic houses. The 1732 Bush-Holley House at 39 Strickland Road in the Cos Cob section of Greenwich (203–869–6899) is notable not just for its antiquity, but for its role as the site of the first Impressionist colony in Connecticut, predating Old Lyme.

Kid stuff. New Haven has the Connecticut Children's Museum at 22 Wall Street (203–562–KIDS; www.childrensbuilding.org) and the 1911 Lighthouse Point Carousel at 2 Lighthouse Road (203–946–8790). Children will also enjoy, and be edified by, Yale's Peabody Museum of Natural History at 170 Whitney Avenue (203–432–5050; www.peabody.yale.edu), featuring dioramas and the Great Hall of Dinosaurs. Bridgeport has not only the Barnum Museum at 820 Main Street (203–331–1104; www.barnum-museum. org), a grandiose self-monument by the nonpareil promoter, but a hands-

Greenwich's Bush-Holley House attracted Impressionists.

on Discovery Museum at 4500 Park Avenue (203–372–3521; www.
discoverymuseum.org) and the Beardsley Zoological Gardens at 1875
Noble Avenue (203–394–6565; www.beardsleyzoo.org).

Nature preserves. Sherwood Island State Park in Westport (203–226–6983)
contains a 1½-mile, swimmable beach where fishing and scuba diving are
allowed and interpretive nature programs are offered. Devil's Den, a Nature
Conservancy property at 33 Pent Road in Weston (203–226–4991;
http://nature.org), covers 1,756 acres with 20 miles of walking trails.

Performing arts. New Haven's Long Wharf Theatre at 222 Sargent Drive
(203–787–4282; www.longwharf.org) has long been a top venue for classic
as well as new plays. The Yale Repertory Theatre at 222 York Street (203–
432–1234; www.yale.edu/yalerep) serves as a showcase for the Yale School
of Drama. New Haven arenas for traveling shows include the Shubert The-

ater at 247 College Street (888–736–2663; www.shubert.com) and the Palace Performing Arts Center at 246 College Street (203–789–2120). Toad's Place at 300 York Street in New Haven (203–624–TOAD; www.toadsplace. com) books some big rock acts for a reasonable cover; the freebie New Haven *Advocate* (www.newhavenadvocate.com) can fill you in on other venues. The Westport Country Playhouse at 25 Powers Court (203–227–4177) has been a notable strawhat theater since the forties. Also in Westport, the Levitt Pavilion for the Performing Arts at 260 Compo Road South (203–226–7600) offers free evening entertainment throughout the summer. The Stamford Center for the Arts at 307 Atlantic Street (203–325–4466; www.onlyatsca.com) attracts notable performers in every genre.

SPECIAL EVENTS

Early April. Film Fest New Haven; (203) 776–6789; www.filmfest.org. A chance to catch the up-and-coming indies.

Late June. International Festival of Arts & Ideas, New Haven; (888) ART–IDEA; www.artidea.org. A cultural free-for-all in various media.

Early August. SoNo Arts Celebration, South Norwalk; (800) 866–7916; www.sonoarts.org. Hundreds of performing and visual artists show their stuff.

OTHER RECOMMENDED RESTAURANTS AND LODGINGS

Greenwich

Baang Café, 1191 East Putnam Avenue; (203) 637–2114. Dynamite Cal-Asian fusion.

Bleu, 339 Greenwich Avenue; (203) 661–9377; http://bleu-cafe.com. A cutting-edge bistro.

Dome, 253 Greenwich Avenue; (203) 661–3443. New American invention in a dramatic tiled vault.

Mediterraneo, 366 Greenwich Avenue; (203) 629–4747. A justly popular spot covering the whole Mediterranean rim—eastern coast as well.

Meli-Melo, 362 Greenwich Avenue; (203) 629–6153. A tiny, creative creperie.

Rebecca's, 265 Glenville Road; (203) 532–9270. Ultra-sophisticated Nouvelle American.

Restaurant Jean-Louis, 61 Lewis Street; (203) 622–8450; www.restaurantjean louis.com. *Maitre cuisinier* Jean-Louis Gerin presents stellar classic/contemporary fare.

64 Greenwich Avenue, 64 Greenwich Avenue; (203) 861–6400. A townhouse with a moneyed air makes a lively setting for New Mediterranean artistry.

New Canaan

Bluewater Cafe, 15 Elm Street; (203) 972–1799. Tiny and just right, a neo-bistro specializing in mostly Mediterranean-style seafood.

Gates, 10 Forest Street; (203) 966–8666. Fun food and a lively crowd.

New Haven

Atticus Bookstore Cafe; 1082 Chapel Street; (203) 776–4040. The ideal place for a bookish nosh.

Frank Pepe Pizzeria Napoletana, 157 Wooster Street; (203) 865–5762. Classic pizza since 1925.

The Inn at Oyster Point, 104 Howard Avenue; (203) 773–334 or 86–OYSTERPT; www.oysterpointinn.com. Luxurious quarters minutes from downtown.

Louis' Lunch, 263 Crown Street; (203) 562–5507. Serving hamburgers—purportedly the first and still resolutely plain, on toast—since 1895.

Roomba, 1044 Chapel Street; (203) 562–7666. Exuberant Latino fare.

Scoozzi, 1104 Chapel Street; (203) 776–8268; www.scoozzi.com. Rich North Italian cuisine, and a Sunday jazz brunch.

Three Chimneys Inn, 1201 Chapel Street; (203) 789–1201 or (800) 443–1554; www.threechimneysinn.com. An 1870 mansion turned luxury urban inn.

Zinc, 964 Chapel Street; (203) 866–0507; www.zincfood.com. Fusion-zapped excitement, by the green.

Ridgefield

Biscotti, 3 Big Shop Lane; (203) 431–3637. An intimate—and popular—rustic-Italian trattoria housed in an eighteenth-century blacksmith shop.

Rowayton

The Restaurant at Rowayton Seafood, 89 Rowayton Avenue; (203) 866–4488; www.rowaytonseafood.com. Nouveau seafood with a water view.

South Norwalk

Barcelona, 63-65 North Main Street; (203) 899–0088. Mediterranean tapas and more.

The Brewhouse, 13 Marshall Street; (203) 866–1339. The New England Brewing Company's spacious brick-walled brewpub offers interesting cuisine, much of it hops-enhanced.

Côte d'Azur, 86 Washington Street; (203) 855–8900. Country-style coastal French.

Habana, 70 North Main Street; (203) 852–9790. A Cuban contender.

Kazu, 64 North Main Street; (203) 866–7492. Japanese delicacies in a festive setting.

Pasta Nostra, 116 Washington Street; (203) 854–9700; www.pastanostra.com. A convivial trattoria.

Stamford

Beacon Restaurant, 183 Harbor Drive; (203) 327–4600. Legendary new York chef Waldy Malouf lends staid Stamford unexpected panache.

Ocean 211, 211 Summer Street; (203) 973–0494. An elegant townhouse dedicated to new-wave seafood.

Weston

Cobb's Mill Inn, 12 Old Mill Road; (203) 227–7221 or (800) 640–9365; www.cobbsmillinn.com. Evolved Continental teasting in an eighteenth-century watermill.

Westport

Acqua, 43 Main Street; (203) 222–8899. Mediterreanean mastery.

Bridge Cafe, 5 Riverside Avenue; (203) 226–4800. Dazzling New American fare, with river views.

DaPietro's, 36 Riverside Avenue; (203) 454–1213. Stellar Italian, on a small scale.

The Inn at Longshore, 260 Compo Road South; (203) 226–3316. This old-fashioned inn on the shore has an exciting Pacific Rim restaurant, Splash (203–454–7798).

Momos, 25 Powers Court; (203) 222–9096. Cool jazz and hot fusion cuisine.

FOR MORE INFORMATION

Coastal Fairfield County Convention & Visitor Bureau, 383 Main Avenue, Norwalk, CT 06581; (203) 840–0770 or (800) 866–7925; www.visit fairfieldco.org.

Connecticut Office of Tourism, 505 Hudson Street, Hartford, CT 06106; (860) 270–8080 or (800) CT–BOUND; www. ctbound.org.

Greater New Haven Convention and Visitors Bureau, 59 Elm Street, New Haven, CT 06510; (203) 777–8550 or (800) 332–STAY; www.new havencvb.org.

NEW YORK
ESCAPE

ESCAPE ONE

NEW YORK

New York City

A PARALLEL UNIVERSE, PLUS

2 NIGHTS

*Hot neighborhoods • Boutique hotels • Low-cost haute couture
Urbane flea markets • First-rank restaurants*

Winged but unbowed, New York is nothing if not resilient. Even in the wake of September 11, the city is flying high and steadily adding to its roster of attractions. It's patently impossible to "do" New York in a weekend, and presumptuous to dictate what warrants doing. Everyone has his or her own New York: favorite haunts, neighborhoods, pursuits. What follows is a précis of my New York—a somewhat haphazard and constantly shifting mix of touristy and recherché, cheapo and luxurious.

DAY 1

Morning

Head out of Boston by about 8:00 A.M. and you can pull into New York in time for lunch: it's only 200 miles. Of the many possible routes, we've found the following the least stressful and most scenic: Take the Mass Pike to I-84 West; follow signs to Route I-91 South just short of Hartford; pick up Route 15 West (the Wilbur Cross Parkway, becoming the Merritt); take the Cross County Parkway a few miles west to the Sawmill Parkway south; then opt for Henry Hudson Parkway, which will take you straight down the western side of Manhattan, along the river. Cars in the city tend to be more bother than boon, so we usually ditch ours on the Upper West Side, where alternate side-of-the-street parking yields spots good for the weekend.

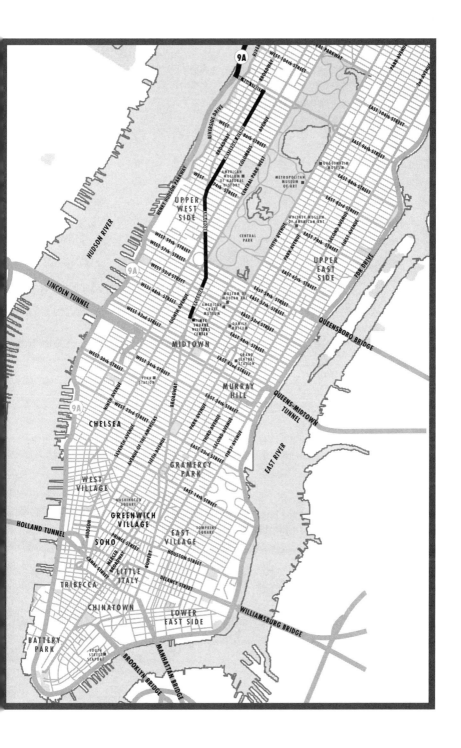

First-timers might want to make a beeline for the **Times Square Visitors Center** housed in the rehabbed 1925 Embassy Theatre at 1560 Broadway near 47th Street (212–768–1560; www.timessquarebid.org). Here you can load up on maps and brochures, pick up a MetroCard (subway/bus pass), and buy full-price theater tickets; discounted day-of-performance counterparts are available at the **TKTS** booth across the street (212–221–0013; www.tdf.org). This area's not really representative of the richness the city has to offer, though, so keep moseying south.

Increasingly strollworthy is **Chelsea,** an area roughly comparable to Boston's South End. Nearly two hundred art galleries have cropped up here, primarily between Tenth and Eleventh Avenues from 22nd to 26th Street. The avant-garde **Dia Center for the Arts** acts as an anchor at 548 West 22nd (212–989–5566; www.diacenter.org); it's open Wednesday through Sunday noon to 6:00 P.M., and boasts a cool rooftop coffee bar. Collectors, serious and otherwise, will want to scan the twelve floors of the **Chelsea Antiques Building** at 110 West 25th Street (212–929–0909; www.chelseaantiques.com), as well as **The Showplace** at number 40 (212–741–8520). **Jeffrey NY** at 449 West 14th Street (212–206–1272) adds a flash of pricy, uptown chic amid the meatpacking district.

Cruising further downtown, you'll pass through **Greenwich Village** into **SoHo**—crassly commercialized since its hippie-era heyday as a low-rent arts frontier, but still great fun to wander around.

LUNCH: Le Pain Quotidien, 100 Grand Street; (212) 625–9009. Pop in for a light meal, haute communal-style.

Afternoon

Just explore the small grid that is SoHo. We usually start with a pilgrimage to the **Earth Room** at 141 Wooster Street (212–229–2744; www.diacenter. org/ltproj/er), a 1977 Walter DeMaria installation that consists of a gallery filled with dirt, pure dirt, and nothing but dirt—it's oddly compelling. Also worth seeking out along Wooster is the **Drawing Center** gallery at number 35 (212–219–2166). One block east, Greene Street offers another vein of recherché shops. Check out **Zona** at number 97 for imaginative home accessories (212–925–6750) and **Vivienne Westwood** at number 71 (212–334–5200) for outrageous tongue-in-chic. The **Painting Center,** upstairs at 52 Greene (212-343-1060; www.thepaintingcenter.com), is another must-see gallery.

Two blocks farther east, at 575 Broadway, you'll find the **Guggenheim Museum SoHo** (212–423–3500; www.guggenheim.org), a satellite open Thursday through Monday from 11:00 A.M. to 6:00 P.M. A few doors up, at number 583, is the **New Museum of Contemporary Art** (212–219–1222; www.newmuseum.org), open Tuesday through Sunday from noon to 6:00 P.M., till 8:00 on Thursday evening (free); it's reliably provocative.

DINNER AND LODGING: Mercer Hotel, 147 Mercer Street; (212) 966-6060. The first boutique hotel to hit SoHo, this 1890 Romanesque Revival building with forties moderne interiors remains *the* place to stay. Handily, the best place to eat is in the basement: in the **Mercer Kitchen** at 99 Prince Street (212-966-5454; www.starchefs.com/jeangeorgesmercer) where superchef Jean-Georges Vongerichten marries SoHo cool and Provençale warmth.

DAY 2

Morning

BREAKFAST: The Mercer Kitchen. The woodstoves have been working all night to yield applewood-smoked bacon and other breakfast delights.

Devote today to an uptown museum crawl, with a sideline of shopping and gawking. If you visit every single venue listed, it may indeed end up a crawl, so peruse the newspaper/magazine listings and choose judiciously. You might start with the small but delightful—and free—**Dahesh Museum,** 601 Fifth Avenue at 48th Street (212–759–0606; www.daheshmuseum.org), which specializes in European academic art and is open Tuesday to Saturday 11:00 A.M. to 6:00 P.M. Then leap into the twentieth century at the **MoMA Design Store,** 44 West 53rd Street (212–767–1050; www.momastore.com); the **Museum of Modern Art** itself has taken up temporary quarters in Queens. Across the street, at 40 West 53rd, is the **American Craft Museum** (212–956–3535; www.americancraftmuseum.org), open daily 10:00 A.M. to 6:00 P.M. Back across the street again, at numer 45, visit the dazzling new headquarters for the **American Folk Art Museum** (212–977–7170; www.folkartmuseum.org), open Tuesday through Sunday 10:00 A.M. to 6:00 P.M., Fridays till 8:00.

After a de rigueur peek into **Henri Bendel,** 712 Fifth Avenue at 56th Street (212–247–1100 or 800–HBENDEL) and the **Tiffany** windows at 727 Fifth (212–755–8000), it's fun to amble up Madison Avenue, drooling over the lineup of luxe emporia, including **Barneys** at number 660 near 61st (212–826–8900).

Jog parkward to take in the **Frick Collection** of priceless paintings at 1 East 70th Street (212–288–0700; www.frick.org). This ultracivilized refuge—complete with garden court—is open Tuesday through Saturday 10:00 A.M. to 6:00 P.M. and Sunday 1:00 to 6:00 P.M.; it's the official start of "Museum Mile." You can do some more window-shopping on your way up to the **Whitney Museum of American Art** at 945 Madison Avenue at 75th Street (212–570–3676 or 877–WHITNEY; www.whitney.org), open Tuesday-Thursday and Saturday-Sunday 11:00 A.M. to 6:00 P.M., and Friday 1:00 to 9:00 P.M.

LUNCH: Sarabeth, 945 Madison Avenue; (212) 570–3670. Grab something quick and luscious in the Whitney's lower level.

Afternoon

With a brief, optional detour to the **Allan Stone Gallery** at 113 East 90th Street (212–987–4997; www.allanstone.com), a rare pocket of skilled realism, zip up to the **Cooper-Hewitt National Museum of Design** at 2 East 91st Street (212–849–8400; www.si.edu/ndm); ever-changing exhibits at the grand gated manse are viewable Tuesday 10:00 A.M. to 9:00 P.M., Wednesday to Saturday 10:00 A.M. to 5:00 P.M., and Sunday noon to 5:00 P.M. Two blocks south, at 1083 Fifth Avenue, the **National Academy of Design** (212–369–4880; www. nationalacademy.org) puts on interesting shows; the hours are Wednesday-Thursday noon to 5:00 P.M., Friday 10:00 A.M. to 6:00 P.M., Saturday-Sunday 10:00 A.M. to 5:00 P.M. Three blocks south is the must-see **Solomon R. Guggenheim Museum** at 1071 Fifth Avenue (212–423–3500; www.guggen heim. org), open Friday and Saturday 9:00 A.M. to 8:00 P.M. and Sunday through Wednesday till 6:00 P.M. Best approach: take the elevator to the top, and swirl down. Open Tuesday through Sunday from 9:30 A.M. to 5:30 P.M., and till 9:00 P.M. on Friday and Saturday, the massive **Metropolitan Museum of Art,** 1000 Fifth Avenue at 82nd Street (212–535–7710; www.metmuseum.org), is worth at least a week's perusal, so do the best you can, before heading toward Times Square, ideally to catch a play.

DINNER: West Bank Cafe, 407 West 42nd Street at Ninth Avenue; (212) 695–6909. Pre- or posttheater, celebrity sightings are virtually guaranteed at this intimate spot, whose excellent fare seems to be priced for struggling thespians. It even has a miniscule theater space downstairs, where moonlighting stars and stars-in-the-making sometimes put on their own shows.

LODGING: The Mansfield, 12 West 44th Street; (212) 944–6050 or (800) 255–5167; www.mansfieldhotel.com. Just enough removed from the din of Times Square, this 1904 Beaux Arts bachelors' club has been beautifully updated.

DAY 3

Morning

BREAKFAST: Sarabeth's Kitchen, 423 Amsterdam Avenue near 80th Street; (212) 496–6280. Head to this cozy storefront on the Upper West Side for the ultimate citified country breakfast, served day-long.

Then run, ride, or skate it off: **Central Park**'s looping scenic drives are closed to traffic on Sunday. Allot a few hours for the **American Museum of Natural History** on Central Park West at West 79th Street (212–769–5100; www. amnh.org), open daily 10:00 A.M. to 6:00 P.M., and till 9:00 P.M. on Friday and Saturday. What with the dinos, gemstones, and dioramas, you'll never manage to see it all, so you'll just have to come back.

LUNCH: Zabar's, 2245 Broadway near 80th Street; (212) 787–2000. Before hitting the West Side Highway to head home the way you came in, pick up a picnic-to-go, as well as longer-term provisions, at the nonpareil deli. Cart your moveable feast to the **Cloisters,** the Metropolitan's medieval repository at 190th Street (212–923–3700; www.metmuseum.org), open Tuesday through Sunday from 9:30 A.M. to 5:00 P.M.; or eat in, at the on-site **New Leaf Cafe** (212–568–5323). Bidding goodbye to Manhattan, enjoy a rarefied section of the Bronx: the **Wave Hill** estate at 675 West 252nd Street in Riverdale (718–549–3200; www.wavehill.org), open Tuesday through Sunday in-season from 9:00 A.M. to 5:30 P.M., proffers twenty-eight acres of glorious gardens. Looming across the Hudson are the enticing green cliffs of the Palisades.

THERE'S MORE

Aerial adventures. Survey the skyscrapers with Liberty Helicopters, out of 30th Street and Twelfth Avenue (212–967–6464; www.libertyhelicopters.com).

Art and antiques. New York's elite do their bidding at Sotheby's, 1334 York Avenue at 72nd Street (212–606–7000; www.sothebys.com) or Christie's at 20 Rockefeller Plaza (212–636–2000; www.christies.com). Lesser mortals—as well as incognito VIPs—spend their weekends picking through the

Annex Antiques Fair & Flea Market at Sixth Avenue between 24th and 27th Street (212–243–5343) and the SoHo Antiques Fair at the corner of Broadway and Grand (212–682–2000).

Bargain shopping. Century 21 at 22 Cortland Street in the Wall Street area (212–227–9092) is a stylish, up-to-the-minute version of Filene's Basement. Sunday is peak browsing time for the hundreds of discount shops, with a sprinkling of boutiques, that constitute the Lower East Side Shopping District; start from the visitor center at 261 Broome Street between Allen and Orchard (212–226–9010; www.lowereastsideny.com).

Comestibles. For a breath of fresh country air, in-season, visit the Union Square Green Market at Broadway and 16th Street (212–477–3220). For a fun, knowledgeable entree to New York's foodie scene, sign on with Maddie Tomei of Savory Sojourns (212–691–7314 or 888–9SAVORY; www. savorysojourns.com).

Family fun. For a free harbor cruise past the Statue of Liberty, hop the Staten Island Ferry at Whitehall and South Streets (718–815–BOAT). South Street Seaport is a Faneuil Hall–style complex near the old Fulton Fish Market; get oriented at the visitors center at 12 Fulton Street (212–SEA-PORT; www.southstseaport.com). You don't really need children as an excuse to visit the Central Park Zoo and Wildlife Center off Fifth Avenue at 64th Street (212–861–6030; www.centralpark.org), but they'll definitely enhance your experience on the nearby Carousel (212–879–0244). The Children's Museum of Manhattan, at 212 West 83rd Street near Broadway (212–721–1223; www.cmom.org), guarantees participatory fun.

Museums. The Smithsonian Institution's National Museum of the American Indian at 1 Bowling Green (212–514–3700; www.si.edu/nmai) occupies a nineteenth-century customs house. To get a tactile sense of what New York was like a century ago, visit the Lower East Side Tenement Museum at 90 Orchard Street near Broome Street (212–431–0233; www.tenement.org). Both the Pierpont Morgan Library at 29 East 36th Street (212–685–0610; www.morganlibrary.org) and the New York Public Library at 455 Fifth Avenue at 40th Street (212–340–0833; www.nypl.org) mount outstanding exhibits. Media mavens will also want to check out the International Center for Photography, 1133 Avenue of the Americas at 43rd Street (212–860–1777; www.icop.org) and the Museum of Television & Radio at 25 West 52nd Street

(212–621–6600; www.mtr.org). The Museum of the City of New York, 1220 Fifth Avenue at 103rd Street (212–534–1672; www.mcny.org), hosts a changing array of fascinating exhibits.

Performing arts. Broadway is, of course, a universal draw, and you can find out about every single production, even those touring, at the Broadway Line: 212–302–4111 or 888–BROADWAY (www.broadway.org). You'll also find all sorts of lively arts flourishing off the Great White Way—way off, in the case of the Brooklyn Academy of Music at 30 Lafayette Avenue (718–636–4100; www.bam.org). Whatever is at the Public Theater at 425 Lafayette Street (212–539–8500; www.publictheater.org) is bound to be interesting; Joe's Pub—named for founder Joseph Papp—hosts up-and-coming entertainers. Other venues to check out include the perennially avant-garde Performing Garage at 33 Wooster Street (212–966–3651; www.thewoostergroup.org) and La MaMa E.T.C. at 74A East 4th Street (212–475–7710; www.lamama.org); the Mamet-inspired Atlantic Theatre at 336 West 20th Street (212–645–1242); the American Place Theatre at 111 West 46th Street (212–239–6200; www.americanplcetheatre.org); the many small theaters clustered along 42nd Street between Ninth and Tenth Avenue; and the Vivian Beaumont Theatre at Lincoln Center, 150 West 65th Street (212–362–7600; www.lct.org). Lincoln Center is also home to the Metropolitan Opera (212–362–6000; www.metopera.org), the New York Philharmonic (212–721–6500; www.newyorkphilharmonic.org) and the New York City Ballet (212–870–5570; www.nycballet.com). The prime spot for modern dance is the Joyce Theater, 175 Eighth Avenue at 19th Street (212–242–0800; www.joyce.org), and its satellite, Joyce SoHo at 155 Mercer Street (212–431–9233). Music-lovers will naturally gravitate to Carnegie Hall, at 57th Street and Seventh Avenue (212–247–7800; www.carnegiehall.org). The 92nd Street Y, at 1395 Lexington Avenue (212–415–5500; www.92ndsty.org), hosts stellar literary readings and a varied roster of performers.

The sporting life. The Hudson River Park Trust (212–661–8740; www.hudsonrivertrust.org) has begun converting 550 acres of riverside, from Battery Park to 59th Street, into a recreational oasis. Chelsea Piers, spanning thirty acres between 17th and 23rd Streets (212–336–6666; www.chelseapiers.com), has facilities for just about every urban and even suburban sport imaginable, from bowling to batting cages. For further bowling, in high ironic style, check out Bowlmor Lanes at 110 University Place in the Village (212–255–8188; www.bowlmor.com). In winter, ice skating— either at Rockefeller Center (212–332–7654) or the Wollman Rink in the southeastern corner of Central Park (212–439–6900)—is a picturesque requirement. For two-wheel transportation, with optional escort, hook up with Central Park Bicycle Tours & Rentals at 2 Columbus Circle (212– 541–8759; www.centralparkbiketour.com). English-style riders will want to explore Central Park's 4½ miles of bridle trails atop a mount from the Claremont Riding Academy at 175 West 89th Street (212–724–5100).

SPECIAL EVENTS

Late May. The New Yorker Festival, Citywide; (212) 286–5486; www. newyorker.com. Readings and gatherings.

Mid-June to August. Shakespeare in the Park; (212) 539–8500; www. publictheater.org. Captivating—and free.

Late September. Broadway Flea Market, Midtown; (212) 840–0770. Shubert Alley turns AIDS-action souk.

OTHER RECOMMENDED RESTAURANTS AND LODGINGS

Lower Manhattan

Alison on Dominick, 38 Dominick Street; (212) 727–1188; www.alisonon dominick.com. *Intime* country-French perfection.

Annisa, 13 Barrow Street; (212) 741–6699. Anita Lo's exquisite fusion.

Babbo, 110 Waverly Place; (212) 777–0303. A handsome, spacious setting for Mario Batali's daring neo-American/Italian artistry.

Balthazar, 80 Spring Street; (212) 965–1414. Keith McNally's madly popular French-feel bistro.

Bayard's, 1 Hanover Square; (212) 514–9454. Classic French cuisine in the elegant 1851 Cotton Exchange.

Bouley, 120 West Broadway; (212) 964–8362. David Bouley's x nonpareil New French cuisine.

Chanterelle, 2 Harrison Street; (212) 966–6960. A temple to evolved New American cuisine.

Danube, 30 Hudson Street; (212) 791–3771. Bouley celestializes Austro-Hungarian cuisine.

Gotham Bar & Grill, 12 East 12th Street; (212) 620–4020. Alfred Portale's breeding ground for brilliant culinary talent.

The Harrison, 355 Greenwich Street; (212) 274–9310. A clubby/romantic cousin of Chelsea's Red Cat.

Home, 20 Cornelia Street; (212) 243–9579. David Paige's cozy pretend farmhouse.

Inside, 9 Jones Street; (212) 229–9999. Anne Rosenzweig whips up deceptively casual food.

James Beard House, 167 West 12th Street; (212) 675–4984 or (800) 36–BEARD, www.jamesbeard.org. Where the toop chefs in the country show their stuff.

Layla, 211 West Broadway; (212) 431–0700; www.myriadrestaurantgroup.com. Drew Nieporent does Middle Eastern.

Lupa, 160 Thompson Street; (212) 982–5089. Babbo's bargain offshoot.

Montrachet, 239 West Broadway; (212) 219–2777; www. myriadrestaurant-group.com. Nieporent's still-stellar 1985 flagship.

Nobu and Next Door Nobu, 105 Hudson Street; (212) 219–0500 and (212) 334–4445; www.myriadrestaurantgroup.com. A modernist setting for Nobu Matasuhisa's spectacular sushi and more.

Odeon, 145 West Broadway; (212) 233–0507. This Americanized art deco bistro has catered to an artsy crowd since 1980.

Pastis, 9 Ninth Avenue; (212) 929–4844. Keith McNally's bistro-*vérité*.

71 Clinton Fresh Food, 71 Clinton Street; (212) 614–5960. A little Lower East side gem, manned by Vongerichten protégé Wylie Dufresne.

60 Thompson, 60 Thompson Street; (212) 431–0400 or (877) 431–0400; www.60thompson.com. A garage turned boutique hotel with a fetching fusion restaurant, Thom (Thai for "soup").

SoHo Grand Hotel, 310 West Broadway; (212) 965-3000 or (800) 965-3000; www.sohogrand.com. Luxury, cachet—plus pampering for pets.

Tribeca Grand Hotel, 2 Avenue of the Americas; (212) 519– 6600 or (877) 519–6600; www.tribecagrand.com. Equally cool.

TriBeCa Grill, 375 Greenwich Street; (212) 941–3900; www.myriadrestaurantgroup.com. A stylish commissary where downtown movie honchos mix with mere mortals.

Vine, 25 Broad Street; (212) 344–8463. Vigorous new American fare near Wall Street.

Downtown (14th to 42nd Streets)

Artisanal, 2 Park Avenue at 32nd Street; (212) 725–8585. Picholine chef Terrance Brennan's artful hommage to aged milk.

AZ, 21 West 17th Street; (212) 691–8888. Glorious fusion from Patricia Yeo.

Beppe, 4 East 22nd Street; (212) 982–8422. Rustic Tuscan to sigh for.

Chicama, 35 East 18th Street; (212) 505–2333. Douglas Rodriguez demonstrates South American flair within the ABC design complex; across the hall, Pipa (212–677–2233) serves tapas.

Commune, 12 East 22nd Street; (212) 777–2600. Global noshing amid sleek mingling.

Craft, 43 East 19th Street; (212) 780–0880; www.craftrestaurant.com. Chef-owner Tom Colicchio adds polish to superb provender.

Eleven Madison Park, 11 Madison Avenue at 24th Street; (212) 889–0905. Danny Meyer's tri-level semi-deco refectory.

Empire Diner, 210 Tenth Avenue at 22nd Street; (212) 243–2736. A 1929 chrome survivor favored by artists and actors; open 24-7.

Gramercy Tavern, 42 East 20th Street; (212) 477–0777; www.gramercytavern.com. Danny Meyer and Tom Colicchio collaborate on luscious, forward-looking fare.

Half King, 505 West 23rd Street; (212) 462–4300. Sebastian (The Perfect Storm) Junger's lit-minded pub.

The Library, 299 Madison Avenue at 41st Street; (877) 793–READ; www.libraryhotel.com. A beautifully restored mansion-style hotel dedicated to the ten major categories of the Dewey Decimal System.

Mesa Grill, 102 Fifth Avenue near 16th Street; (212) 807–7400; www.mesagrill.com. Bobby Flay's signature restaurant, the site of some bold southwestern experimentation.

Morgans Hotel, 237 Madison Avenue near 37th Street; (212) 686–0300. Ian Schrager's groundbreaking boutique hotel shelters Asia de Cuba (212–736–7755), featuring jazzy Asian/Latino food.

The Park, 118 Tenth Avenue near 17th Street; (212) 352–3313. A mad amalgam of environments makes for a lively bar scene, and the food's fine, too.

The Red Cat, 117 Tenth Avenue near 23rd Street; (212) 242–1122. An exuberant cafe to suit resurgent Chelsea.

The Roger Williams, 131 Madison Avenue at 31st Street; (212) 448–7000 or (888) 448–7788; www.rogerwilliamshotel.com. Naturalist rooms, plus a grand modern lobby.

Union Square Cafe, 21 East 16th Street; (212) 243–4020. Danny Meyer's Cal/Ital standout, an enduring and invariably dazzling delight.

Verbena, 54 Irving Place near 17th Street; (212) 260–5454; www.verbenarestaurant.com. Lovely food, plus the city's most romantic patio.

W New York-The Court, 130 East 39th Street; (212) 685–1100, www.whotels.com. Luxe minimalism, accompanied by Drew Nieporent's scene-setter restaurant Icon (212–592–8888).

Midtown (42nd to 59th Streets)

Alain Ducasse at the Essex House, 155 West 58th Street; (212) 265–7300. A quirky U.S. foothold for the celebrated French chef.

The Algonquin, 59 West 44th Street; (212) 840–6800. Still attracting litterateurs, as well as cabaret fans.

Beacon, 25 West 56th Street; (212) 332–0500; www.beaconnyc.com. Waldy Malouf's open kitchen occupies the heart of this sleek international bistro.

The Benjamin, 125 East 50th Street; (212) 320–8002 or (888) 4–BENJAMIN; www.thebenjamin.com. This boutique hotel hosts Larry Forgione's lead restaurant, An American Place (212–888–5650).

Bryant Park Hotel, 40 West 40th Street; (212) 869–0100 or 877–640–9300, www. bryantparkhotel.com. This snazzy black-brick boutique hotel has a handsome, hip restaurant, Ilo (212–642–2255).

Chambers Hotel, 15 West 56th Street; (212) 974–5656, www.chambers-hotel. com. The minimalist rooms may look like a rich kids' dorm, but the in-house restaurant, Town (212–582–4445), is modern elegance incarnate.

Citarella the Restaurant, 1240 Avenue of the Americas at 49th Street; (212) 332–1515; www.citarella.com. For fans of the gourmet groceries–especially the fish.

DB Bistro Moderne, 55 West 44th Street; (212) 391–2400; www.danielnyc. com. At Daniel Boulud's theatre district eatery, the house hamburger comes with foie gras and truffles.

Esca, 402 West 43rd St; (212) 564–7272. Superb, understated Mediterranean seafood.

The Fairmont Plaza, Fifth Avenue at 59th Street; (212) 759–3000; www.fair-mont.com. The height of luxury as of 1907 and still inimitable—like its fictional *enfant terrible* in residence, Eloise.

Felidia, 243 East 58th Street; (212) 758–1479; www.lidiasitaly.com. Featuring Lidia Bastianich's award-garnering Listrian cuisine.

Flatotel, 135 West 52nd Street; (212) 887–9400 or (800) FLATOTEL; www. flatotel.com. Spacious Europeanate "flats" with every comfort, including Airon chairs and mini-microwaves.

The Four Seasons, 99 East 52nd Street; (212) 754–9494; http://fourseasons. citysearch.com. *The* place for power lunching, designed by Philip Johnson in 1959.

Four Seasons Hotel, 57 East 57th Street; (212) 758–5700; www.fourseasons. com/newyorkfs. A dazzlingly urbane 1993 Pei design, incorporating the restaurant Fifty Seven Fifty Seven (212–748–5757).

Hotel Elysée, 60 East 54th Street; (212) 753–1066. A Europeanate gem and home to the Monkey Bar (212–838–2600), a forties-style supper club.

Hudson, 356 West 58th Street; (212) 554–6000 or (800) 444–4786, www.
hudsonhotel.com. Another Schrager/Starck hotel/playground, apotheo-
sized in the neo-communal Hudson Cafeteria (212–554–6500).

The Iroquois New York, 49 West 44 Street; (212) 840–3080 or (800) 332–7220;
www.iriquoisny.com. A theatre district oldie, updated and treated to a
seductive little restaurant, Triomphe (212–453–4233).

Le Bernardin, 155 West 55th Street; (212) 489–1515; www.le-bernardin.com.
Clarion seafoods.

Lutece, 249 East 50th Street; (212) 752–2225. Exquisite nouvelleries in an
ivory-toned pretend garden.

The Michelangelo, 152 West 51st Street at Seventh Avenue; (212) 765–1900
or (800) 237–0990; www.michelangelohotel.com. Italianate luxury.

The Muse Hotel, 130 West 46th Street; (212) 485–2400 or (877) NYCMUSE,
www.themusehotel.com. Coccoonish rooms and Sam DeMarco's subtly
theatre-themed restaurant, District (212–485–2999).

The New York Palace, 455 Madison Avenue at 50th Street; (212) 888–7000;
www.newyorkpalace.com. The elegant home of Le Cirque 2000 (212–
794–9292; www.lecirque.com).

Oceana, 55 East 54th Street; (212) 759–5941; www.oceanarestaurant.com.
Spectacular seafood in a 1920s townhouse.

Oyster Bar, 42nd Street and Vanderbilt Avenue; (212) 490–6650; www.oyster
barny.com. An alluring underground vault amid the gloriously renovated
1913 Grand Central Station.

The Paramount Hotel, 235 West 46th Street; (212) 764–5500. A hip Times
Square nexus with small but well-priced rooms.

Le Parker Meridien, 118 West 57th Street; (212) 245–5000 or (800) 543–4300;
www.parkermeridien.com. Vaster than ours, with a park-view penthouse
pool; modernist Norma's serves fabulous breakfasts.

Le Perigord, 405 East 52nd Street; (212) 755–6244, www.leperigord.com.
French wizardry on Sutton Place.

The Royalton, 44 West 44th Street; (212) 869–4400 or (800) 950–1363. The
city's first Schrager/Starck hotel remains a style-setters' scene.

Russian Tea Room, 150 West 57th Street; (212) 974–2111. The star-spotter's spot, splashier than ever.

The St. Regis, 2 East 55th Street; (212) 753–4500 or (800) 759–7550. John Jacob Astor IV's lavish 1904 Beaux Arts beauty provides the ultimate in pampering, plus the legendary restaurant Lespinasse (212–339–6719).

"21," West 52nd Street; (212) 582–7200; www.21club.com. Indefatigably in.

Vong, 200 East 54th Street; (212) 486–9592. A showcase for Vongerichten's Gallic/Thai wizardry.

Upper East Side

Aureole, 34 East 61st Street; (212) 319–1660. Charlie Palmer's "progressive American" hideaway with courtyard garden.

Barbizon Hotel, 140 East 63rd Street at Lexington Avenue; (212) 838–5700 or (888) 227–2496. The 1927 haven for career girls has been transformed into a luxurious, modern, unisex retreat.

Boathouse Cafe, Central Park near 72nd Street; (212) 517–2233. A pastoral setting for impressive fusion cuisine.

Cello, 53 East 77th Street; (212) 517–1200. Cozy, calm, masterful French nouvellerie.

Commissary, 1030 Third Avenue at 61st Street; (212) 339–9955. Matthew Kenney's eclectic Mediterraneanean dishes in a sleek black-and-white space.

Daniel, 60 East 65th Street; (212) 288–0333; www.danielnyc.com. Boulud's elegant shrine to evolved French cuisine.

The Dining Room, 154 East 79th Street: (212) 327–2500. Slick—and dazzling—contemporary American.

E.A.T., 1064 Madison Avenue at 80th Street; (212) 772–0022. The East Side version of Zabar's.

The Franklin, 164 East 87th Street; (212) 369–1000 or (877) 847–4444; www.franklinhotel.com. Deco meets of-the-moment.

Guastavino's, 409 East 59th Street; (212) 980–2455. Sir Terence Conran's stylish "American brasserie" occupies a tiled vault beneath the Queensboro Bridge.

JoJo, 160 East 64th Street; (212) 223–5656. A Belle Epoque-style townhouse provides the perfect playground for Jean-Georges Vongerichten.

Park Avenue Café, 100 East 63rd Street; (212) 644–1900. Artful Americana.

Payard Patisserie & Bistro, 1032 Lexington Avenue near 73rd Street; (212) 717–5252. Bistro classics pave the way for exceptional pastry.

The Regency, 540 Park Avenue at 61st Street; (212) 759–4100 or (800) 235–6397. A Hollywood favorite; the Regency Room, home of the original power breakfast, doubles as Michael Feinstein's nightclub.

The Stanhope, 995 Fifth Avenue at 81st Street; (212) 774–1234; www.hyatt.com. An ideal perch for descending on the Met.

Surrey Hotel, 20 East 76th Street; (212) 288-3700 or (800) MESUITE; www.mesuitc.com. A fine hotel, and home to Cafe Boulud (212–772–2600), where chef Daniel installs his most promising protégés.

Sylvia's Restaurant, 328 Lenox Avenue at 127th Street; (212) 996–0660. The fabled soul-food destination (line up for the Sunday gospel brunch).

Urban Jem Guest House, 2005 Fifth Avenue at 125th Street; (212) 831–6029, www.urbanjem.com. A brownstone embodying the New Harlem.

Upper West Side

Boat Basin Cafe, West 79th Street at the Hudson River Basin; (212) 496–5542. The West Side's backyard barbecue.

Cafe des Artistes, 1 West 67th Street; (212) 877–3500; www.cafedes.com. For steeped-in-the-past romance.

Café Luxembourg, 200 West 70th Street: (212) 873–7411, www.cafeluxembourg.com. Congenial and accomplished.

Jean-Georges, 1 Central Park West, at 60th Street; (212) 299–3900. Further virtuosity from Jean-Georges Vongerichten.

New York International AYH-Hostel, 891 Amsterdam Avenue at 103rd Street; (212) 932–2300; www.hiayh.org. Plain but cheap.

Ouest, 2315 Broadway at 84th Street; (212) 580–8700. American bistro fare in a snappy setting.

Picholine, 35 West 64th Street; (212) 724–8585. French/Mediterranean artistry near Lincoln Center.

Tavern on the Green, Central Park at West 67th Street; (212) 873–3200; www.tavernonthegreen.com. A long-time tourist mecca with—surprise!—exciting cuisine.

FOR MORE INFORMATION

New York Convention and Visitors Bureau, 810 Seventh Avenue at 53rd Street, New York, NY 10019; (212) 484–1200 or (800) NYC–VISIT; www.nycvisit.com.

INDEX

Forbidden Fruit, 71
Forks, The, 143
Four Seas, 52
Franconia, 181–83
Franconia Notch, 183
Freeport, 120
Frick Collection, 306
Frog Hollow Vermont State Craft
  Center, 224, 233
Frost Place, 182
Fruitlands Museums, 15
Funicular, 195

G

Gallery 7, 107
Gallery North Star, 235
Garden House, 280
Gelston House, 267
Giardelli/Antonelli Studio
  Showroom, 70
Gillette Castle, 266
Glissades de la Terrasse, 195
Gloucester, 5–7
Goodspeed Opera House, 269
Goldenrod, 104
Grafton Historical Society
  Museum, 235
Grafton Nature Museum, 235
Grafton (New Hampshire), 168
Grafton (Vermont), 235
Grafton Ponds Nordic Ski & Mountain
  Bike Center, 235
Granary Gallery at the Red Barn
  Emporium, 83
Grand View Inn & Resort, The, 158
Grapevine, The, 4
Green Animals Topiary Gardens, 250
Green Mountain Audubon Nature
  Center, 209
Green Mountain Chocolate
  Company, 208
Green Mountain Cultural
  Center, 209

Green Mountain National
  Forest, 224
Green Mountain Spinnery, 236
Greenfields Mercantile, 224
Greenvale Vineyards, 250
Greenwich, 293
Greenwich Village, 304
Greystone Gardens, 29
Griswold Inn, 268
Goodspeed Opera House, 267
Guggenheim Museum SoHo, 305
Guida's Coast Cuisine, 14

H

H. Richard Strand Antiques, 40
H.O.M.E. Co-op, 129
Hadwen House, 92
Halcyon Gallery, 70
Halibut Point State Park and
  Reservation, 5
Hall Tavern, 15
Hallet's, 54
Hallowell, 143
Hammond Castle, 4
Hancock, 160
Hancock Shaker Village, 26
Hanover, 168–69
Hanover Inn, 169
Harden Studios, 54
Harney & Sons, 281
Harraseeket Inn, 120
Harraseeket Lunch & Lobster
  Company, 120
Harriet Beecher Stowe House, 278
Harris Center for Conservation
  Education, 160
Harrisville, 158–59
Harrisville Designs Weaving
  Center, 159
Hart Gallery, 16
Hartford, 276–78
Harwich Port, 57
Hatch's, 68

ABOUT THE AUTHOR

Sandy MacDonald grew up in Riverdale, near New York City, and spent winter vacations skiing in Vermont and several summers ensconced in an island lighthouse off Blue Hill, Maine. Over the past two decades, she has contributed to dozens of magazines and numerous guidebooks. She and her husband, John Devaney, a painter, share an 1860s townhouse in Cambridge, Massachusetts, and a fledgling family compound on Nantucket.